Politics and Development of Contemporary China

Series Editors
Kevin G. Cai
University of Waterloo
Renison University College
Waterloo, ON, Canada

Pan Guang
Shanghai Center for International Studies
Shanghai Academy of Social Sciences
Shanghai, China

Daniel C. Lynch
School of International Relations
University of Southern California
Los Angeles, CA, USA

As China's power grows, the search has begun in earnest for what superpower status will mean for the People's Republic of China as a nation as well as the impact of its new-found influence on the Asia-Pacific region and the global international order at large. By providing a venue for exciting and ground-breaking titles, the aim of this series is to explore the domestic and international implications of China's rise and transformation through a number of key areas including politics, development and foreign policy. The series will also give a strong voice to non-western perspectives on China's rise in order to provide a forum that connects and compares the views of academics from both the east and west reflecting the truly international nature of the discipline.

More information about this series at
http://www.palgrave.com/gp/series/14541

Olayiwola Abegunrin • Charity Manyeruke

China's Power in Africa

A New Global Order

Olayiwola Abegunrin
Howard University and
University of Maryland
Hyattsville, MD, USA

Charity Manyeruke
University of Zimbabwe
Harare, Zimbabwe

Politics and Development of Contemporary China
ISBN 978-3-030-21993-2   ISBN 978-3-030-21994-9   (eBook)
https://doi.org/10.1007/978-3-030-21994-9

© The Editor(s) (if applicable) and The Author(s), under exclusive licence to Springer Nature Switzerland AG 2020
This work is subject to copyright. All rights are solely and exclusively licensed by the Publisher, whether the whole or part of the material is concerned, specifically the rights of translation, reprinting, reuse of illustrations, recitation, broadcasting, reproduction on microfilms or in any other physical way, and transmission or information storage and retrieval, electronic adaptation, computer software, or by similar or dissimilar methodology now known or hereafter developed.
The use of general descriptive names, registered names, trademarks, service marks, etc. in this publication does not imply, even in the absence of a specific statement, that such names are exempt from the relevant protective laws and regulations and therefore free for general use.
The publisher, the authors and the editors are safe to assume that the advice and information in this book are believed to be true and accurate at the date of publication. Neither the publisher nor the authors or the editors give a warranty, express or implied, with respect to the material contained herein or for any errors or omissions that may have been made. The publisher remains neutral with regard to jurisdictional claims in published maps and institutional affiliations.

This Palgrave Macmillan imprint is published by the registered company Springer Nature Switzerland AG.
The registered company address is: Gewerbestrasse 11, 6330 Cham, Switzerland

ACKNOWLEDGMENTS

Every serious work of research owes a considerable debt to the many who have, even without their knowledge, contributed to shaping it. Our primary indebtedness is to the forerunners among scholars, of whom there are too many to name, whose ideas, theories, and hypotheses are tested, while examining the relevant sources they cite, and others who one encounters along the way. Next are archivists and librarians; they often work unobtrusively but show geniality and willingness to oblige and facilitate work through a maze of diverse sources from the ever-intense students anxious to see as many sources as are relevant or which might shed light on just a single point, including those which are peripheral to the study.

In writing this book, we give very special thanks and love to our two families—Olayiwola Abegunrin's wife, Mrs. Funmilola Atoke Abegunrin, and the children, and to Charity Manyeruke's husband, Mr. Shingirai Manyeruke and their children for their moral support throughout the period of working on this book. Our deepest gratitude to Professor Abiodun Alao, School of Global Affairs, King's College, London, and Professor Ezra Chitando, University of Zimbabwe, and Zimbabwe National Defence College, Harare, Zimbabwe, for their wonderful and timely commendations. We thank the United States Office of Energy Information Administration, Washington DC, for providing us sources and materials on African trade with China. We thank the Staff of the African and Middle Eastern Division, especially Angel Batiste of the Library of Congress, Washington DC, for making available to us very useful documents and materials on Sino-African Relations and China's economic engagement with Africa, and we thank the staff of Howard

vi ACKNOWLEDGMENTS

University Library, Washington DC. We also thank the publisher, Palgrave Macmillan, especially Alina Yurova, Editor for Regional Politics and Development Studies, and Politics & International Studies. Finally, we are responsible for the ideas expressed in this book.

Hyattsville, MD, USA   Olayiwola Abegunrin
Harare, Zimbabwe   Charity Manyeruke
March 2019

ALSO BY OLAYIWOLA ABEGUNRIN

1. Olayiwola Abegunrin, (authored), *Nigeria-United States Relations, 1960–2016*, MD, Lanham: Lexington Books, 2018
2. Olayiwola Abegunrin, and Sabella O. Abidde (co-editor), *African Intellectuals and the State of the Continent: Essays in Honor of Professor Sulayman S. Nyang*, London: Cambridge Scholars Publishing, 2018
3. Olayiwola Abegunrin, (authored), *Nigeria, Africa, and the United States: Challenges of Governance, Development and Security*, Lanham, MD: Lexington Books, 2016
4. Olayiwola Abegunrin, and Sabella O. Abidde (co-editor), *Pan-Africanism in Modern Times: Challenges, Concerns, and Constraints*, Lanham, MD: Lexington Books, 2016
5. Olayiwola Abegunrin, (Authored), *The Political Philosophy of Chief Obafemi Awolowo*, Lanham, MD: Lexington Books, 2015
6. Olayiwola Abegunrin, (editor), *Africa in the New World Order: Peace and Security Challenges in the Twenty-First Century*, Lanham, MD: Lexington Books, 2014
7. Olayiwola Abegunrin, (editor), *AFRICA: The State of the Continent Fifty Years After the Liberation*, New York: Nova Publishers, 2013
8. Olayiwola Abegunrin, (Authored) *Africa in Global Politics in the Twenty-First Century: A Pan-African Perspective*, New York: Palgrave Macmillan, 2009
9. Olayiwola Abegunrin, and Olusoji Akomolafe (co-editor), *Nigeria in Global Politics: Twentieth Century and Beyond; Essays in Honor of Professor Olajide Aluko*, Nova Publishers, 2006

10. **Olayiwola Abegunrin**, (Authored) *Nigerian Foreign Policy under Military Rule, 1966–1999,* Westport, CT: Praeger Publishers, 2003)
11. **Olayiwola Abegunrin**, and Franklin Vivekananda (co-editor), *The Political Economy of South-South Cooperation: Towards A New International Economic Order,* Stockholm, Sweden: Bethany Books, 1998
12. **Olayiwola Abegunrin**, (Authored) *Nigeria and the Struggle for the Liberation of Zimbabwe: A Study of Foreign Policy Decision Making of An Emerging Nation,* Stockholm, Sweden: Bethany Books, 1992
13. **Olayiwola Abegunrin**, (Authored) *Economic Dependence and Regional Cooperation in Southern Africa: SADCC and South Africa in Confrontation,* Lewiston, New York: Edwin Mellen Press, 1990
14. **Olayiwola Abegunrin**, and H.E. Newsum (Co-authored), *United States Foreign Policy Towards Southern Africa: Andrew Young and Beyond,* London & New York: Macmillan and St. Martin's, 1987
15. **Olayiwola Abegunrin**, Ralph Onwuka and Dhajoo Ghista (co-editor), *African Development: OAU/ECA Lagos Plan of Action and Beyond,* Brunswick Publishing Company, 1985

CONTENTS

1 Introduction   1

2 Sino-Africa Relations: An Overview   9

3 China's Economic Engagement in Africa   27

4 China and Resource (Oil) Diplomacy in Africa   59

5 China's Involvement in Southern African Liberation Struggles   75

6 China-Zimbabwe Relations: A Strategic Partnership?   95

7 Zambia's Bilateral Relations with China   115

8 Ethiopia-China Relations: A Focus on Factors Driving Investment Inflows and the Socioeconomic Impact   131

9 China and Regional Integration in Africa   151

10 China's Military Involvement and Peacekeeping in Africa   173

ix

x   CONTENTS

11	China's One Belt One Road Initiative in Africa	187
12	Conclusion	207
	Selected Bibliography	217
	Index	225

About the Authors

Olayiwola Abegunrin is Professor of International Relations, African Studies, and Political Economy, Howard University and University of Maryland. He was formerly Chair, Department of International Relations, Obafemi Awolowo University, Ile-Ife, Nigeria. He is a Carnegie Mellon Foundation Fellow and a Distinguished Professor in teaching and service in African Studies. He is author, co-author, editor, and co-editor of fifteen books, several book chapters, and many articles in referred journals. He was a recipient of Howard University's Distinguished Faculty Author for scholarly work published during 1998–2000 and 2002–2003 academic year. His latest book is *Nigeria—United States Relations, 1960–2016* (2018). He is Series Editor, Cambridge Scholars Publishing, editor and consultant to publishers and journals, and consultant to international organizations. He is a member of the Honor Society of International Scholars and the Academic Advisory Board for Global Studies: AFRICA.

Charity Manyeruke is a professor of political science and international relations, and the Dean of the Faculty of Social Studies at the University of Zimbabwe. She has taught both undergraduate and postgraduate courses in Politics and Governance in Africa, International Relations, Political Science, Strategic Studies, Conflict Management, and International Organizations over the years. She has published books and book chapters on politics, women, land, trade, and elections, and many referred articles. Manyeruke is also the former Chairperson of the Department of Politics and Administrative Studies at the University of Zimbabwe. She is a member of the International Political Science Association and the South African Association of Political Studies.

ABBREVIATIONS

ACFTA	African Continental Free Trade Area
ADB	African Development Bank
AFRICOM	U.S. African Command
AGOA	African Growth Opportunity Act
AIIB	Asian Infrastructure Investment Bank
ANC	African National Congress (of South Africa)
ANLF	Algeria National Liberation Front
AU	African Union
AUCC	African Union Conference Center
BRF	Belt and Road Forum
BRI	Belt and Road Initiative
CAC	China Africa Cooperation
CADF	China-Africa Development Fund
CADRG	China Architecture and Design Research Group
CAF	Central African Federation
CATIC	China Aero Technology Import-Export Cooperation
CCB	China Construction Bank
CCECC	China Civil Engineering Construction Corporation
CCP	Chinese Communist Party
CCPIT	China's Council for the Promotion of International Trade
CCTV	China Central Television
CCYL	Chinese Communist Youth League
CDB	Chinese Development Bank
CET	Common External Tariff
CGTN (TV)	China Global Television Network
CIA	Central Intelligence Agency

xiii

xiv ABBREVIATIONS

CIF	Chinese Investment Fund
CJTF-HOA	Joint Task Force for the Horn of Africa
CMBIC	China Machine Building International Corporation
CMC	Central Military Commission
CMHI	China Merchant Holdings International
CNBC	Chinese National Broadcasting Corporation
CNBS	China's National Bureau of Statistics
CNMC	China Non-Ferrous Metals Group Company
CNOC	Chinese National Oil Companies
CNOOC	China National Offshore Oil Corporation
CNPC	Chinese National Peoples' Congress
COMESA	Common Market for Eastern and Southern Africa States
COREMO	Mozambique Revolutionary Committee
CPC	Communist Party of China
CPLA	Chinese People's Liberation Army
CPWF	Communist Party's Women Federation
CREC	China Railway Engineering Corporation
CSCE	China State Construction Engineering
DPFZA	Djibouti Ports and Free Zone Authority
DRC	Democratic Republic of the Congo
EAC	East African Community
ECOWAS	Economic Community of West African States
EIBC	Export-Import Bank of China
EITI	Extractive Industry Transparency Initiative
EPA	Economic Partnership Agreements
ESAP	Economic Structural Adjustment Program
ETCZ	Economic and Trade Cooperation Zones
EU	European Union
EXIM BANK of China	Export-Import Bank of China
FDI	Foreign Direct Investment
FOCAC	Forum on China-Africa Cooperation
FRELIMO	(Frente de Libertacaio de Mozambique) Front for the Liberation of Mozambique
FTLRP	Fast Track Land Reform Program
GDP	Gross Domestic Products
GNPOC	Greater Nile Petroleum Operating Company
GWIC	Great Wall Industry Corporation
HUAWEI	Huawei Technologies Limited
ICC	International Criminal Court
ICT	Information and Communication Technology
IEA	International Energy Agency

IFI	International Financial Institution
IMF	International Monetary Fund
IOM	International Organization of Migrants
LDC	Less Developing Countries
MFEZ	Multi-Facility Economic Zones
MNR (RENAMO)	Mozambique National Resistance
MOFCOM	Ministry of Commerce of the People's Republic of China
MPLA	Popular Movement for the Liberation of Angola
MSR	Maritime Silk Road
NAASP	New Asian-African Strategic Partnership
NEPAD	New Partnership for African Development
NFCA	Non-Ferrous Metals Corporation of Africa
NICTIB	National Information and Communication Technology Infrastructure Backbone
OAU	Organization of African Unity
OBORI	One Belt One Road Initiative
OECD	Organization of Economic Cooperation and development
PAC	Pan-Africanist Congress of South Africa
PAIGC	Partido Africano do Independencia da Guine e Cabo Verde
PIDA	Program for Infrastructure Development for Africa
PKO	Peacekeeping Operation
PLA	People's Liberation Army
PRC	People's Republic of China
REC	Regional Economic Communities
ROC	Republic of China (Taiwan)
SACP	South African Communist Party
SACU	Southern African Customs Union
SADC	Southern African Development Community
SADCC	Southern Development Coordination Conference
SALM	South African Liberation Movement
SEZ	Special Economic Zone
SGR	Standard Gauge Railway
SIRI	Stockholm International Research Institute
SIRPA	School of International Relations and Public Affairs, (China Fudan University)
SOE	State-owned Enterprises
SREB	Silk Road Economic Belt
SSA	Sub-Saharan Africa
UDHR	Universal Declaration of Human Rights

xvi ABBREVIATIONS

UN	United Nations
UNCTAD	United Nations Conference on Trade and Development
UNECA	United Nations Economic Commission for Africa
UNITA	National Union for the Total Independence of Angola
UNSC	United Nations Security Council
USSR	Union of Soviet Socialist Republics
WAEC	West African Economic Community
WB	World Bank
WTO	World Trade Organization
ZANLA	Zimbabwean African National Liberation Army
ZANU-PF	Zimbabwean African National Union-Patriotic Front
ZAPU	Zimbabwean African People's Union
ZCCZ	Zambia-China Cooperation Zone
ZESA	Zimbabwean Electricity State Association
ZESCO	Zambian Electricity Supply Corporation
ZISCO	Zimbabwean Iron and Steel Company
ZNPU	Zambian National Power Utility
ZRDA	Zambia Road Development Agency
ZREA	Zimbabwean Rural Electrification Agency

LIST OF TABLES

Table 3.1	Sino-African trade 2003	33
Table 3.2	Trans-African highway network route	51
Table 4.1	Major African sources of oil for China	62
Table 4.2	Other African sources of oil for China	64
Table 4.3	China foreign direct investment top destinations in Africa 2005–2017	71
Table 8.1	Chinese Exports to Ethiopia (1995–2015)	139
Table 8.2	Chinese Imports from Ethiopia (2005–2015)	140
Table 8.3	Top 10 Recipients of Chinese Developmental Assistance (2000–2014)	142

xvii

CHAPTER 1

Introduction

The rapid increase of China's economic and political involvement in Africa is the most momentous development on the continent of Africa since the end of the Cold War. China is aptly referred to as *new imperialist, new actor, giant economy, and emerging power*, but China is not very new to the African continent. However, in recent years, particularly since the end of the Cold War, China's presence in Africa has grown immensely, and China's renewed engagement with Africa has come at a time when the business climate has improved across Africa and interest in Africa as a market has grown tremendously.

The first mention of Africa in Chinese sources was in the Yu-yang-tsa-tsu by Tuan Ch'eng-shih (died in 863), a compendium of general knowledge, where he wrote about the land of Po-pa-li, referring to Somalia of modern time.[1] The Yuan Dynasty's Zhu Siben made the first known Chinese voyage to the Atlantic Ocean, while the Ming Dynasty's Admiral Zheng He and his fleet of more than 300 ships made seven separate voyages to areas around the Indian Ocean and landed on the coast of East Africa.[2]

However, the modern Sino-Africa relations began with Premier Zhou Enlai's first tour of Africa, popularly known as *Zhuo's African Safari* was a series of state visits to ten independent African countries, undertaken between December 1963 and February 1964. Premier Zhou Enlai's primary goal in Africa was to raise China's profile on the continent at a time when it was beginning to challenge the former Soviet Union openly over

© The Author(s) 2020   1
O. Abegunrin, C. Manyeruke, *China's Power in Africa*,
Politics and Development of Contemporary China,
https://doi.org/10.1007/978-3-030-21994-9_1

the direction of the global Communist movement. This visit was much on ideological struggles, unlike the current emphasis on economic development and investments in Africa today. The ideological emphasis was on agreement on opposing imperialism, colonialism, racism, and expansionism, safeguarding world peace, and strengthening unity between China and African countries. The current Chinese policy toward Africa is part of the Open Door Policy engineered by the Deng Xiaoping reforms in virtually all aspects of China's political, economic, and social life, starting from 1978, restoring the country to domestic stability and economic growth after the excesses of the Cultural Revolution and cementing an inequality gap as well. Deng Xiaoping guided China out of its decades-long isolation and economic stagnation. On economic development, he emphasized that:

> Modernization does represent a great new revolution. The aim of our revolution is to liberate and expand the productive forces. Without expanding the productive forces, making our country prosperous and powerful, and improving the living standard of the people, our revolution is just empty talk. We oppose the old society and the old system because they oppressed the people and fettered the productive forces. We are clear about this problem now.[3]

Deng Xiaoping sent many people abroad to familiarize themselves with and learn about the outside world. He said that China cannot develop by closing its door, sticking to the beaten track and being self-complacent.[4]

While there is a growing list of literature on China's relations with other parts of the world, there is a lack of books on Sino-Africa relations; thus, this book intends to fill that gap and:

> (1) examine the historical background of the ongoing Sino-Africa relationship; (2) report on what is going on in Africa's political, economic, military/security, cultural and social space vis-à-vis Chine's; (3) China's involvement in African liberation, and particularly Southern African liberation struggles; (4) Where the Sino-Africa relationship is heading; and (5) what are the immediate and long-term problems and prospects of the said relations. Thus, the central question to be answered in this book is whether the relationship between Africa and China is a mutually benefitting relationship or is China the new imperial power or friend of Africa?

After the devastating effects of the Cultural Revolution and the death of the country's revered leader Chairman Mao Zedong in 1977,[5] deep pockets of ultra-leftist thinking remained, and reformers determined to help bring the Chinese economy and industry out of its backward state faced the challenge of a lifetime. Nevertheless, against tremendous odds and resistance, a determined team of reformers, led by Deng Xiaoping, guided China out of its decades-long international isolation and economic stagnation.

Perhaps no leader in the twentieth century had a greater long-term impact on world history than Chairman Deng Xiaoping. He was China's boldest strategist; he was once described by Chairman Mao Zedong as a "Needle inside a ball of cotton."[6] He was a pragmatic and disciplined driving force behind China's radical transformation in the late twentieth century. He boldly confronted the damage wrought by the Cultural Revolution, dissolved Mao's cult of personality, especially the Gang of Four,[7] and loosened the economic and social policies that had stunted China's growth. He was obsessed with modernization and technology, and opened trade relations with the West (the arch enemy of communism), which lifted hundreds of millions of his country-citizens out of poverty. "Yet at the same time he answered to his authoritarian roots, most notably when he ordered the crack-down in June 1989 at Tiananmen Square."[8] Deng Xiaoping's youthful commitment to the Communist Party was cemented in Paris in the early 1920s, among a group of Chinese student-workers that also included Zhou Enlai. Deng Xiaoping returned home in 1927 to join the Chinese Revolution on the ground floor. In the fifty years of his tumultuous rise to power between 1927 and 1977, he endured accusations, purges, and even exile, before becoming China's preeminent leader from 1978.

Jiang Zemin replaced—Deng Xiaoping in 1992 and was the President of China until 2002. He promoted his *Three Represents*, which was basically a continuation of China's economic development, with the maintenance of people's mandate and development of cultural identity. Hu Jintao, who also received political tutelage under Deng Xiaoping, became the President of China from 2002 to 2012. His contribution was a continuation of the reform policies set in motion by Jiang Zemin. Xi Jinping, the current President of China, assumed office in 2013. His policy is characterized as economically liberal but politically conservative.[9]

As of now, Africa is transforming rapidly, and the United States' approach to Africa is not keeping pace. While China has jumped at opportunities to invest in growing African economies, the United States is struggling to keep up. China's commitments to the 2018 Forum on China-Africa Cooperation (FOCAC) Summit, during which China and African countries strengthened cooperation on the Chinese One Belt One Road Initiative, signed several bilateral agreements, and signed a communiqué calling for a stronger community with a shared future between China and Africa.[10]

Since launching its (Open Policy) open-up reform four decades ago (in 1978), the economic volume of the People's Republic of China has leapfrogged to the second place in the world,[11] with its industrialization gradually reaching the mature stage and its sophisticated manufacturing capacities. The story of China's economic success in recent decades is something that is possible in many African countries and it is through platforms such as the Forum on China-Africa Cooperation that such aspirations can be pursued better. With the African continent's abundant natural resources, plentiful and cheap human labor, and large market potential, Africa is at the starting stage of industrialization and China is willing and is the ideal partner in the process of industrialization of Africa.

As a way for fostering such partnership, the Forum on China-Africa Cooperation Summit will help build consensus on China-Africa cooperation and align the Chinese development agenda with that of Africa. Our thinking is that, through helping the sustainable development of Africa, China itself would realize better development domestically; this is true and should be encouraged as Africa would largely benefit from the advantage of Chinese equipment, technology and finance. For instance, many African countries are undergoing a stage that China has only previously experienced and there is plenty of experience to share. For example, while most of the African countries are working tirelessly to achieve industrialization and modernization, China is undergoing structural economic adjustment for the transformation and up-grading of its industrialization. Therefore, the high degree of complementarity between China and Africa provides an important opportunity for the strategic alignment of the Sino-Africa development agenda. However, to take that complementarity to high levels, there is a need for more cooperation, including upgrading the existing common trade relations to industrial cooperation and technological transfer, to help propel Africa's nascent manufacturing base.

We also believe that through making full use of the political mutual trust and economic complementarity, this can turn the Chinese-African traditional friendship into a strong force to propel development and help turn the potential of African plentiful labor resources and abundant natural resources into strengths of economic development and fruitful outcomes, benefitting not only African but Chinese peoples as well.

It should be noted that the 2015 Johannesburg Forum on China-Africa Cooperation Summit emphasized the China-Africa cooperation in various fields, especially industrial and agricultural modernization cooperation, which are a top priority for most African countries. The Johannesburg summit also strengthened the solidarity between the developing countries at a time when the world is at the critical stage of big development, reform, and adjustment. While at the 2018 Beijing Forum on China-Africa Cooperation and Ministerial Conference, President Xi Jinping pledged $60 billion in financing for projects in Africa in the form of assistance, investment, and loans, as China furthers its efforts to link the African continent's economic prospects to its own. The theme of the 2018 Beijing Forum on China-Africa Cooperation Summit was *Walk together towards prosperity*, and President Xi Jinping emphasized the priority areas of China's engagement with Africa in the next three years, 2018–2021. Thus, he announced *Eight Actions Plan* to succeed his 2015 *Ten Cooperation Plans*. The three-year Eight Actions Plan (eight major initiatives) with African countries, covering fields such as industrial promotion, infrastructure connectivity, trade facilitation, and green development.[12]

China's new plan involved the One Belt One Road Initiative (OBORI)[13] established by China in 2013 as the centerpiece of President Xi Jinping's foreign and economic policy. It is made up of a "*belt*" of overland corridors and a maritime "*road*" of shipping lanes. It has been referred to as the Chinese Marshal Plan, backed by the state, which is campaigning for its global dominance. This is a trillion-dollar plan that aims to connect more than seventy countries in Asia, Africa, and Europe, and account for half of the world's population and a quarter of the world's GDP. "In Africa, infrastructural projects have been established in Egypt, Djibouti and Kenya, and more significantly for geo-political reasons."[14] This initiative is Beijing's consensus for Africa, which is replacing the failed Washington consensus. The Beijing consensus is an antithesis of the Washington consensus.

With the rise of developing countries, China and Africa occupy a very critical position in that discourse, whereby China is the world's largest developing country and Africa the continent with the highest concentration of developing countries. Also considering that the total combined population of China and Africa is 2.5 billion (Africa 1.2 billion and China 1.3 billion)[15]—accounting for one-third of the world's population—the China-Africa partnership can also be an alliance to safeguard the rights and interests of the developing countries to foster a more balanced international order. Therefore, these are all grounds upon which we can construct a stronger foundation for developing cooperation and the Forum on China-Africa Cooperation Summit will reflect the solidarity among developing nations and show a new vision of common development to the world.

NOTES

1. "China-Africa Relations," Ministry of Foreign Affairs of the People's Republic of China, April 25, 2002. http://www.fmprc.gov.cn/eng/ziliao/3602/3604/t18059.htm. Retrieved July 24, 2018.
2. Yuan Wu, *La Chine et l'Afrique, 1956–2006*, China Intercontinental Press, 2006.
3. Committee for the Party Literature, Central Committee of the Communist Party of China. *Selected Works of Deng Xiaoping*, Volume II, Beijing: Foreign Languages Press, 1995.
4. Ibid., p. 143.
5. Li, Langqing, *Breaking Through: The Birth of China's Opening-Up Policy*, New York, NY: Oxford University Press, 2009.
6. Ezra F. Vogel, *Deng Xiaoping and the Transformation of China*, Cambridge, MA: The Belknap Press of Harvard University Press, 2011.
7. The Gang of Four, or Siren Bang, was a group of four influential Chinese Communist Party figures during the latter years of Chairman Mao Zedong's rule. The Gang consisted of Mao's wife, Jiang Qing, and her associates Wang Hongwen, Yao Wenyuan, and Zhang Chunqiao. Wang, Yao, and Zhang were all major Communist Party officials from Shanghai. They rose to prominence during the Cultural Revolution 1966–1976, pushing Mao's policies in Shanghai. When the Chairman's health began to decline over that decade, the Gang of Four gained control of major government functions. Kallie Szczepanski, "What was the Gang of Four in China?" *ThoughtCo.*, April 14, 2018. For details on the Gang of Four, see Ezra F. Vogel, *Deng Xiaoping and the Transformation of China*, Cambridge, MA: The Belknap Press of Harvard University Press, 2011, pp. 175–180.
8. Ibid.
9. "Leaders of the People's Republic of China." www.chinasage.info/leaders.htm. Accessed December 9, 2018.
10. Reuben Brigety, "A Post-American Africa: The U.S. Falling Behind," *Reuter International*, August 28, 2018.
11. For details on economic transformation of the People's Republic of China to World Second Economic Power see the following books; Ezra F. Vogel, *Deng Xiaoping and the Transformation of China*, Cambridge, MA: The Belknap Press of Harvard University Press, 2011. Also see Li, Langqing, *Breaking Through: The Birth of China's Opening-Up Policy*, New York, NY: Oxford University Press, 2009.
12. For full details on three years' eight major initiatives with African countries in the next three years and beyond, covering fields such as industrial promotion, infrastructure connectivity, trade facilitation, and green development, Liangyu, "Xi Jinping Says China to Implement Eight Major Initiatives with African Countries," https://www.xinhuanet.com, September 3, 2018.

13. Hong Kong Trade Development Council, "The Belt and Road Initiative: Six Economic Corridors Spanning Asia, Europe and Africa." *Resource Portal on Belt and Road*, May 3, 2018.
14. Ibid.
15. For details see Rand McNally, *The World, Afghanistan to Zimbabwe*, New York: Map and Atlas Publishing, 1996, pp. 16–17.

CHAPTER 2

Sino-Africa Relations: An Overview

INTRODUCTION

Sino-Africa relations refer to the historical, political, economic, military, social, and cultural connections between China and the African continent. Little is known about ancient relations between the African continent and China, although there is some evidence of early trade connections. For instance, highlights of medieval time contacts were the fourteenth century-journey of Ibn Battuta, the Moroccan scholar and traveler, to parts of China[1]; the fourteenth-century journey of Said of Mogadishu, the Somali scholar and explorer, to China; and the fifteenth-century Ming Dynasty voyages of Chinese Admiral Zheng He and his fleet, which rounded the coast of Somalia passing the Ajuran Sultanate, and followed the coast down to the Mozambique Channel[2] in Southern Africa.

There are traces and evidence of Chinese activity in Africa dating back as far as the Tang Dynasty. Chinese porcelain was found along the coasts of Egypt in North Africa.[3] Chinese coins, dating back to the ninth century, have been discovered in Kenya, Zanzibar, and Somalia. The Song Dynasty established maritime trade with the Ajuran Empire in the mid-twelfth century. "China and Africa have a history of trade relations sometimes through third parties, dating back as far as 202 BC and 220 AD. In the medieval times, the Somalia Empire (Ajuran Empire) dominated the Indian Ocean trade. This empire belonged to the Somalia Muslim Sultanate."[4]

© The Author(s) 2020
O. Abegunrin, C. Manyeruke, *China's Power in Africa*,
Politics and Development of Contemporary China,
https://doi.org/10.1007/978-3-030-21994-9_2

According to available information and evidences, ancient Sino-Africa official contacts were not widespread. Most Chinese emissaries are believed to have stopped before ever reaching Europe or Africa, probably travelling as far as the eastern provinces of the Roman and later Byzantine empires. However, some did reach Africa. For instance, in one of the only two instances when China was ruled by a foreign dynasty, Yuan Dynasty ambassadors, this time Mongols, traveled to Madagascar in East Africa. In addition, "Zhu Siben of the Yuan Dynasty made a map of the African continent at the time. Southern Africa was included on the map. Zhu Siben also traveled along West Africa's coasts drawing a more precise map of Africa's triangular shape."[5]

However, between 1405 and 1433, the Yongle Emperor of the Ming Dynasty sponsored a series of naval expeditions, with Zheng He as the leader. He was placed in control of a massive fleet of ships, which numbered as many as 300 ships with at least 28,000 men.[6] Among the many places the Zheng He fleet traveled were Arabia, Somalia, India, Indonesia, Thailand, and East Africa. On their return, the fleet brought back from Africa lions, rhinoceros, ostriches, giraffes, et cetera, to the great joy of the Ming Dynasty.[7] The modern Chinese version is that the European mercantilism in the so-called age of discovery (age of exploitation of Africa by colonial powers) aggressively ended Sino-Africa relations. This point of view enforces the rhetoric of the blood brother relations of China and Africa.[8]

PREMIER ZHOU ENLAI AND MODERN SINO-AFRICA RELATIONS

The current/modern Sino-Africa relations began in the 1950s under the leadership of Mao Zedong, when Zhou Enlai, the first Premier of the People's Republic of China, visited Africa and signed bilateral agreements with several African states. This was Premier Zhou Enlai's first visit to Africa, popularly known as Zhou's *African Safari* was a series of state visits to ten independent African countries, undertaken between December 1963 and February 1964 by the Chinese Premier. These visits occurred during the period when African countries were gaining independence from colonial powers, and marked as the first time any high-ranking Chinese Communist leader had traveled to Africa.[9]

Premier Zhou Enlai was a very skilled and experienced diplomat who was the Chinese Foreign Minister when the People's Republic of China was founded on October 1, 1949 and served in that position until 1958.

Advocating peaceful coexistence with the West after the stalemated Korean War of 1950–1953, he participated in the 1954 Geneva Conference on Indochina, and the 1955 Bandung Asian-African Conference/Afro-Asian Conference, and orchestrated President Richard Nixon's 1972 visit to China that led to the opening up of China to the United States.[10]

Premier Zhou Enlai's original plan on his 1963–1964 Africa tour was to visit every country on the continent that had established formal diplomatic relations with Beijing. He led a delegation of more than fifty people, including Chinese Foreign Minister Chen Yi to Africa.[11] The delegation began their Africa tour in Egypt, which was the first country in Africa to recognize the Communist government in Beijing. During the journey, the itinerary was amended several times to add Tunisia, whose government planned to recognize communist China. Tanganyika (now Tanzania), which was undergoing the Zanzibar Revolution, was removed from the itinerary and Ethiopia was added, even though Ethiopia did not recognize the Communist government in Beijing until 1970.[12]

In the end, the ten countries visited were as follows: Egypt, Algeria, Morocco, Tunisia, Ghana, Mali, Guinea, Sudan, Ethiopia, and Somalia. Premier Zhou Enlai's primary goal in going to Africa was to raise China's profile on the continent at a time when China was beginning to challenge the former Soviet Union (now the Russian Federation) openly over the direction of the global Communist movement. While Premier Zhou received a warm reception in countries with left-wing governments, such as Algeria, Mali, Egypt, and Ghana, he faced more hostile encounters with leaders who were adamantly anti-communist, especially in Tunisia and Ethiopia.[13]

In response to those anti-communist African governments, Premier Zhou Enlai consistently asserted that China could maintain friendly relations with countries with different *political systems*. And rather than focus on the problems of postcolonial governments, he mainly restricted himself to call for African countries still under colonial rule to gain independence. However, he was very careful and did not employ potentially inflammatory Marxist rhetoric in several of his speeches in Africa. For example, in a farewell address in Mogadishu, the capital of Somalia, before returning to China, he pledged that China would support *revolutionary struggles* throughout the continent of Africa and oppose both foreign intervention and native *reactionaries*.[14]

The second important goal of Premier Zhou Enlai's trip to Africa was to drum up enthusiasm for holding a second Afro-Asian Conference in Algeria in 1965, a decade after the first Asian-African (Afro-Asian) Conference was held in Bandung, Indonesia in 1955.[15] The Bandung Afro-Asian Conference symbolized the People's Republic of China's recognition that China and African countries shared an important common interest in their struggles for liberation from colonial rule, and equally more important, there were no basic conflicts of interest between Africa and China. Zhou Enlai was especially concerned to make sure that the Soviet Union not be invited to send a delegate to the conference, because it would make it more difficult for the Chinese government to present itself as the only truly anti-imperialist Marxist power. Zhou Enlai made a second but shorter trip to Africa in June 1965 to lobby several African leaders to support his vision for the second Afro-Asian Conference. Unfortunately, the conference was canceled soon thereafter in the wake of the overthrow of Algerian President Ahmed Ben Bella.[16]

RESTORING ORDER AND SETTING THINGS RIGHT

From the Chinese perspective, major changes took place on the world stage in the 1970s, and Chairman Mao Zedong's diplomatic philosophy played a major role in it. For instance, a major diplomatic achievement for China led by Premier Zhou Enlai was, on October 25, 1971, the 26th Session of the United Nations General Assembly passed with an overwhelming majority vote the resolution to restore People's Republic of China to all its lawful rights in the United Nations. In addition, according to former Vice-Premier of China, Li Langqing:

> United States President Richard Nixon's historic China visit, which began on February 21, 1972, culminated in the now-famous meeting between the American President and Chairman Mao. On February 28, based on repeated consultations between Premier Zhou Enlai and President Nixon on the normalization of bilateral diplomatic relations and other issues of common concerns, the joint Communique of the United States of America and the People's Republic of China was signed in Shanghai. The Communique emphasized that both nations agreed to handle international relations based on the Five Principles of Peaceful Coexistence. The Chinese side reaffirmed its solemn, principled stand on the Taiwan issue, while the US side declared, the United States acknowledges that all Chinese on either side of the Taiwan Straits maintain there is but one China and that Taiwan is a part of China. The United States Government does not challenge that position. The Communique also stipulated that both sides will facilitate the gradual conduct of Sino-US trade, as well as contact and exchanges between the two

2 SINO-AFRICA RELATIONS: AN OVERVIEW 13

nations in such areas as science, technology, culture, sports, and the press. The Nixon visit and the conclusion of the Shanghai Communique (also known as the Shanghai Accord) were milestones in the annals of Sino-American relations. They marked the beginning of normalized relations between the two countries, and laid the cornerstone for further improvement and growth in Sino-U.S. relations.[17]

In relation to One China Policy as it relates to Africa, Taiwan (Republic of China) now has one diplomatic ally left in Africa. For Taiwan (ROC), the list of its diplomatic allies in Africa has dwindled to all but one nation. In August 2018, Burkina Faso cut its ties with the island nation Taiwan, joining a growing list of countries cowering to increasing pressure from China (the People's Republic of China) to cut their ties with the island nation. Under its *One-China Policy*, China refuses to maintain diplomatic relations with any nation that recognizes Taiwan, a self-governed island off its southeastern coast which Beijing considers an integral part of its territory.

This leaves Swaziland (eSwatini) as the only African country with formal relations with Taiwan, along with eighteen other allies around the world, and mostly smaller and poorer nations in the Pacific and the Caribbean. The Burkinabe Foreign Ministry justified its decision of breaking diplomatic ties with Taiwan by saying, "the evolution of the world and the socioeconomic challenges of our country and region push us to reconsider our position."[18] This is the second time Burkina Faso has cut ties with Taiwan, the last time it did so was in 1973, before resuming relations again with Taipei in 1994. Consequently, Taiwanese President Tsai Ing-Wen lashed out at China following the diplomatic fallout with Burkina Faso, saying the country was using dollar diplomacy to lure away its supporters. Thus, Taipei said it would end its assistance to Burkina Faso, halt all bilateral cooperative projects, and close its embassy there. Swaziland Foreign Minister, Mgwagwa Gamedze, reemphasized the kingdom's commitment to Taiwan, warning China that Beijing "must not play mind games because our relationship with Taiwan is over 50 years so we will not dump them. We have no desire to change camps since Taiwan has been good to us."[19]

The breakup with Burkina Faso comes just a few weeks after the Dominican Republic cut off ties with Taiwan following reports that the People's Republic of China (PRC) had offered loans and investments worth $3.1 billion. In 2017, Nigeria ordered Taiwan's trade mission (embassy) to move out of the nation's capital Abuja, after getting a $40 million pledge from China. And in December 2016, Sao Tome and Principe also bid Taipei goodbye after a two-decade diplomatic relationship. In September 2018, the Vatican and China reached an Accord to normalize their ties. Thus, the Vatican might break ties with Taiwan.[20]

Nevertheless, President Tsai Ing-wen has so far remained steadfast, saying China's *pressure* will only push Taiwan to get closer with its allies. However, the diplomatic split might still undermine her leadership, especially given that it took place just a few weeks after she made her maiden trip to Africa in a bid to keep its now only one remaining African ally-eSwatini (formerly Swaziland) on its side.[21]

For the past decade, support for Taiwan has dwindled as billions of dollars in Chinese investments have flowed into the African continent. Sino-Africa relations have also soared, as China dishes out loans to African countries, and provides investments in infrastructure, construction, energy, transportation, and more. As economic engagement with Africa has increased, China has also expanded its diplomatic and military footprint and provided thousands of scholarships to African students every year to study in China.

DENG XIAOPING: THE MODERN-DAY CHINA'S REFORMER

Modern-day China's reformer, Deng Xiaoping, was born on August 22, 1904 in Guang'an, part of Sichuan Province of China. The son of a well-to-do landowner, Deng Xiaoping joined the Chinese Communist Party in High School at a young age and traveled to France in 1920, and later to Moscow. Deng studied and worked in France in the 1920s, where he became a follower of Marxism-Leninism, before returning to his home country in 1926. Deng Xiaoping joined China's burgeoning Communist Revolution led by Chairman Mao Zedong, as a political and military organizer. He cut his revolutionary teeth on the fabled *Long March* of 1934–1935, when the fledging Chinese Communist Movement escaped capture by the Nationalist Chinese Army. War broke out against Japan in 1937, and Deng Xiaoping served as educational leader of the Chinese Revolutionary Army, helping it to grow into a large military machine during the Communist Revolution of 1946–1949.[22]

Initially, Chairman Mao Zedong praised Deng Xiaoping for his organizing skills, but he fell out of favor with Mao Zedong in the 1960s, during the Cultural Revolution. Deng Xiaoping's emphasis on individual self-interest did not sit well with Chairman Mao Zedong's egalitarian policies. Consequently, Deng Xiaoping was eventually stripped of all his posts within the Communist Party, and with his family, was exiled to the rural Jiangxi Province to undergo reeducation. However, in 1973, Chinese Premier Zhou Enlai felt China needed Deng Xiaoping's organizational skills to improve the Chinese economy. Deng Xiaoping was reinstated and carried out a major reorganization of the government. Thus, he was soon elevated to the Politburo. Deng Xiaoping was widely considered to be Zhou Enlai's successor. However, upon Zhou Enlai's death, in 1976, the Gang of Four managed to purge Deng Xiaoping from leadership.[23]

The Gang of Four, also known as *Siren Bang*, was a group of four influential Chinese Communist Party members during the latter years of Chairman Mao Zedong's rule. The Gang consisted of Mao's wife, Jiang Qing, and her three associates, Wang Hongwen, Yao Wenyuan, and Zhang Chunqiao. Wang, Yao, and Zhang were all major Communist Party officials from Shanghai. They rose to prominence during the Cultural Revolution 1966–1976, pushing Mao's policies in Shanghai. When the Chairman's health began to decline over that decade, the Gang of Four gained control of major government functions.[24]

However, after the death of Chairman Mao Zedong in 1977, the Gang of Four itself was purged and Deng Xiaoping again, for the third time, made a political comeback. The Third Plenary Session of the Tenth Party Central Committee of the Communist Party (July 16–21, 1977) in Beijing, "unanimously endorsed the Resolution to restore Comrade Deng Xiaoping to his posts.

This act reinstalled Deng as Politburo Member and Standing Committee Member, Vice Chairman of the Party Central Committee and of the Military Commission, Vice Premier of the State Council and Chief of the General Staff of the People's Liberation Army."[25] In his speech to the session,

Deng said:
It is a personal pleasure for me, in the few years left in my lifetime, to do what a veteran Communist is supposed to do for the Party, the nation and the people. Anyone setting out to work may take one of two attitudes, to be a bureaucrat or to get something done. I say to myself, who was it that turned me into a Communist? It was none other than me. Now that I have chosen to be a Communist, it makes no sense for me to indulge in official-dom and selfish thinking. I have no choice but to be humble while fulfilling my obligations as a Party member and to obey the Party's arrangements.[26]

Thus, Deng Xiaoping downgraded Chairman Mao's legacy, and he defeated his opponents and banned unofficial organizations. Consequently, Deng Xiaoping solidified his power and quickly instituted new economic policies—the New China, *China Open Door Policy*, opening China to international trade and investment.[27] This led to a peace treaty with Japan, improved relations with the former Union of Soviet Socialist Republics (USSR), and official recognition by the United States, and return of control over the British colony of Hong Kong.[28] In 1992, Deng Xiaoping said firmly, "We would come to a dead end should we fail to adhere to socialism, reform and opening up, develop the economy, and improve people's livelihood, and the fundamental policies must be maintained for 100 years, unswervingly."[29] These resounding statements fully demonstrated Deng Xiaoping's firm determination on China's socialist reform, opening-up and modernization drive. "Deng Xiaoping's heroic spirit despite of formidable obstacles will forever encourage the Chinese people in their efforts to build socialism with Chinese characteristics, a fundamental policy of the Communist Party."[30]

Many changes were made and implemented under Deng Xiaoping, for instance, China's economy grew and standards of living increased under a Communist government committed to one-party rule. Andrew Moody described, Deng Xiaoping's initiative; "that not only transformed China—turning it from a largely agrarian and poor society to the second-largest economy in the world—but in doing so changed the world itself. Shifting its center of gravity eastward."[31] Thus the 1978 reform and opening-up of China has had a profound influence on the landscape of the global economy. The economy was liberalized but a one-party state was maintained under Communist Party government.[32] Thus, the shift to a less ideological approach to the economy was not without difficulty, and it involved considerable political efforts on the part of Deng Xiaoping to maintain the perception of a coherent national direction. However, Philip Snow describes the situation thus: "A continual attempt to sustain a rhetorical unity which has sometimes disguised the pursuit of profoundly different goals."[33]

DIPLOMATIC OPENING, 1949–1980

After the establishment of the People's Republic of China (PRC) following the Communist Party victory over the Nationalist Chinese Army in 1949, some Chinese fled, eventually landing/ended in Africa. By the 1950s, there were Chinese communities amounting to more than 100,000 people existing in South Africa, Madagascar, and Mauritius. Small Chinese communities in other parts of Africa later became the cornerstone of the post-1980 growth in dealings between China and Africa. However, at the time, many lived lives centered on local agriculture and probably had little or no contact with China. Precise statistics of the Chinese presence in Africa are difficult to obtain, since both Chinese and African officials have remained discreet about this issue.[34]

A new Chinese trade began in the industrial era. European colonization of Africa and the abolition of slavery in France caused major workforce shortages in European colonies. Europe looked for a way to fill the gap with low-cost workers from abroad, namely, India and China. Beginning in the 1880s, tens of thousands of Chinese Coolies were sent overseas to work in the mines, railroads, and plantations of the colonial powers. The exploitation of inland resources, such as copper mines, also led to the presence of relatively large, isolated Chinese populations in landlocked countries, such as Botswana and Zambia. For instance, Jean Ping, born on November 24, 1942,[35] is a Gabonese diplomat and politician; he was the Minister of Foreign Affairs of Gabon, and former Chairperson of the African Union Commission 2008–2012, and a Sino-African descendant was born from a marriage of an African mother and a Chinese father in Gabon. His Chinese father Cheng Zhiping, a Chinese from Wenzhou, China, and a Gabonese mother, Germaine Anina. Jean Ping was born in Omboue, Etimbwe Department, Ogooue-Maritime Province in Gabon. His father, Cheng, had immigrated to French Equatorial Africa in the 1930s as a trader and later married Germaine Anina, a local Gabonese Princess, a daughter of a local chief in Gabon. Because of his good relationship with the Gabonese people, Cheng, Jean Ping's father, got involved in local politics, and was elected to the local Assembly in Gabon three times.[36]

The newly established People's Republic of China (PRC) actively began supporting the decolonization movements in Africa from the 1950s (e.g. support to African Liberation Movements in Southern Africa), and the Pacific. This period is especially important in the Sino-Africa movement, as both the PRC and many of the decolonized African nations shared a victim background, the perception that they were humiliated, dehumanized, and taken advantage of by imperialistic nations such as Japan and European states.[37]

The growing Sino-Soviet split of the 1950s and 1960s allowed the PRC to get United States' support and return to the international scene in 1971. The Nationalist China (Taiwan's seat) in the UN Security Council was expelled by General Assembly Resolution 2758 of 1971[38] and replaced in all the United Nations organs with the People's Republic of China. For instance, with growing opposition between the PRC and the USSR in the 1960s, China was expanding its own program of diplomacy, sometimes supporting capitalist factions within some countries against USSR backed factions, for example, Ethiopia and the African National Congress (ANC) fighting for their liberation in apartheid South Africa.[39]

At the 1955 Bandung Afro-Asian Conference, China showed an interest in becoming the leader of the *Developing World*. Chinese Premier Zhou Enlai made an extensive African tour between 1963 and 1964, to strengthen the Sino-African friendship. Hundreds of Chinese Medical Doctors and engineers were sent to Africa and infrastructural projects were planned. The iconic 1160 miles Tanzam railroad, between Tanzania and Zambia, built by 50,000 Chinese workers, was completed in 1976. A former diplomat, Professor M. Xinghua, referred to this era as the *golden age* of Sino-Africa relations.[40] Growing numbers of African countries switched their recognition from the Nationalist Republic of China (Taiwan) to the People's Republic of China (PRC), starting from 1971. Most specifically, 1976 marked the deaths of Premier Zhou Enlai and 1977 Chairman Mao Zedong, bringing the era of ideology symbolically to a close and leaving power in the pragmatic hands of Deng Xiaoping.[41]

Against tremendous odds and resistance, a determined team of reformers, led by Deng Xiaoping, guided China out of its decades-long international isolation and economic stagnation. People witnessing this astonishing national transformation over the past four decades are familiar with general outlines of the story of China's economic miracle. Many scholars, especially Americans and Europeans, are very critical of China's rapid transformation. The New York Times columnist Thomas Friedman predicted in 1998 that; "when China will need a government that is legitimate....When China's 900 million villagers get phones, and start calling each other, China will inevitably become a more open country."[42] A majority of the Americans shared Friedman's predictions that China's economic ascent under authoritarian rule could not last; eventually, and inescapably, further, economic development would bring about democratization. However, two decades after Friedman's prophecy, China has morphed into the world's second largest economy. Though, growth has slowed recently, but only because it leveled off when China reached middle-income status, not as Friedman predicted. Today, communications technology rapidly spreading, 600 million Chinese citizens own smartphones and 750 million use the internet, and the much-anticipated tsunami of political liberalization predicted by some Western scholars and press has not happened.[43]

PRESIDENT XI JINPING'S SPEECH AT THE OPENING CEREMONY OF 2018 FORUM ON CHINA-AFRICA COOPERATION BEIJING SUMMIT

President Xi Jinping said; "According to ancient Chinese scholar; only with deep roots can a tree yield rich and only with oil can a lamp burn brightly."[44] With similar history and fate in the past and a common mission, China and Africa have a long history and extended sympathy to and helped each other throughout all the years. China and Africa have embarked on a distinctive path of win-win cooperation. China is following this principle, with real results, amity and good faith and the principle of pursuing the greater good and shared interests. China has stood with African countries even during the struggles for liberation in the 1950s and 1960s.[45]

China values sincerity, friendship, and equality in pursuing cooperation. The over 1.3 billion Chinese people have been with the over 1.2 billion African peoples in pursuing a shared future. President Xi Jinping spelt out Chinese views of Africa thus:

We respect Africa, love Africa and support Africa. We follow a five-no approach in our relations with Africa:

(1) No interference in African countries' pursuit of development paths that fit their national conditions
(2) No interference in countries' internal affairs in Africa
(3) No imposition of our will on African countries
(4) No attachment of political strings to assistance to Africa, and
(5) No seeking of selfish political gains in investment and financing cooperation with Africa.

We hope this five-no approach could apply to other countries as they deal with matters regarding Africa. For China, we are always Africa's good friend, good partner, and good brother. No one could undermine the great unity between the Chinese people and the African peoples.[46]

Our world is undergoing profound changes unseen in a century; the surging trend toward multipolarity, economic globalization, Information Technology application, and cultural diversity accelerated transformation of the global governance system and international order, rapid rise of emerging markets and developing countries, and greater balance in global power configuration. The well-being of people in all countries has never been so closely interwoven as ever. The world is now a global village. Therefore, to respond for the call of the times; "China is ready to jointly promote the One Belt One Road Initiative with international partners. We hope to create new driver to power common development through this new platform of international cooperation, and we hope to turn it into a road of peace, prosperity, openness, green development and innovation and a road that brings together different civilizations."[47]

In his speech titled *"Work Together for Common Development and a Shared Future,"* at the 2018 Summit of the Forum on China-Africa Cooperation, held at the Great Hall of the People in Beijing; President Xi Jinping said; "China will implement eight major initiatives with African countries in the next three years (2019–2021) and beyond, covering fields such as industrial promotion, infrastructure connectivity, trade facilitation, and green development."[48] In addition, President Xi Jinping went further and spelt out the following eight points:

First, on industrial promotion, a China-Africa economic and trade Expo (exhibition) will be set up in China and Chinese companies are encouraged to increase investment in Africa. China will carry out 50 agricultural assistance programs, provide emergency humanitarian food aid amounting to one billion Yuan ($147 million) to African countries affected by natural disasters and send 500 Senior Chinese agricultural experts to Africa.

Second, on infrastructure connectivity, China will work with the African Union to formulate a China-Africa infrastructure cooperation plan and support Chinese companies in taking part in Africa's infrastructure development by way of investment construction-operation or through other models.

Third, on trade facilitation, China will increase imports, especially non-resource products from Africa and support African countries in participating in China International Import Expo. However, the least developed African countries will be exempted from paying exhibition stand fees.

Fourth, on green development, China will undertake fifty aid projects on green development, and ecological and environmental protection, with a focus on climate change, ocean, desertification prevention and control, and wildlife protection.

Fifth, for capacity building, China will set up *10 Luban Workshops*[49] in Africa to offer vocational training for young Africans. In addition, China will also train 1000 High-Caliber Africans, provide Africa with 50,000 Government Scholarships, sponsor seminar and workshop opportunities for 50,000 Africans, and invite 2000 African youths to visit China for exchanges.

Sixth, for health care, China will upgrade fifty medical and health Aid Programs for Africa, with a focus on Flagship Projects, such as the Headquarters of the African Center for Disease Control and Prevention, and China-Africa Friendship Hospitals.

Seventh, People to People exchanges, China will set up an Institute of African Studies and enhance exchanges with Africa on civilization. China welcomes Africa's participation in the Silk Road International League of Theaters, the Silk Road International Museum Alliance, and the Network of Silk Road Art Festivals.

Eighth, concerning peace and security, China will set up a China-Africa Peace and Security Fund and continue providing free military aid to the African Union. And a total of fifty security assistance programs will be carried out in the fields including United Nations peacekeeping missions, fighting piracy, and combating terrorism.[50]

THE NEW AFRICAN UNION HEADQUARTERS AND CHINA'S INFLUENCE IN AFRICA

The African Union Conference Center (AUCC) and Office Complex Building in Addis Ababa, Ethiopia was designed and built by a collaboration of Tongji University, China State Construction Engineering (CSCE) and the China Architecture and Design Research Group (CADRG), with the $200 million budget donated by the Chinese government.[51] The design of the site of current African Union building resembles two hands in embrace, symbolizing Africa-China relations, and includes both traditional African art and modern Pan-African symbology, with the height of the main building/tower 99.9 meters (328 feet) tall, a reference to adoption of the Sirte, Libya Declaration of September 1999, founding of the African Union.[52] However, "the majority of the materials used in the construction were Chinese, and the art on the walls was produced in China. And the construction of the building took three years with a workforce of

1,200, and roughly half of whom were Ethiopian and half of whom were Chinese."[53] The building was officially open on January 28, 2012.

The unfortunate event happened in January 2018, just six years after the opening of the African Union Conference Center (AUCC), it was reported by the African edition of a French newspaper-*Le Monde*, and confirmed by the *Financial Times*, that:

> The African Union's IT Department had discovered in early 2017 that the site's computer systems were connecting nightly to servers in Shanghai and uploading African Union files as well as recordings from microphones embedded in the walls and furniture. The building's computer was subsequently removed, and the African Union refused a Chinese offer to configure the replacement system.[54]

Consequently, the African Union has accused China of hacking its headquarters. What does this accusation portend for Sino-Africa relations? The intention of these allegations was to create a rift between Beijing and the African continent. The age of colonial domination is over. Thus, African leaders and their policy makers must be very strategic in their thinking and vision and develop a clear road-map of where they are going and what they want, before negotiating any agreements and/or contracts with China, and with any advanced powers in the world, be it Western powers, China, India, Brazil, or Russia.

NOTES

1. Gin Ooi Keat, SouthEast Asia: A Historical Encyclopedia, From Angkor War to East Timor, ABC-CLIO, 2004, p. 626.
2. Charles Parker and Jerry H. Bentley, Between the Middle Ages and Modernity: Individual and Community in the Early, p. 160.
3. Yuan Wu, *La Chine et l'Afrique, 1956–2006*, China Intercontinental Press, 2006.
4. Ibid., pp, 87–88.
5. Ibid.
6. "Archived copy" http://web.archiev.org/web/20080827195453/ http://www.travel-skillroad.com/english/marine/ZhengHe.htm. August 27, 2008. Retrieved August 3, 2018.
7. Yuan Wu, op. cit.
8. Michael, Serge; Beuret, Michael; Wood, Paolo, *La Chinafrique: Pékin a la conquête du continent noir*, Grasset and Fasquelle, 2008, pp. 305–306.

9. "Zhou Enlai's African Safari," www.blackpast.org. Retrieved July 24, 2018. Also see Bruce Larkin, China and Africa, 1949–1970: *The Foreign Policy of the People's Republic of China*, Berkeley, CA: University of California Press, 1971.

10. Marilyn Young, *The Vietnam Wars: 1945–1990*, New York: Harper Perennial, 1991, p. 41. "Indochina- Midway in the Geneva Conference: Address by the Secretary of State," Avalon Project, Yale Law School, May 7, 1954. Also see Bruce Larkin, *China and Africa, 1949–1970: The Foreign Policy of the People's Republic of China*, Berkeley, CA: University of California Press, 1971.

11. "Zhou Enlai's African Safari," www.blackpast.org. Retrieved July 24, 2018.

12. Ibid.

13. For example, Ethiopia did not recognize the Communist government in Beijing until 1970.

14. Bruce Larkin, China and Africa, 1949–1970: *The Foreign Policy of the People's Republic of China*, Berkeley, CA: University of California Press, 1971.

15. George McTurnan, Kahin. *The Asian-African Conference: Bandung, Indonesia, April 1955*. Port Washington, NY: Kennikat Press, 1956. Twenty-nine Asian and African countries attended this conference, including: Afghanistan, Burma, Cambodia, Sri Lanka, Communist China, India, Indonesia, Iran, Iraq, Japan, Jordan, Laos, Lebanon, Nepal, Pakistan, the Philippines, Saudi Arabia, Syria, Thailand, Turkey, North Vietnam, South Vietnam, Yemen, Egypt, Ethiopia, the Gold Coast, Libya, and Sudan. Also see Bandung Conference of 1955 and the Resurgence of Asia and Africa. https://www.dailynews.lk/2005/04/21/fea01htm. Archived. Retrieved October 2, 2018.

16. Ibid.

17. Li, Langqing, *Breaking Through: The Birth of China's Opening-Up Policy*, New York, NY: Oxford University Press, 2009, pp. 38–39.

18. Abdi Latif Dahir, "Taiwan Now Has One Diplomatic Ally Left in Africa," *Quartz Africa Weekly Brief*, May 28, 2018.

19. Sebastiane Ebatamehi, "As African countries jostle for a piece of the $60 billion promised by China during the FOCAC Summit, eSwatini remains resolute in her stance not to have relationship with China." *IOL, African liberty*, October 4, 2018.

20. Victor Gaetan, "The Vatican and China Reach a Promising Accord," *Foreign Affairs*, Washington, DC, 2017. www.foreignaffairs.com/articles/2017-03-27/vatican-and-china-reach-promising-accord. Retrieved September 24, 2018.

21. Ibid.

22. Ezra F. Vogel, *Deng Xiaoping and the Transformation of China*, Cambridge, MA: The Belknap Press of Harvard University Press, 2011, pp. 33–37.

23. The Gang of Four, or Siren Bang, was a group of four influential Chinese Communist Party figures during the latter years of Chairman Mao Zedong's rule. The Gang consisted of Mao's wife, Jiang Qing, and her associates Wang Hongwen, Yao Wenyuan, and Zhang Chunqiao. Wang, Yao, and Zhang were all major Communist Party officials from Shanghai. They rose to prominence during the Cultural Revolution 1966–1976, pushing Mao's policies in Shanghai. When the Chairman's health began to decline over that decade, the Gang of Four gained control of major government functions. Kallie Szczepanski, "What was the Gang of Four in China?" *ThoughtCo.*, April 14, 2018. For details on the Gang of Four, see Ezra F. Vogel, *Deng Xiaoping and the Transformation of China*, Cambridge, MA: The Belknap Press of Harvard University Press, 2011, pp. 175–180.
24. Ibid.
25. Li Lanqing, op. cit. p. 30.
26. Ibid., pp. 30–31.
27. Abdi Latif Dahir, "Taiwan Now Has One Diplomatic Ally Left in Africa," *Quartz Africa Weekly Brief*, May 28, 2018, pp. 28–32.
28. Ibid.
29. Li Lanqing, op. cit., pp. 426–427.
30. Ibid., p. 427.
31. Andrew Moody. "Four Decades that Changed Country," *Chinawatch, China Daily*, People's Republic of China, December 19, 2018.
32. Ibid., pp. 425–427.
33. Ibid., pp. 40–42.
34. https://www.archive.org/web/20090311160010/.html. Retrieved August 7, 2018.
35. United Nations Profile Page https://www.un.org/ga/president/59/office/president.htm. Retrieved August 6, 2018.
36. "Jean Ping, Ministre des Affaires Étrangères, de la Cooperation et de la Francophonie," https://www.jeuneafrique.com/jeune_afrique/article_jeune_afrique.asp?art_cle=LIN05013jeanpeinohp0 (Jeune Afrique), African Journal January 5, 2003. Retrieved August 6, 2018.
37. See the following books on colonialism and decolonization, Howard W. French, *Everything Under the Heavens: How the Past Helps Shape China's Push for Global Power*, New York, NY: Alfred A. Knopf, 2017; Also, by Howard W. French *China's Second Continent How A Million Migrants Are Building A New Empire in Africa*, New York, NY: Vintage Books, 2014.
38. Ibid., p. 67.
39. See the following books Kenneth W. Grundy, *Confrontation and Accommodation in Southern Africa: The Limit of Independence*, Berkeley and Los Angeles, CA: University of California Press, 1973; Janice Love, *Southern Africa in World Politics: Local Aspirations and Global Entanglements*, Denver, CO: Westview Press, 2005; also see Raymond Suttner, *The ANC*

Underground in South Africa, 1950- 1976, Boulder, CO: First Forum Press, 2009.

40. Donghai Yu, "Why the Chinese Sponsored the TAZARA: An Investigation About the People's Republic of China's African Policy in the Regional Context, 1955–1970," University at Buffalo, State University of New York, 2012.

41. https://www.statssa.gov.za/PublicationsHTML/PO302200/html/P03022007.html. pp. 109–110. Retrieved August 7, 2018.

42. China Reckoning, Foreign Affairs, February 13, 2018. https://www.foreignaffairs.com/articles/united-states/2018-02-13/china-reckoning. Retrieved August 16, 2018.

43. Ibid.

44. Liangvu, "Full Text of Chinese President Xi Jinping's Speech at Opening Ceremony of 2018 FOCAC Beijing Summit." September 9, 2018. Also see https://www.xinhuanet.com.

45. Olayiwola Abegunrin, "Soviet and Chinese Military Involvement in Southern Africa," A *Current Bibliography on African Affairs,* Washington, DC: 6, 3, 1983–1984.

46. Liangu, op cit.

47. Ibid.

48. Liangyu, "Xi Jinping Says China to Implement Eight Major Initiatives with African Countries," https://www.xinhuanet.com, September 3, 2018.

49. Luban is the largest classical art Antiques Furniture Professional Company in China, established in 1998.

50. For full details on three years eight major initiatives with African countries in the next three years and beyond, covering fields such as industrial promotion, infrastructure connectivity, trade facilitation, and green development, Liangyu, "Xi Jinping Says China to Implement Eight Major Initiatives with African Countries," https://www.xinhuanet.com, September 3, 2018.

51. "African Union opens Chinese-funded Headquarter in Ethiopia," https://www.bbc.co.uk/news/world-africa-16770932. BBC News Online, January 28, 2012. Retrieved October 1, 2018.

52. The role and contributions of Muammar Ghaddafi, the former Leader of Libya should not be forgotten in founding of the African Union as we know it today. For details see Olayiwola Abegunrin, *Africa in Global Politics in the Twenty-First Century: A Pan-African Perspective,* New York: Palgrave Macmillan, 2009, pp. 161–166.

53. Sophie Grove, "Special Relations," https://monocle.com/magazine/issues/52/special-relations, April 2012. Retrieved October 1, 2018.

54. John Aglionby, Emily Feng, and Yuan Yang, "African Union Accuses China of Hacking Headquarters," *Financial Times,* January 29, 2018. https://www.ft.com/content/c26a9214-04f2-11e8-9650-9c0ad2d7c5b5. Retrieved October 1, 2018.

CHAPTER 3

China's Economic Engagement in Africa

INTRODUCTION

China and Africa have a history of trade relations, sometimes through third parties, dating back as far as 202 BC and 220 AD. Speaking before the Summit of the Heads of State and Government of the African Union, in Addis Ababa, Ethiopia in May 1996, former Chinese President Jiang Zemin said:

> We had a memorable yesterday... We enjoy a splendid today. The flower of Sino-African friendship is blooming with the care and nurturing of the Chinese and African peoples. We will greet a flourishing tomorrow... China, the biggest developing country in the world, is ready to join hands with Africa, the biggest developing continent in the world, to...march into the twenty-first century full of confidence.[1]

Africa-China relations began centuries ago and continue through the present day. Currently, China is seeking resources for its growing economy and consumption, and African countries are seeking funds to develop their infrastructures. Large-scale structural projects, often accompanied by soft loans, are proposed to African countries rich in natural resources. China commonly funds the construction of infrastructure such as roads and railroads, dams, ports, and airports. While relations are mainly conducted through diplomacy and trade, military support via provision of arms and other modern technological equipment is also a major component.

© The Author(s) 2020
O. Abegunrin, C. Manyeruke, *China's Power in Africa*,
Politics and Development of Contemporary China,
https://doi.org/10.1007/978-3-030-21994-9_3

In the diplomatic and economic rush into Africa, the United States, the United Kingdom, Germany, France, and Taiwan are China's main competitors. China overtook and surpassed the United States in 2009 to become the largest trading partner of Africa.[2] Bilateral trade agreements have been signed between China and 40 countries in the continent of Africa. In 2000, China-Africa Trade was $10 billion, and by 2014 it had grown to $220 billion.[3]

The People's Republic of China began to pursue market socialism in the late 1970s under the leadership of Deng Xiaoping. Deng Xiaoping's period as the President of the People's Republic China (PRC) marked the change to limited capitalist practices as the foundation of the PRC's socioeconomic development, a process initiated several decades earlier following the aftermath of the Great Leap Forward. Beginning in 1980, the PRC initiated a policy of rapid modernization and industrialization, resulting in reduced poverty and developing the base of a powerful industrial economy. As of 2011, the People's Republic of China had the second largest GDP in the world, at $6.5 trillion, and the second largest GDP by purchasing power parity at $11.1 trillion.[4]

Africa is the second largest continent, with Asia as the largest. Africa has a population of 1.2 billion (a landmass of 30,221,532 km) and 11.7 million square miles in size, and the Gross Domestic Products (GDP) of $1.2 trillion. The partition of Africa at the Berlin conference of November 1884 to February 1885 by the European powers brought on the violence and division of Africa.[5] Africa, being a major source of raw materials, saw the colonial powers vie for influence among the newly independent nations, with former colonial powers establishing special relations with their colonies, and often by offering economic aid and alliances for access to the vast resources of their former colonies. Today the presence of all these resources, such as diamonds, gold, silver, uranium, cobalt, coltan, and large oil reserves have brought Africa to the forefront of industrial development, with many of the world's economic powers building relations with Africa's resource rich nations.[6]

China and Africa have proclaimed a new and mutually beneficial economic, political, and regional alliance. China has seen Africa as a source of raw materials and energy, desperately needed to support its rapid industrial and economic growth. Success in this quest means high employment and a higher quality of life for Chinese citizens, as well as increasing social stability and political security for Chinese elites.

African countries partnering with China today are signing with a future world superpower. In Africa, this hope shows African elites an model of success, which they may take as an example and it can thus be said that the Chinese alliance provides strong psychological consequences. It provides economic prospects of their own future. Harry Broadman pointed out that, "if Chinese investments in key sectors of infrastructure, telecommunication, manufacturing, foods, and textiles radically alter the African continent, the main change will have taken place in African minds."[7] With the recent growth and economic improvement, more African students are returning to Africa after studies abroad to bring their skills and industry home.

CHINESE ECONOMIC EXPANSION, 1980 TO THE PRESENT

China awakened from its decades-old period of semi-isolation after 1976, when Deng Xiaoping took over as the new leader of the People's Republic of China. The country was boosted by internal reforms, growing foreign investments, and dramatic expansion of its work-force. China once more turned to Africa, now looking to the African continent both as a source of key natural resources, and as a market for its low-cost consumer goods. R. Marchal identifies the key resources and key events that have had a bearing on the Sino-Africa relations. First, the Tiananmen Square; the spectacle consolidated opposition to what was perceived as the PRC's violent opposition of demonstrators. Economically developed nations threatened to enforce economic sanctions, while African countries kept silent, either to conceal their own harsh policies or to further their ties with China. Indeed, that was the result as China strengthened its cooperation with African countries.[8] The growing alliance between China and Africa was more and more needed for both sides. Second, China's growing industry resulted in a rapidly expanding and seemingly inexhaustible demand for resources. Meanwhile, in the relative calm ushered in by the end of the Cold War, concerns about Human rights issues in China, further isolated the mix of rogue and pariah states.[9]

In 1995, President Jiang Zemin pushed the pace of Chinese economic growth faster. Under his leadership, China pursued broad reforms with confidence, and he declared to Chinese entrepreneurs, *Go Out* encouraging businessmen to conquer world markets.[10] And in the late 1990s, Chinese bids were heavily supported by the government and local embassies, with government-owned Exim Bank of China providing needed finances at low rates. The advantages provided by the PRC allowed Chinese enterprises to win many bids on the world market.

People's Republic of China officials described the period as a *Sane adjustment*, and the "sane development of economic and commercial Sino-African relations."[11] Still, Chinese and African diplomacy continued to invoke the imagery of the past ideological period: the shared history of victimization at the hand of nineteenth-century Westerners and the common fight for autonomy and independence. To those, China made significant progress to the fight toward progress in a world unfairly government-backed Chinese companies are equally or more successful than many Western companies.

One international relations analyst on Asia, Parag Khanna, states that by making massive trade and investment deals with Latin America and Africa, China established its presence as a superpower along with the European Union and the United States.[12] China's rise is demonstrated by its ballooning share of trade in its gross domestic product. Khanna believed that China's consultative style has allowed it to develop political and economic ties with many countries including those viewed as rogue states by Western powers.

China's rise in the world market led the Chinese diaspora in Africa to make contact with relatives in their homeland. Renewed relations created a portal through which African demand for low-price consumer goods could flow. Chinese businessmen in Africa, with contacts in China, brought in skilled industrial engineers and technicians such as mechanics, electricians, carpenters, to build African industry from the ground up. The 1995 official *Go Out Global* declaration and the 2001 Chinese entry into the World Trade Organization (WTO) paved the way for private citizens in China to increasingly connect with, import from, and export to the budding Sino-African markets.[13]

The Effects of the Global Economic Crisis (2007–2009)

China's Economic Interests in Africa

Today, China has bilateral and multilateral agreements with nearly all African countries. China's feat and level of influence, since the end of the Cold War, has become a source of concern not just for the Europeans but also for the United States, which sees herself as the world's preeminent power and the so-called policeman of the world. China's power and influence, according to many scholars, have been built by knowing how to play *better politics* and having a better understanding of the psyche of African leaders and her elites. Indeed, there are African leaders, and a growing number of diplomats, observers, and scholars who believe firmly in the long-term commitment and righteousness of the Chinese government and firms. But China, many scholars have also argued, has not come to Africa with bags full of free goodies and free of conditionalities and preferences. What we have now, according to these scholars, is a relationship that is profoundly unequal and troubling—with China gaining the most from barter trade-transactions, which basically involve natural resources in exchange for low-interest loans and cheap infrastructures.

China's economic and political involvement in Africa is the most momentous development on the continent of Africa since the end of the Cold War. China is aptly referred to as *new actor, giant economy, and emerging power* that is not very new to the African continent. However, in recent years, particularly since the end of the Cold War, China's presence in Africa has grown immensely. Irene Yuan Sun, a leading expert on the Africa-China economic relationship said:

> China is now the biggest foreign player in Africa. It's Africa's largest trade partner, the largest infrastructure financier, and the fastest-growing source of foreign direct investment. Chinese entrepreneurs are flooding into the continent, investing in long-term assets such as factories and heavy equipment.[14]

China's renewed engagement with Africa has come at a time when the business climate has improved across Africa and interest in Africa as a market has grown tremendously. China's transformation is without parallel in economic history. Since the beginning of the twenty-first century, China has experienced an eightfold increase in Gross Domestic Products (GDP), enabling it to serve as the primary engineer of global economic growth in the early twenty-first century. It has leapfrogged from sixth to second place among the world's economies, rivaling only the United States in absolute economic size. In addition, China has become the world's leading trading state and is now the second largest source of outward foreign direct investment.[15]

The Forum on China-African Cooperation held in Beijing in November 2006 was attended by 48 African heads of state and government.[16] The forum was given wide global prominence as a pointer to several of the Sino-Africa relations dynamic. The Summit approved a three-year action plan to create a *new strategic partnership* between China and Africa based on equality and mutual benefit. The Plan included a doubling of aid to Africa from 2006 levels by 2009, a $5 billion China-Africa Development Fund (CADF), debt cancellations, a further opening of the Chinese markets to exports from Africa by increasing from 190 to 400 products. There was also an increase in the number of products receiving zero-tariff treatment, and pledged to build 30 hospitals, 30 malaria treatment centers, and 100 rural schools in African countries.[17]

During his visit to Africa in January 2007, Chinese President Hu Jintao offered $3 billion in credit to African countries along with additional aid and interest-free loans. "He emphasized that the money comes with none of the political conditions attached to aid from Western governments."[18] Chinese trade with Africa valued at $3 billion in 1995, has grown to $55 billion in 2007. Chinese trade with Africa has increased fivefold since 2001, and represents more trade than Africa does with the European Union. It has been predicted that Chinese trade with Africa will continue to increase.[19]

OVERVIEW OF TRADE

Chinese world trade has grown rapidly over the last decades. Total trade was roughly $100 billion in 1990, $500 billion in 2000, $850 billion in 2004, 1400 billion in 2005, and 2200 billion in 2007. That computes to an over twenty-fold increase in under 20 years and an annualized growth rate of nearly eighteen percent. More remarkably, most of China's growth has taken place in the past, especially in 2000–2010 decade; in other words, not only is the size of China's trade growing, the rate of growth is accelerating. Thanks to the decades-old Chinese diaspora, the economic dynamism of People's Republic of China embassies, China's low-cost manufacturing industry, an efficient export engine, and an exchange rate of 16.4 percent that until 2010 had been held deliberately low, China's global trade has thrived.[20]

In the context of China's total trade, Africa comprises only a small part. For instance, in 2007, Sino-African trade rose to $73 billion, 3.4 percent of China's $217 billion total, far lower than that of the European Union at $356 billion, 16.4 percent, the United States at $302 billion, 13.9 percent, and Japan at $236, 10.9 percent. China is Africa's first trading partner since it surpassed the United States in 2009.[21]

Chinese Exports to Africa

The Chinese diaspora first reactivated its familial links to import low-priced goods such as cups, forks, cellular phones, radio, television sets and umbrellas to Africa. Indeed, African society has a ready need for cheap goods in large quantities. China's manufacturing industry is truly complementary to African markets, often producing more cheaply than most African manufacturers can, and with better quality. Cheap Chinese clothes and cheap Chinese cars at half the price of Western products allow African customers to suddenly raise their purchasing power.[22]

In Africa, China may sell its own low-quality or overproduced goods and inventory, a key outlet which helps maintain China's economic and social stability. Chinese shop-owners in Africa can sell Chinese-built, Chinese-shipped goods for a profit. A negative consequence of China's low-cost consumer goods trade is that it only goes one way. China does not purchase manufactured products from Africa, while cheap Chinese imports flood the local African marketplace, making it difficult for local industries to compete. A noticeable case is the Chinese textile industry, which has hit Africa like a tsunami. In many countries, textiles are one of the first manufacturing industries to develop, but the African textile industry has been crippled by Chinese competition (see Table 3.1 on Sino-African Trade). The consequences are not easily resolved: African consumers give praise to Chinese textiles, and they are often the first

Table 3.1 Sino-African trade 2003

Country	To China	From China	Total
South Africa	2.02	1.84	3.86
Angola	0.14	22	2.34
Sudan	0.47	1.44	1.91
Nigeria	1.78	0.07	1.85
Egypt	0.93	0.15	1.08
Congo Brazzaville	0.06	0.81	0.87
Morocco	0.69	0.16	0.85
Algeria	0.64	0.09	0.73
Benin	0.47	0.07	0.54
Others	2.93	1.52	4.45
Total	10.13	8.35	18.48

Source: Africa-China Economic Relations. Lafargue, Francois, "China's Presence in Africa," *China Perspective*, https://chinaperspectives.revues.org/document519.html. Retrieved August 8, 2018

clothes they can afford to buy new; yet local manufactures are badly wounded, raising opposition and concern over the loss of local jobs.

Thus, Africa is seen by Chinese businessmen as one billion plus potential customers in a fast-growing market.[23] Perhaps, more importantly, African societies are far from market saturation, like their Western counterparts. Thus, in Africa, China finds not only an ample supply of potential new customers but far less competition from other nations. A few examples of products imported from China in African countries in 2014: Benin bought $411 million worth of wigs and fake bears from China, eighty-eight percent of South Africa's imported male underpants were from China, Mauritius spent $438,929 on Chinese soy sauce, Kenya spent $8,197,499 on plastic toilet seats, Nigeria spent $9,372,920 on Chinese toothbrushes, Togo bought $193,818,756 worth of Chinese motorbikes and Niger $450,012,993.[24]

African Exports to China

In the other direction, China's growing thirst for raw materials has led Chinese State-owned Enterprises to African countries with natural resources, such as minerals, timber, and wood. By the end of the 1990s, China had become interested in African oil. Over time, African laws adapted to China's demand, laws intended to force the local transformation of raw materials for export. This has led to a new kind of manufacturing in Africa, and managed by the Chinese, with African workers producing exports for Chinese, as well as European, American and Japanese customers. African leaders have pursued an increase of the share of raw material transformation both to add value to their exports and to provide manufacturing jobs for local Africans.

China's oil purchases have raised oil prices, boosting the government revenues of oil exporters, like Angola, Gabon, and Nigeria, while hurting the other oil-importing African countries. At the same time, China's raw materials purchases have increased prices for copper, timber, and nickel, which benefits many African countries as well. While African growth from 2000 to 2005 averaged 4.7 percent per year, almost twice the growth has come from petroleum exporting countries (2005: 7.4 percent; 2006: 6.7 percent; 2007: 9.1 percent) than from petroleum importing countries (2005: 4.5 percent; 2006: 4.8 percent; 2007: 4.5 percent).[25]

During the year 2011, trade between Africa and China increased a staggering thirty-three percent from the previous year to $166 billion. This included Chinese imports from Africa equaling $93 billion, consisting mostly of mineral ores, petroleum, and agricultural products and Chinese exports to Africa totaling $93 billion, consisting mostly of manufactured goods.[26] Outlining the rapidly expanding trade between the African continent and China, trade between the two areas of the world increased further by over twenty-two percent year-over-year to $80.5 billion during the first five months of 2012. Imports from Africa were up by 25.5 percent to $49.6 billion during these first five months of 2012 and exports of Chinese-made products, such as machinery, electrical, and consumer goods and clothing, and footwear increased 17.5 percent to reach $30.9 billion.[27] China remained Africa's largest trading partner during the year 2012 for the fifth consecutive year, starting in 2008. To put the entire trade between China and Africa into perspective, during the early 1960s, trade between these two large parts of the world were in the mere hundreds of millions of dollars back then. In those days, Europe dominated African trade during these formative years of the European decolonization process in the African continent. Even as early as the 1980s, trade between China and Africa was minuscule. Trade between China and Africa grew exponentially following China's joining of the World Trade Organization (WTO) in 2001, and the opening-up of China to emigration of Chinese people to Africa and free movement of companies, peoples, and products both to and from the African continent starting from the early 2000 onwards.

CHINESE BANKS

The Exim Bank of China (Eximbank) is a government bank under the direct leadership of the State Council, operating both in China and Overseas. For its overseas actions, EximBank has hundreds of offices across the world, with three key representatives in Paris in France, Petersburg in the Russian Federation, and Johannesburg in South Africa.[28] This bank is a major force in Chinese foreign trade, aiming to catalyze import-export initiatives.

Chinese Eximbank offers enterprises and allies with a complete set of financial products. Low-rate loans and associations with skilled Chinese building companies are guided toward building or rebuilding local infrastructure, equipment, and offshore stations which meet a dual Chinese and African interest.[29] Eximbank can provide loans for roads, railroads, electricity and telecommunication systems, pipelines, hospitals, and various other needed facilities. It is the sole lending bank for Chinese Government Concessional Loans entrusted by the Chinese Government.

The objectives of Eximbank are to officially promote the development of Chinese export-oriented economy, to help provide China with raw materials, and facilitate the selling of Chinese goods abroad. Eximbank also helps to invest in underdeveloped countries, allowing them to both produce and export more raw materials to Chinese industries, and to allow African societies to expand their own markets. In 2006, Eximbank alone pledged $20 billion in development funds for 2007 through 2010; this is more than all Western funding.[30] Several other Chinese banks also provide African governments and enterprises with similar agreements. China has shown itself to be more competitive, less bureaucratic, and better adapted to doing business in Africa. Between 2009 and 2010, China Development Bank (CDB) and Eximbank publicly offered around $110 billion worth of loans to Emerging markets. Beating the World Bank's record of offering just over $100 billion between 2008 and 2010.[31]

Chinese Embassies and Their Economic Engagement in Africa

The Chinese government helps her diplomatic officials, "by providing information, legal counsel, low-rate loans, and upon return to China, cheaper land in return for all the services provided to the Chinese nation in Africa."[32] The People's Republic of China Embassies are full-time supporters of Chinese economic progress in Africa, widely using the numerous and well-organized pioneer Chinese businessmen in the diaspora. The Chinese government, well informed by the local businessmen about regional conditions, is equipped with thousands of skilled engineers and workers ready to leave China, as well as by experienced bankers (from Eximbank), and large reserves of U.S. dollars; as of 2008, approximately $1.4 trillion.[33] Thus, the Chinese government is ready to take on large-scale investments and projects and, if approved, to lead them to completion.

In pursuing economic progress in Africa, the Chinese diaspora and Chinese producers have been actively assisted by People's Republic of China embassies. Michael and Beuret noted that People's Republic of China embassies and local Chinese businessmen have frequent meetings and actively provide mutual assistance and information. For an African requesting PRC Visas for China, the embassy may request further information about the local businessmen often about his wealth.[34] When confirmed, the African businessmen or consumer gets his visa agreement.

First Chinese Major Project in Africa

"In December 1961 former Tanganyika (now Tanzania) became the tenth African state to recognize the People's Republic of China, and the first to do so within a few days of independence. Shortly afterwards a Chinese Embassy and an office of the New China News Agency were opened in Dar-es-Salaam."[35] By 1965, Tanzania had become the center of China's Africa policy.[36]

TAZARA RAILWAY (Tanzam Railway): Also known as *Uhuru Railway*, Swahili for Freedom Railway was designed and constructed between 1968 and 1976. The actual construction between 1970 and 1975 by the Tanzania-Zambia Railway Authority (TAZARA)[37] or (TANZAM) was conceived to provide the critical outlet to the sea that landlocked Zambia needed to break free from its dependency on the former Southern Rhodesia (now Zimbabwe), Angola, and South Africa rails and ports. The TAZARA was therefore a transnational as well as Pan-African project intended to serve as a symbol of revolutionary Developing World solidarity and resistance to the forces of colonialism, neocolonialism, and imperialism. The Chinese Participation in this and other projects, which also included sending technical experts and doctors to Africa and granting African students with scholarships to study in China, had less to do at the time with economic considerations than with political ones: it formed an obvious part of Beijing's ideological strategy to counter the influence of the former Soviet Union (now the Russian Federation) in East Africa. Moreover, the support of African countries was sought and needed to bolster Beijing's attempts to reclaim its seat in the United Nations Security Council.

A link between British colony of Northern Rhodesia (Zambia) and German colony of Tanganyika (Tanzania) was originally conceived by a British imperialist, Cecil Rhodes, but this imperial dream was never realized. In fact, this was part of a much larger effort of Cecil Rhodes' vision of a Cape to Cairo Railway through former British colonies, from Southern Africa to Northern Africa.[38] However, between 1963 and 1966 several feasibility studies for the construction of the railroad were conducted and requests for finance were submitted to Britain, the United States, Canada, France, Germany, the former Soviet Union (now the Russian Federation), the World Bank, and African Development Bank. But no firm offers were received from any of these countries and International Institutions. President Nyerere of Tanzania and President Kaunda of Zambia pursued different avenues for the construction of an alternative rail route.

During his first visit to China in 1965, President Nyerere signed a Treaty of Friendship with Beijing.[39] This Treaty of Friendship between China and Tanzania provided support that symbolized China's support to the revolutionist comrades in Africa. Thus, the Treaty paved the way for China's considerations and commitment on the Tanzania-Zambia railway construction. Thereupon, President Nyerere accepted a team of Chinese surveyors, who produced a report in October 1966. President Kaunda was more skeptical of communist involvement and pursued Western backing. The resulting Canadian-British aerial survey produced a favorable report in July 1966, but at the end Western funding was not forthcoming.[40]

Chinese Chairman Mao Zedong supported the funding of the railway, initially estimated at $1 billion, to secure votes against the former Soviet Union planning to attend the second Afro-Asian Summit in Algiers, Algeria in 1965. After his visit to China in January 1967, President Kaunda dropped his objections to the Chinese building the railways. Consequently, in September 1967, a tripartite agreement between China, Tanzania, and Zambia was signed in Beijing, under which China undertook to make a full survey of the rail-line and formally committed itself to build and finance the railway. Further negotiations between the three countries in April 1968 in Dar-es-Salaam and November 1969 in Lusaka led to the signing of the final agreement in July 1970 in Beijing.[41]

On July 12, 1975, President Julius Nyerere of Tanzania, accompanied by Fang Yi, the Chinese Minister of the Commission of Foreign Aid, witnessed the official opening of the TAZARA railroad, signaling the formal completion and operation of the single largest overseas investment in Chinese history in Africa. The total length of the railroad is 1160 miles and cost $570 million,[42] more than other Chinese-sponsored overseas projects combined prior to 1975.

China is building a new port in the tiny village of Bagamoyo in Tanzania. This is set to become Africa's largest port in a $10 billion Chinese development project in Africa. "In a decade, however, the mud-and-thatch homes of Mlingotini, and a further four villages along this coastline 30 miles north of Dar-es-Salaam, will be gone-razed to make space for a $10 billion Chinese-built mega-port and a special economic zone in Tanzania backed by an Omani sovereign wealth fund."[43]

THE ESTABLISHMENT OF FORUM ON CHINA-AFRICA COOPERATION (FOCAC)

The Forum on China-Africa Cooperation is a consultative forum and dialogue mechanism launched by China in 2000 to strengthen Chinese cooperation with Africa in various sectors.[44] The International situation has undergone tremendous changes since the Forum on China-Africa Cooperation (FOCAC) was established in 2006. When it was initially conceived in 2000 the Forum was known as The Ministerial Conference.[45] Thus, the first Ministerial Conference was held in Beijing from October 10 to 12, 2000. President Jiang Zemin, Premier Zho Rongji of the Council of State, and Vice-President Hu Jintao of the People's Republic of China participated in the conference. More than 80 Ministers from China and delegates from 44 countries, and representatives from 17 International and Regional Organizations attended this meeting. African attendees included President Gnassingbe Eyadema of Togo, President Abdelaziz Bouteflika of Algeria, President Frederick Chiluba of Zambia, President Benjamin William Mkapa of Tanzania, and Secretary-General Salim Ahmed Salim of the Organization of African Unity (now African Union). The conference passed the *Beijing Declaration of the Forum on China-Africa Cooperation and the Programme for China-Africa Cooperation in Economic and Social Development.*[46]

The second Ministerial Conference was held in Addis Ababa, Ethiopia, from December 15 to 16, 2003. Chinese Premier Wen Jiabao, Ethiopian Prime Minister Meles Zenawi, six African Presidents, three Vice Presidents, two Prime Ministers, and one President of the Senate as well as President Lapha Oumar Konare the Chair of the African Union Commission, and the representative of the United Nations Secretary General attended the opening ceremony and delivered speeches. More than 70 ministers from China and 44 African countries attended the conference. The Conference passed the *Addis Ababa Action Plan, 2004–2006.*[47]

Over the years, Summit on China and Africa have played bigger roles in the international political and economic landscape. And starting from 2006, the Ministerial Conference became known as the Forum on China-Africa Cooperation (FOCAC). The Forum meets every three years in China and in different African countries, but most of the time in China. The Forum on China-Africa Cooperation Summit is always a grand family gathering for China and African countries.[48]

The First Forum on China-Africa Cooperation Summit, and which was the Third Ministerial Conference, was held in Beijing, China November 3–5, 2006. This third Ministerial Conference was styled as the first Forum on China-Africa Cooperation Summit was attended by President of the People's Republic of China, Hu Jintao, and heads of state and government from 35 African countries. China's President, Hu Jintao, announced $5 billion worth of concessionary loans to Africa during the summit. As one of the *Eight Measures* for Sino-Africa relations, President Hu Jintao announced the creation of the China-Africa Development Fund (CADF) to further Chinese investment in Africa with $1 billion of initial funding with its fund expected to grow to $5 billion in the future.[49]

THE 2009 SHARM EL-SHEIKH, EGYPT FORUM ON CHINA-AFRICA COOPERATION SUMMIT

The Fourth Ministerial Conference and the Second Forum on China-African Cooperation Summit was held at Soho-Square, in the Egyptian Resort of Sharm El-Sheikh November 8–9, 2009. The meeting reviewed how the consensus of the Beijing Summit of 2006 has been implemented. It also adopted a *Sharm el-Sheikh Declaration and an action plan* for 2010–2012 to chart the path for further China-Africa cooperation. Chinese Premier Wen Jiabao, former Egyptian President Hosni Mubarak and African heads of state and government from 49 countries attended the opening ceremony of this summit. Chinese Foreign Minister, Yang Jiechi and Minister of Commerce Chen Deming led the Chinese delegation to attend the meeting.[50]

At the 2009 Summit, a $10 billion low-cost loan was announced on the last day of the summit on November 9, 2009, this doubled the $5 billion loan announced and implemented at the 2006 Beijing Summit. A $1 billion special loan for small and medium-sized African business was also established. China also announced eight new policy measures aimed at strengthening relations with Africa that were "more focused on improving people's livelihoods."[51] Premier Wen Jiabao announced that China will write off the debt of some of the poorest African nations. He also said China will construct 100 new clean-energy projects on the African continent covering solar power, bio-gas, and small hydro-power and gradually lower customs duties on ninety-five percent of products from African countries with which China has diplomatic ties.[52] In addition, he stated

3 CHINA'S ECONOMIC ENGAGEMENT IN AFRICA   41

that China would undertake 100 joint demonstration projects on scientific and technological research, receive 100 African post-doctoral fellows to conduct scientific research in China and assist them in going back and serving their home countries in Africa. The numbers of agricultural demonstration centers built by China in Africa will be increased to 20, and 50 agricultural teams would be sent to Africa and 2000 agricultural technology personnel would be trained for Africa, to help strengthen Africa's ability to ensure food security.[53]

China will provide medical equipment and anti-malaria materials worth 500 million Yuan (Chinese currency) to 30 hospitals and 30 malaria prevention and treatment centers built by China and train 3000 doctors and nurses for Africa. Premier Wen Jiabao further stated that China will build 50 China-Africa friendship schools and train 1500 school principals and teachers for African countries and increase the number of Chinese government scholarships for Africa to 5500 by 2012. China will also train a total of 20,000 professionals in various fields for Africa over the next three years, 2012–2015.[54]

The 2012 Beijing Forum on China-Africa Cooperation Summit

The 2012 Forum on China-Africa Cooperation Summit was held on July 19–20, 2012 in Beijing. This forum adopted the theme *Beijing Action Plan 2013–2015*, outlining ways to improve Sino-African cooperation. The Beijing Action Plan laid out the following: first, strengthening relations with the African Union and implementing supporting measures for regional integration and sustainable development through the African Union and the New Partnership for Africa's Development (NEPAD). Second, the plan emphasized the need to prioritize agriculture and food security in cooperation efforts through capacity building, technology transfer, foreign direct investment, and improved market access. Third, it established a China-Africa energy forum, and enhanced capacity for improving energy production and efficient resource use. Fourth, it called to strengthening of South-South cooperation to ensure that international commitments are met and adequately implemented to ensure advances in development. Addressing the 2012 Beijing Forum on China-Africa Cooperation Conference, United Nations Secretary-General Ban Ki-moon "emphasized that while North-South cooperation to advance development is necessary, South-South cooperation is important to complement these developments, citing Forum on China-Africa Cooperation as a successful example of South-South cooperation."[55]

THE 2015 JOHANNESBURG, SOUTH AFRICA FORUM ON CHINA-AFRICA COOPERATION SUMMIT

The Johannesburg, South Africa Summit and Ministerial Conference of the Forum on China-Africa Cooperation (FOCAC) was held from December 3 to 5, 2015.[56] Over 50 heads of state and government attended, including the Chairperson of the African Union Commission and the United Nations Secretary-General attended the opening ceremony of this Summit. The summit was cochaired by Chinese President Xi Jinping and South African President Jacob Zuma. The 2015 Johannesburg Forum on China-Africa Cooperation conference was held with China-Africa agreeing to upgrade the Ministerial session of the Forum on China-Africa Cooperation to a Summit level, with the intention of promoting the development of China-Africa relationship.

Under the theme, *China-Africa Progressing Together: Win-Win Cooperation for Common Development,* Johannesburg summit inspired the ideas and solutions to address current and emerging global challenges. The founding of the Forum on China-Africa Cooperation in 2000, as a triannual collective dialogue platform for cooperation between China and Africa, was seen as a signal of the dynamic and expanding nature of Sino-Africa relations.[57] Fifteen years later (after founding of the FOCAC), that signal has grown clearer and stronger and the significance of the 2015 Johannesburg Summit was an evidence to that fact.

The Johannesburg 2015, the Forum on China-Africa Cooperation helped enhance investor confidence in Africa from the international community and attracted more attention and greater input into the continent of Africa at a time of greater need for investment to create more jobs. It has been noted by many observers that the Forum on China-Africa Cooperation is an exemplary form of South-South cooperation, demonstrating the strengths of utilizing an incremental and practical approach to tackling development issues of mutual concern.[58]

Since launching its (Open Policy) open-up reform (over four decades ago), since 1978, the economic volume of the People's Republic of China has leapfrogged to second place in the world, with its industrialization

3 CHINA'S ECONOMIC ENGAGEMENT IN AFRICA   43

gradually reaching the mature stage and its sophisticated manufacturing capacities. The story of China's economic success in recent decades is something that is possible in many African countries and it is through platforms such as the Forum on China-Africa Cooperation that such aspirations can be pursued better. With the African continent's abundant natural resources, plentiful and cheap human labor, and large market potential, Africa is at the starting stage of industrialization, and China is willing and is the ideal partner in the process of industrialization of Africa.

As a way of fostering such partnership, the Forum on China-Africa Cooperation (FOCAC) Summit will help build consensus on China-Africa cooperation and align the Chinese development agenda with that of Africa. The thinking is that, through helping the sustainable development of Africa, China itself would realize better development; this is true and should be encouraged, as Africa would largely benefit from the advantage of Chinese equipment, technology, and finance. For instance, many African countries are undergoing a stage that China has only previously experienced and there is plenty of experience to share. For instance, while most of Africa is working tirelessly to achieve industrialization and modernization, China is undergoing structural economic adjustment for her transformation and upgrading of its industrialization. Therefore, the high degree of complementarity between China and Africa provides an important opportunity for the strategic alignment of the Sino-Africa development agenda. However, to take that complementarity to high levels, there is a need for more cooperation, including upgrading the existing common trade relations to industrial cooperation and technological transfer to help propel Africa's nascent manufacturing base, and thus:

> We also believe that through making full use of our political mutual trust and economic complementarity, we can turn our (Chinese-African) traditional friendship into a strong force to propel development and help turn the potential of African plentiful labor resources and abundant natural resources into strengths of economic development and fruitful outcomes benefitting not only African peoples but Chinese peoples as well.[59]

It should be noted that the 2015 Johannesburg (FOCAC) Summit emphasized the China-Africa cooperation in various fields, especially industrial and agricultural modernization cooperation, which are a top priority for most African countries. The Johannesburg summit also strengthened the solidarity between the developing countries at a time when the world is at the critical stage of big development, reform, and adjustment. With the rise of developing countries, China and Africa occupy a very critical position in that discourse, whereby China is the world's largest developing country and Africa the continent with the highest concentration of developing countries. Also considering that the total population of China and Africa is 2.5 billion (Africa 1.2 billion and China 1.3 billion)—accounting for one-third of the world population—the China-Africa partnership can therefore also be an alliance to safeguard the rights and interests of the developing countries to foster a more balanced international order. Therefore, these are all grounds upon which we can construct a stronger foundation for development cooperation and the Forum on China-Africa Cooperation Summit will reflect the solidarity among developing nations and show a new vision of common development to the world.[60]

The two sides (China and Africa) at the Johannesburg Summit reviewed with satisfaction the development of relations between China and Africa and applauded the positive contribution the Forum on China-Africa Cooperation had made over the past fifteen years since its inception in advancing the comprehensive and in-depth development of China-Africa relations, and agreed that FOCAC had become both a key platform for collective dialogue between China and African countries and an effective mechanism for practical cooperation.[61]

The two sides share the view that, as China works for the two Centenary Goals and as Africa implements African Union Agenda 2063[62] and its First Ten-Year Implementation Plan, the current development strategies of China and Africa are highly compatible. "The two sides shall make full use of their comparative advantages to transform and upgrade mutually beneficial cooperation focusing on better quality and higher efficiency to ensure the common prosperity of our peoples."[63]

The two sides are satisfied with the effective implementation of the Forum on China-Africa Cooperation *Beijing Action Plan*, 2013–2015, adopted at the 5th Ministerial Conference of FOCAC, and decided in the spirit of the Johannesburg Declaration of the 2015 Summit of the Forum on China-Africa Cooperation, to jointly establish and develop comprehensive and cooperative partnership between China and Africa, featuring political equality and mutual trust, economic cooperation for win-win results, exchange and mutual learning between Chinese and African civilizations, mutual assistance in security affairs, as well as solidarity and cooperation in international affairs.

To implement the outcomes of the Johannesburg 2015 FOCAC Summit and Ministerial Conference and chart the course of China-Africa friendly and mutually beneficial cooperation in all fields in the next three years under the theme of "China-Africa Progressing Together; win-win Cooperation for Common Development," the two sides jointly formulated and adopted with consensus this Action Plan with the following:

1. Political Cooperation and High-level Visits and Dialogue. The two sides will continue to encourage high-levels visits and dialogue to consolidate traditional friendship, enhance political mutual trust and deepen strategic consensus and coordination.
2. Consultation and Cooperation Mechanism. To enhance the planning and implementation of relations and cooperation between China and African countries, the two sides agreed to improve and encourage mechanisms such as bilateral joint commissions, strategic dialogue, foreign ministries' political consultations, and joint commissions on economic and trade cooperation.
3. The two sides will continue to strengthen the mechanism of regular political consultations between Chinese and African Foreign Ministers.
4. Exchanges between Legislatures, Consultative Bodies, Political Parties, and Local Governments.
5. The two sides will enhance exchanges and cooperation between the National People's Congress of China and African National Parliaments, Regional Parliaments, the Pan-African Parliament, and the African Parliamentary Union, to consolidate the traditional China-Africa friendship and promote mutually beneficial cooperation.[64]

In announcing the $60 billion for development projects in Africa over the next three years (2015–2018) at the 2015 Johannesburg, South Africa FOCAC Summit, President Xi Jinping called "for a lift in China-Africa relations to promote a mutually beneficial partnership. It is a familiar routine, since the Forum on China-Africa Cooperation began in 2000 with a summit held every three years, Chinese leaders have pledged funding and commitment to building a win, win relationship with the African continent."[65] Critics are saying trade ties between China and African countries mostly benefit Chinese Businesses and investors. There are obvious growing tensions between African workers and Chinese managers as well as between African and Chinese migrants.

There are claims that, because of growing grievances between African workers and the Chinese managers, Beijing has more than doubled its financing pledges to Africa since 2006. Many observers are wondering whether the pattern would continue, given China's slowing economy since the world-wide economic crisis of 2008.[66] The promised funds include zero interest loans as well as export credits and concessional loans to African countries. The pledge is another way that Beijing is making efforts to assuage African leaders that investment will continue. Consequently, at the 2015 Johannesburg Summit, President Xi Jinping promised Africa that "China would train 200,000 African technicians, bringing some of them to China, and that China and Africa share a common future. We Chinese and Africans have forged a profound friendship through our common historical experience and our common struggles."[67] President Xi Jinping went further, and highlighted China's difference with Western partners that "China supports the resolution of African issues by Africans in the African way."[68]

THE 2018 BEIJING FORUM ON CHINA-AFRICA COOPERATION SUMMIT

Chinese officials defined the September 3 to 4, 2018 Beijing Summit of the Forum on China-Africa Cooperation as the most important home diplomatic event of the year, held at the Great Wall Hall of the People; and 53 African countries were represented, leaving out only Swaziland, which still maintains diplomatic relations with Taiwan.[69] The Chairperson of the African Union Commission and United Nations Secretary-General Antonio Guterres attended the opening ceremony of the Summit.

At the September 2018 Beijing Forum on China-Africa Cooperation Summit and Ministerial Conference, President Xi Jinping pledged $60 billion in financing for projects in Africa in the form of assistance, investment, and loans, as China furthers its efforts to link the African continent's economic prospects to its own.[70] In his keynote address at the summit themed *Walk together towards prosperity*, President Xi Jinping illustrated the priority areas of China's engagement with Africa in the next years-2018–2021. In his speech, President Xi Jinping announced *Eight Actions Plan* to succeed his 2015 *Ten Cooperation Plans* at the Johannesburg Forum on China-Africa Cooperation Summit. He renewed another financing commitment of $60 billion to Africa, although the changing composition of the committed financing reflects key recalibration by China. President Xi Jinping in his keynote speech to the opening ceremony of the 2018 FOCAC Summit said: "China stands ready to strengthen comprehensive cooperation with the African countries to build a road of high-quality development that is suited to national conditions, inclusive, and beneficial to all."[71]

ONE BELT ONE ROAD INITIATIVE

Launched in 2013, China's One Belt One Road Initiative (OBORI) strives to improve infrastructure, trade, financial integration, and people-to-people bonds across more than 70 countries in Asia, Africa, and Europe. And its digital dimensions are far-reaching, including fiber optic cables, 5G networks, satellites, and devices that connect to these systems.[72] It is made up of a "*belt*" of overland corridors and a maritime "*road*" of shipping lanes. It has been referred to as the Chinese Marshal Plan, backed by the state, which is campaigning for its global dominance. This is a trillion-dollar plan that aims to connect more than 70 countries in Asia, Africa, and Europe, and account for half of the world's population and a quarter of the world's GDP.

However, there is ever-growing criticisms of China's One Belt One Road Initiative (OBORI) by the Western powers, and especially by the United States, "such as being neo-colonialism or a giant debt trap for the recipient countries, have raised doubts about the massive Chinese economic and infrastructure campaign, leading to the cancellation or down-sizing of major projects in Pakistan, Malaysia and Myanmar."[73] Thus, at this critical juncture, the Forum on China-Africa Cooperation serves as the key event to repair and restore China's tarnished reputation and recon-solidate its message. On this One Belt One Road Initiative and including China's economic engagement in Africa, African countries should and must demand total and complete transparency and accountability and not allow a new version of colonialism or neocolonialism.

STAGNATING FINANCIAL PLEDGE AND DECREASING CONCESSIONALITY

Traditionally, China had a pattern of doubling or tripling recent Forum on China-Africa Cooperation pledges: from $5 billion in 2006 to $10 billion in 2009, to $20 billion in 2012, and to $60 billion in 2015. Deviating from this pattern, China's financing pledge at the Beijing Summit of 2018 remains the same as in 2015, $60 billion. No one should expect China's financing pledges to continue to double or triple indefinitely, the stagnation of any growth indirectly reflects a cautious attitude on the part of China. However, this could be attributed to a few factors, such as including the negative impact of the trade war on the Chinese economy, the rising concern over its capital outflow, the continued growth of bad debt in China, as well as the domestic criticism of Beijing squandering taxpayers' money to buy foreign affinity; and the slowing down of its economy since 2016.[74]

The most noticeable change to Beijing's financing pledges lies in its composition. For instance, Judging by the language alone, the overall level of concessionality and preferentiality of the Chinese financing is decreasing. To begin with, the amount for grants, zero-interest loans, concessional loans, and credit lines have decreased from the $40 billion in the 2015 commitment to $35 billion. Concessional loans, which were combined with exports credits to reach $35 billion in 2015, are now put in the same category with grants and zero-interest loans in 2018. Although the total of these three items (grants and zero-interest loans, and concessional loans) reaches $15 billion, it remains a question whether the free grants and zero-interest loans will match the 2015 level of $15 billion. Although China still pledges $20 billion of credit lines, the credit is no longer specifically confined to or meant for the export credit as it was in 2015, and there is no mentioning of such credits being preferential. In addition, the specification from 2015 on the enhancement of the concessionality of the concessional loans is removed from China's pledges in 2018.[75] This could be the most indicative of China's heightened concerns about the returns and commercial viability of the Chinese financing.

Transforming from Loans to Investment

China is committed to set up a $10 billion special fund for development financing, reflecting China's changing model of financial engagement in Africa. Evolving away from the previous resources for infrastructure model, China has been increasingly keen on utilizing financing provided by Chinese development finance institutions, such as China Development Bank (CDB) and China-Africa Development Fund (CADF), to support Chinese companies' equity investment in Africa.

To diversify the pool of Chinese investors in Africa, Beijing has pledged "to encourage Chinese companies to make at least $10 billion of investment in Africa in the next three years (between 2018 and 2021)."[76] In the past, this was not included in China's Forum on China-Africa Cooperation commitments, illustrating a conscious push by the Chinese government for more Chinese companies, including private investors, to invest in Africa. The $10 billion is included in the $60 billion of support China pledged, but the specification is that such investment will be made by Chinese companies. And most likely, Chinese state financial institutions will encourage and induce such investment by contributing to or jointly funding such projects.

The new commitment to boost Chinese investment to Africa inadvertently reveals an inconvenient truth in China's economic engagement in Africa. Despite all the enthusiasm about China investing more in Africa, the actual volume of Chinese investment in Africa remains small, both in absolute terms and in comparison with other regions. For example, in 2017, China's foreign direct investment toward Africa was $3.1 billion, 2.5 percent of China's global foreign direct investment that year, the smallest among all continents. In comparison, Chinese Companies' acquisition in Latin America in 2017 alone was $18 billion. In terms of investment stock, Chinese investment in Latin America has surpassed $200 billion by the end of 2017, twice that of Chinese investment in Africa, which surpassed $100 billion by the end of 2017.[77]

The composition of Chinese financing also reveals another, perhaps deeper, inconvenient truth. Given that China pronounces that it has fulfilled its pledged of $60 billion of financing to Africa under the 2015 FOCAC commitment, including $5 billion for grants and zero-interest loans, and given the Chinese foreign direct investment to Africa in 2016 was $3.3 billion, and in 2017 $3.1 billion totaled $6.4 billion, what the number does manifest is that:

> Most of the Chinese financing to Africa are neither grants nor investment, but loans of various forms. However, China may not be the biggest creditor of Africa, but this serves to substantiate the wide-spread conviction that China is creating more debt for Africa, although the Chinese counterargument has been that the long-term economic capacity building effect of the Chinese loans significantly outweighs their downsides.[78]

The Beijing Summit of 2018 also includes a $5 billion special fund for financing Chinese imports from Africa. Indeed, in the *Trade Facilitation* action, China declares its decision to increase imports, particularly nonresource products from Africa. This has consistently been a claim by the Chinese government, but its ability to increase nonresource imports from Africa also depends on the region's ability to generate such products. Chinese official statistics no longer provide a detailed breakdown of categories of Chinese imports from Africa. However, the top African exporters to China are indeed resource-rich African nations, ranking down from South Africa to Angola, Zambia, Republic of Congo, and Democratic Republic of Congo (DRC) in 2017. If South Africa, China's biggest trading partner on the continent of Africa and the largest African exporter to China, could serve as an example, according to data from China's Ministry of Commerce, natural resources (mineral resources and base metals) together accounted for 86.2 percent of the South African's exports to China in 2017, up from the 83.7 percent in 2016.[79]

INFRASTRUCTURE AND TRANS-AFRICAN HIGHWAY NETWORK ROUTE

For years, business in Africa was hampered by poor transportation between countries and regions. Chinese-African Associations have worked toward ending this unproductive situation. China provides infrastructure funding and workforce in exchange for immediate preferential relations including lower resource prices or shares of African resources. As a secondary effect, this infrastructure allows Africa to increase her production and exports, improve the quality of life and enhance the condition of millions of Africans, who will one day become many millions of potential buyers of Chinese goods.

There has been an official plan for a Pan-African road network since 1971, with the United Nations Economic Commission for Africa envisioning significant boost to Continental trade. The Trans-African Highway is an ambitious network of nine highways traversing the continent for 60,000 kilometers. They include routes from Dakar to Cairo 8636 kilometers, Lagos to Mombasa 6260 kilometers and from Cape Town to Cairo 8860 kilometers (for details see Table 3.2). If these Trans-African Highway Network Routes are completed, the Chinese government, in line with its One Belt One Road Initiative, sees the potential and opportunity of 54 countries/markets, with more than one billion people and with more accessible consumers. China has helped complete 4500 kilometers through seven countries from Dakar, Senegal to N'Djamena in Chad.

Table 3.2 Trans-African highway network route

Countries	Distance
Tripoli-Windhoek	9610 km
Cairo-Gaborone-Cape Town	8860 km
Cairo-Dakar	8636 km
Lagos-Mombasa	6260 km
Dakar-Lagos	4760 km
Algiers-Lagos	4504 km
Dakar-N'Djamena-(complete)	4500 km
N'Djamena-Djibouti	4220 km
Beira, Mozambique-Lobito, Angola	3520 km

Source: United Nations Economic Commission for Africa. www.uneca.com

The idea that African countries and cities should be connected with better transportation networks, particularly by road and rail, is one of Pan-African vision of independence struggle. This idea has roots in colonialists' vision for connecting the territories they ruled. For instance, in the early twentieth century, the racist colonial leader of the former Rhodesia—Cecil Rhodes envisioned a railroad from the Cape in South Africa to Cairo in Egypt.[80] Governments, multilateral organizations, and development agencies, financing officials are usually clear about the huge economic potential that could be unlocked by getting Africa better connected across her often-arbitrary colonial-era borders. However, doing this is easier said than done among a continent of 54 countries spread across a land mass that could take in China, India, the United States of America mainland and the whole of Western Europe.[81]

According to Cobus Van Staden of the South African Institute of International Affairs; "African development hinges on a maddening paradox: Its greatest asset-the sheer size and diversity of its landscape is also the greatest barrier to its development on the possibility of an East-West transport link Africa. The difficulty of moving goods weighs down trade on the continent. And it also curtails most of the benefits of international trade."[82] The cost of transportation and poor infrastructure also is on average of fifty percent to 175 percent more than in many parts of the world due to poor infrastructure also means the impact of years of trade liberalization and tariff reductions has been significantly limited by the cost of moving goods within African countries and between the neighboring cities. The high cost of moving goods from or to ports affects the benefits of free and lower-tariff trade.

Many analysts are rightly concerned about African governments' rising debt to China, a topic that was topmost in the minds of many African leaders when Chinese President Xi Jinping visited four countries in Africa in July 2018. These concerns are weighed against the potential economic return of better infrastructure, rather than whether these network highways fulfill the long-held Pan-African dream. As a sign of commitment to help in financing the part of Trans-African Highways, President Xi Jinping signed up Senegal as the first West African country to be part of the Chinese One Belt One Road Initiative.[83] Before President Xi Jinping's visit to Senegal in July 2018, the Chinese focus has been on Africa's East Coast, as strategically important for China's transporting of goods. Thus, Senegalese Minister for Chinese Affairs, Ibrahim Diong, said to CNBC that; "his country's Western location is great for exports, and for any Chinese companies that would like to export to the United States, you cannot get better than Senegal."[84]

There is still a long way to go for the diversification of African exports to China. Judging from the volume and composition of China's 2018 Forum on China-Africa Cooperation Summit and financial pledges to Africa, China's commitment remains strong, but appears to be more cautious and calculating than its pledges from the past summit. The concessional side of Chinese financing is being moderated, while China has grown visibly more focused on the commercial and viability aspects. From the traditional model of resources for infrastructure, China appears to be morphing toward the next stage; equity investment by a more diverse group of investors supported by state development finance. Meanwhile, Africa still has major catching up to do to attract more Chinese investment and to diversify its trade relations with China.

Notes

1. President Jiang Zemin, Speech to the African Union, Addis Ababa, Ethiopia, May 13, 1996, *China Africa*, 66 June 1996, p. 24.
2. Martin Jacques, When China Rules the World: The End of the Western World and the Birth of a New Global Order, New York, NY: Penguin books, 2012. Also see Philippe Le Corre and Jonathan D. Pollack, *China's Global Rise: Can the EU and U.S. Pursue a Coordinated Strategy?* Washington, DC: Brookings Institution, October 2016.
3. China-Africa Trade Relations, Euroasian Times. Retrieved August 3, 2018.

4. Now the People's Republic of China faces a growing shortage of raw materials such as oil, wood, copper, and aluminum, all of which are needed to support its economic expansion and the production of manufactured goods, International Monetary Fund (IMF), http://www.imf.org/external/pubs/ft/weo/2011/01/weodata/weorept.aspx. Retrieved August 3, 2018.
5. Thomas Pakenham, *The Scramble for Africa: White Man's Conquest of the Dark Continent From 1876 to 1912.* New York; NY: Avon Books, 1991, pp. 239–255. Also see The United Nations, Department of Economic and Social Affairs, New York, NY: Population Division, June 6, 2012.
6. Irene Yuan Sun, *The Next Factory of the World: How Chinese Investment is Reshaping Africa,* Boston, MA: Harvard Business Review Press, 2017. Also see Kasahun Woldemariam, *The Chinese Eldorado and the Prospects for African Development,* Trenton, NJ: Africa World Press, 2016.
7. Chris Alden, Daniel Large, and Ricardo Soares De Oliveira, Editors, *China Returns to Africa: A Rising Power and a Continent Embrace,* London: Hurst & Company, 2008.
   Https://www.statssa.gov.za/PublicationsHTML/PO302200/html/P03022007.html. pp. 109–110. Retrieved August 7, 2018, pp.111–112.
8. The CIA World Fact-Book 2010, Central Intelligence Agency (CIA), New York, NY: Skyhorse Publishing, 2009, pp. 143–145. https://www.statssa.gov.za/PublicationsHTML/PO302200/html/P03022007.html. pp. 109–110. Retrieved August 7, 2018.
9. Chris Alden, Daniel Large, and Ricardo Soares De Oliveira, Editors, *China Returns to Africa: A Rising Power and a Continent Embrace,* London: Hurst & Company, 2008. https://www.statssa.gov.za/PublicationsHTML/PO302200/html/P03022007.html. pp. 109–110. Retrieved August 7, 2018, pp.111–112.
10. Li Lanqing, Breaking Through: The Birth of China's Opening-up Policy, New York, NY: Oxford University Press, 2009.
11. Ibid.
12. Parag Khanna, *The Future is Asian:* Commerce, Conflict, and Culture in the 21st Century. New York: Simon & Schuster, 2019.
13. Li Lanqing, Breaking Through: The Birth of China's Opening-up Policy, New York, NY: Oxford University Press, 2009.
14. Irene Yuan Sun, *The Next Factory of the World: How Chinese Investment is Reshaping Africa,* Boston, MA: Harvard Business Review Press, 2017.
15. Philippe Le Corre and Jonathan D. Pollack, *China's Global Rise: Can the EU and U.S. Pursue a Coordinated Strategy?* Washington, DC: Brookings Institution, October 2016.
16. Edwin Madunagu, "China's Return to Africa," *The Guardian,* Lagos, December 14, 2006.

17. "China-Africa Relations: A win win Strategy," *African Business*, London, March 2007, p. 4.
18. Chris McGreal, "Hu Jintao Starts Africa Tour with Loans Promise," *Guardian News*. London, January 31, 2007.
19. Graig Timberg, "Hu Jintao Defends China's Role in Africa," *The Washington Post*, February 8, 2007.
20. Ernest, J. Wilson III, *China's Role in the World: Is China A Responsible Stakeholder in Africa?* The U.S.-China Economic and Security Review Commission; Center for International Development and Conflict Management, University of Maryland, College Park, MD: August 3–4, 2006, p. 10. https://www.uscc.gov/hearings/2006hearings/written_testimonies/06_08_3_4_wilson_ernest_statement.pdf) (PDF). U.S. Congress.
21. Kingsley Ighobor, "China in the Heart of Africa," *Africa Renewal Magazine*, New York, NY: United Nations, January 2013, https://www.un.org/africarenewal/magazine/january-2013/china-heart-africa. Retrieved August 8, 2018.
22. Ernest, J. Wilson III, *China's Role in8, 2018 the World: Is China A Responsible Stakeholder in Africa?* The U.S.-China Economic and Security Review Commission; Center for International Development and Conflict Management, University of Maryland, College Park, MD: August 3–4, 2006, p. 10. https://www.uscc.gov/hearings/2006hearings/written_testimonies/06_08_3_4_wilson_ernest_statement.pdf) (PDF). U.S. Congress.
23. Lafargue, Francois, "China's Presence in Africa," *China Perspective*, https://chinaperspectives.revues.org/document519.html. Retrieved August 8, 2018.
24. Sam Piranty, "Seven surprising numbers from China-Africa Trade," BBC World News, Africa, December 5, 2015, https://www.bbc.com/news/world-africa-35007900, Retrieved August 8, 2018.
25. Thomas R. Yager; Omayra Bermudez-Lugo; Philip M. Mobbs; Harold R. Newman; David R. Wilburn, "The Mineral Industries of Africa," *U.S. Geological Survey: Introduction*, Mineral Yearbook, 2005.
26. "China and Africa Trade," https://www.joc.com/global-trade/china-africa-trade-booms. Retrieved August 9, 2018.
27. Ibid.
28. China EximBank: Introduction, https://www.english.eximbank.gov/cn/profile/introduction.jsp. Retrieved August 9, 2018.
29. China EximBank: Introduction, https://www.english.eximbank.gov/cn/profile/introduction.jsp. Retrieved August 9, 2018.
30. Ibid.
31. BBC NEWS, "China Banks Lend More Than World Bank, Report," January 18, 2011. https://www.bbc.co.uk/news/world-asia-pacific-12212936. Retrieved August 9, 2018.
32. Ibid.

3 CHINA'S ECONOMIC ENGAGEMENT IN AFRICA   55

33. Michael, Serge; Beuret, Michael; Wood, Paolo, *La Chinafrique: Pékin a la conquête du continent noir*, Grasset & Fasquelle, 2008, p. 316.
34. Ibid.
35. Martin Bailey, "Tanzania and China," *African Affairs*, Volume 74, No. 294, January 1975, p. 39.
36. Ibid.
37. Media Reports, "TAZARA: How the Great Uhuru Railway was Built." Embassy of the People's Republic of China in Tanzania, Dar-es-Salaam. Also see Tanzania-Zambia Railroad Authority. *Ten Years of TAZARA Operations Review Perspective*, Dar-es-Salaam Head Office, 1986.
38. "Death of Mr. Rhodes." *The Times*, London: March 27, 1902, p. 7. Also see Anthony Thomas, Rhodes: *The Race for Africa*, London: Bridge, 1927.
39. David H. Shinn and Joshua Eisenman, *China and Africa: A Century of Engagement*. Philadelphia, PA: University of Pennsylvania Press, 2012, p. 69.
40. Hilal K. Sued, Embassy of the People's Republic of China in the United Republic of Tanzania, "TAZARA: How the Great Uhuru Railway was Built," *The African*, April 7, 2012.
41. Ibid.
42. Yu, Donghai, "Why the Chinese Sponsored the TAZARA: An Investigation About the People's Republic of China's African Policy in the Regional Context, 1955–1970," University of Buffalo, State University of New York, Tonawanda, New York, 1970.
43. Nick Van Mead, "China in Africa: Win-Win Development, or A New Colonialism?" *The Guardian*, September 28, 2018. www.theguardian.com.
44. Kate Louw, *International Institute of Development Studies*, Cape Town: July 2012.
45. "The 1st Ministerial Conference," *Xinhua News*, October 26, 2006, p. 1. www.xinhuanet.com, www.xinhuanews.com.
46. Ibid.
47. Osamu Kawakami, "China Rivalry Marks TICAD IV/ Government Seeks African Support on Climate Change, United Nations Security Council Membership," Daily Yomiuri, May 2008.
48. Ibid.
49. Zhou Yan, "China-African Development Fund to Boost Footprint in Africa," *China Daily*, May 28, 2010. https://www.chinadaily.com.cn/bizchina/2010-05/28/content_9903203.htm. Retrieved September 1, 2018.
50. https://www.news.xinhuanet.com/english/2009-10/27/content_12341880.htm. Retrieved September 1, 2018.
51. Barney Jopson and Jamil Anderlini, "China Pledges $10 billion in low-cost loans to Africa," *The Washington Post*, November 9, 2009.

56 O. ABEGUNRIN AND C. MANYERUKE

52. "Full Text of Wen Jiabao's Speech at 4th Ministerial Conference of Forum on China-Africa Cooperation (FOCAC)-China.org.cn." https://www.china.org.cn/world/2009-11/09/content_18849890htm. Retrieved September 1, 2018.
53. Ibid.
54. Ibid.
55. Kate Louw, "Ministers Adopted Beijing Action Plan for 2013–2015," July 31, 2012.
56. Peterson Tumwebaze, "Johannesburg Summit of FOCAC 2015 Will Deepen Sino-African Cooperation," *The New Times*, Johannesburg, November 28, 2015.
57. Ibid.
58. Ibid.
59. Ibid.
60. Ibid.
61. The Forum on China-Africa Cooperation Johannesburg Action Plan, Beijing, 2016–2018.
62. African Union Agenda 2063 is a strategic framework for the socioeconomic transformation of the African continent over the next 50 years. It builds on and seeks to accelerate the implementation of past and existing continental initiatives for growth and sustainable development.
63. Peterson Tumwebaze, "Johannesburg Summit of FOCAC 2015 Will Deepen Sino-African Cooperation," *The New Times*, Johannesburg, November 28, 2015.
64. Ibid.
65. Lily Kuo, "China's Xi Jinping Pledges $60 billion to Help Africa Solve Its Problems Its Own Way," *Quartz Weekly*, December 4, 2015.
66. Ibid.
67. Ibid.
68. Ibid.
69. Yun Sun, "China's 2018 Financial Commitments to Africa: Adjustment and Recalibration," *Africa in Focus*, September 5, 2018.
70. "China Raises Fears of New Colonialism with $60 billion Investment Across Africa," *The Telegraph*, London, September 3, 2018.
71. Yao Dawei, "China Supports Africa Building Belt and Road," *Xinhua*, September 3, 2018. www.xinhuanet.com.
72. China's Digital Silk Road. Csis.org/events/china's-digital-silk-road. Retrieved February 5, 2019.
73. Ibid.
74. Ibid.
75. See the speech of President xi Jinping in pledging the $60 billion at the 2018 Forum on China-Africa Cooperation (FOCAC).

76. Yun Sun, "China's 2018 Financial Commitments to Africa: Adjustment and Recalibration," *Africa in Focus,* September 5, 2018.
77. Ibid.
78. Ibid.
79. Ibid.
80. "Death of Mr. Rhodes," *The Times,* London: March 27, 1902, p. 7. Also see Anthony Thomas, *Rhodes: The Race for Africa,* London, Bridge, 1997.
81. Fischetti, "Observations: Africa is Way Bigger Than You Think," Africa is Bigger Than China, India, the Contiguous United States and most of Europe-combined, *Scientific American, A Division of Nature America,* Inc., 2018.
82. Cobus Van Staden, "The Possibility of an East-West Transport Link in Africa," *South African Institute of International Affairs,* Johannesburg, July 31, 2018. Also see Mark Fischetti, "Observations: Africa is Way Bigger Than You Think," Africa is Bigger Than China, India, the Contiguous United States and most of Europe-combined, *Scientific American, A Division of Nature America,* Inc., 2018.
83. Yinka Adegoke, "African Countries Know They Need Better Road Networks but Not Know How to Pay for Them," *Quartz Africa Weekly Brief,* July 31, 2018.
84. Ibid.

CHAPTER 4

China and Resource (Oil) Diplomacy in Africa

INTRODUCTION

Africa is the second largest continent in the world, with 30 million square kilometers (11.6 million miles) of land, population 1.2 billion, and contains a vast quantity of natural resources. This trait, together with the continent's relatively low population density and small manufacturing sector, has made Africa a key target for Chinese imports. Africa ranks first or second in abundance globally, for the following minerals—bauxite, cobalt, diamonds, phosphate rocks, platinum group metals, coltan, vermiculite, and zirconium.[1] And many other minerals are also present in large quantities, such as gold, copper, coal, petroleum, et cetera. This chapter offers an overview of the Sino-African oil relationship to provide a foundation for future analyses.

Many African countries are mostly dependent on exports of minerals. Mineral fuels such as coal and petroleum account for more than ninety percent of export earnings for Algeria, Equatorial Guinea, Libya, and Nigeria.[2] Various minerals account for eighty percent for Botswana, in order of value led by diamonds, copper, nickel, soda ash, and gold; Congo, diamonds, petroleum, cobalt, and copper; Gabon, petroleum and manganese; Guinea, bauxite, alumina, gold, and diamonds; Sierra Leone, diamonds; and Sudan, petroleum and gold. Minerals and mineral fuels and gold accounted for more than fifty percent of the export earnings of Mali; Mauritania, iron ore; Mozambique, aluminum; Namibia, diamonds,

© The Author(s) 2020
O. Abegunrin, C. Manyeruke, *China's Power in Africa*,
Politics and Development of Contemporary China,
https://doi.org/10.1007/978-3-030-21994-9_4

59

uranium, gold and zinc; and Zambia, copper and cobalt.[3] China's ongoing mining projects of more than $1 billion are taking place in South Africa, platinum and gold; in Guinea bauxite and aluminum; in Madagascar nickel; in Mozambique coal; in Congo and Zambia cobalt and copper; in Nigeria and Sudan crude petroleum; and in Senegal iron ore.

CHINA'S GROWING ENERGY NEEDS

Since the mid-1950s and 1980s, China has expanded its relations with Africa as part of its broader strategy of developing friendly relations with the developing world. In recent years, China has achieved deeper and closer ties with many African countries, and the issue of Chinese energy security and geopolitics in Africa has received more attention. China's pursuit of energy resources had generated great interest in the last decade, and energy concerns are indeed a vital national security interest for China to sustain both economic growth and economic development.[4]

According to the International Energy Agency (IEA), for the month of July 2010, China surpassed the United States as the world's largest energy consumer.[5] Analysts say that, for China, energy security is crucial for its economic health and directly relates to the legitimacy and survival of the Communist Party. China's push to secure energy resources and raw materials is part of its energy security diversification strategy, which is also evidenced in other regions such as the Middle East, Latin America, and Central Asia. Oil is only one component of the energy resource picture, though an increasingly important one. China remains dependent on fossil fuels such as coal, oil, and natural gas; China's oil consumption made up just twenty percent of China's total energy use.

China is currently the second-largest consumer of oil in the world next to the United States, and more than half of its crude oil is imported. By 2020, official sources estimate that China will import about sixty-five percent of its crude oil. China does not produce enough oil domestically, though, in 1993, China became a net importer of oil and has since increased its dependency on foreign import. According to the International Energy Agency (IEA), China was the second largest net oil importer in the world in 2009; and official statistics also record China's oil imports at 204 million tons in 2009, and crude oil accounting for fifty-two percent of China's oil consumption.[6]

Major African Sources of Oil for China

China's presence in Africa to secure oil resources has been increasing. However, it is important to contextualize these relationships and overestimate China's oil demands. For example,

1. China still produces much of the oil it consumes.
2. China imports most of its oil from the Middle East, from Saudi Arabia, Iran, and Iraq, and from, Africa, as well as Asia (Russia), Latin America (Brazil and Venezuela), and North America (Canada).
3. Africa reportedly only accounts for nine percent to ten percent of global oil reserves.
4. China imports an estimated one-third of its oil from Africa, mostly from Angola, Sudan, Republic of Congo, Equatorial Guinea, and Nigeria (see Table 4.1).[7]
   For China, the Middle East remains the most important source for oil. While Chinese oil imports from the Middle East are projected to increase in the future, China also seeks to reduce its dependence on the Middle Eastern oil. While African countries are neither the top oil producers nor the top oil-exporting countries in the world, there are opportunities for future expansion and production. In discussing Sino-Africa relations, there is a tendency to consider the African continent as one entity. While we can make broader observations about China's relations with Africa, there is also much diversity and complexity in the many countries with which China has oil relationships. Table 4.1 shows some of the important points in contextualizing the China-Africa oil relationship.

While a country may have large oil reserves, they may not be developed, or internal conflict may prevent stability of development and production, for example, South Sudan. While the presence of Chinese National Oil Companies (CNOCS) is expanding in Africa overall, it should be considered relative to Western presence and not overestimate their influence. It would be an overstatement to say that Chinese oil companies would supplant Western presence in the near-term. Oil is one component of China's growing reach into Africa. Other resource extraction includes copper from Zambia, cobalt from the Democratic Republic of Congo (DRC), and Iron from Liberia.

Table 4.1 Major African sources of oil for China

Country	OPEC members	Oil resources	Oil exported to China	Major deals and partnerships
Angola	Yes	Largest source of oil in Africa (about eighty percent) Largest crude oil exporter in Africa in 2009 *Largest Investors* ChevronTexaco & ExxonMobil (United States) BP (UK), Total (France)	Largest African Oil provider to China	2004: $2 billion loans and aid 2005: Nine agreements signed, including long-term oil supply
Sudan	No	Oil Export account for ninety percent of country's total Revenue *Largest Investor* China National Petroleum Company (entered 1996). U.S. companies not allowed to invest	Second largest oil provider to China (sixty percent of its oil goes to China)	1997–2007: Interest free loans for building construction 2008: $2.8 billion humanitarian aid package
Republic of Congo (Congo Brazzaville)	No	*Largest Investor* Total (France) and Eni (Italy). Around 20 U.S. companies including Chevron and Murphy Oil	China is largest importer of Dar Blend (High-acid crude oil) Third Largest Oil provider to China (around fifty percent of its oil goes to China)	2006: Cooperation to build airport and infrastructure 2010: Chinese Development Bank to help create SEZs
Equatorial Guinea	No	Oil accounts for over eighty percent of total Revenue *Largest Investors* ExxonMobil, Hess and Marathon (U.S)	Around twelve percent of its oil exports go to China	2009: China gained exploration and drilling Rights in this country
Nigeria	Yes	Second largest Oil Reserves in Africa: Oil accounts for over ninety percent of country's export, and eighty percent of total Revenue *Largest Investors* Royal Dutch Shell (British/Dutch) ChevronTexaco, ExxonMobil (United States), Agip (Italy), Total (France)	Small amount of oil export to China (in 2009, 28,000 barrels per day)	2006: $4 billion in oil and infrastructure projects in exchange for drilling licenses 2010: $23 billion to build oil Refineries and infrastructure

Source: Shelly Zhao, "The Geopolitics of China-African Oil," April 13, 2011. China Briefing, https://www.china-briefing.com/news/2011/04/13/the-geopolitics-of-china-africa-oil.html

The Sino-African oil relationship can become complex due to other linked areas of concern. Oil, as part of China's desire to acquire more natural resources, has brought criticism of China's neocolonialist presence in Africa, and questions whether China's presence benefits governance and the African people. Some of the related areas of interest include:

Foreign Aid: Chinese aid to developing countries can be attractive because of their no-strings attached conditions in contrast with aid from Western countries or institutions such as the World Bank. The tied aid from Western lenders may involve economic, political, social, or environmental penalties, as well as other strings such as democracy promotion and human rights concerns. Chinese loan policies also tend to be less transparent and easier for recipients to use.

Infrastructure: Linked with aid, China's infrastructure projects in Africa can involve concessional or low-interest loans as well as direct financing. In addition, China can promote economic projects in areas in Africa deemed too risky or unfeasible by other governments or multinational corporations.

Table 4.1 provides information on the five African countries that are China's largest sources of oil in Africa, and Table 4.2 shows other African sources of oil for China. Except for Sudan, Western oil companies are the largest players, as shown in these two tables. In these cases, oil relationships point to comprehensive arrangements that involve trade and infrastructure, as well as oil extraction and export.

Africa produced about 10.7 million barrels of oil per day in 2005, which is twelve percent of the 84 million barrels per day produced world-wide.[8] About one half of that is produced in North Africa, which has Preferential trade agreements with Europe.[9] The Sub-Saharan African countries' oil producers include by global rank and produce millions of barrels per day. Nigeria, ranked 13th world producer, produces 2.35 million barrels per day; Angola, ranked 16th, produces 1.91 million barrels per day; Sudan, ranked 31st, produces 0.47 million barrels per day; Guinea, ranked 33rd, Congo ranked 38th, and Chad ranked 45th also have notable output.[10]

In 2005, thirty-five percent of exported African oil went to the European Union, thirty-two percent to the United States and ten percent to China, while one percent of African gas goes to other Asian countries.[11] North African countries were preferentially exporting their oil to Western countries—European Union sixty-four percent, the United States eighteen percent, and all others eighteen percent[12]; and sixty percent of African wood goes to China, from where it is manufactured

64 O. ABEGUNRIN AND C. MANYERUKE

Table 4.2 Other African sources of oil for China

Country	OPEC members	Oil resources and Chinese involvement
Gabon	No	Oil export account for about half of total revenue in Gabon: eighty-one percent of exports and forty-three percent of GDP. Gabon signed oil deals with China in 2004 for drilling and exploration project worth $7 billion, $9 billion in 2009
Algeria	No	Algeria has significant oil and gas Resources, a reported 10 billion barrels of oil. China's reach into Algeria has involved infrastructure and oil exploration projects. CNPC signed a $31 million oil and gas contract with Algeria in 2003, found a major reserve in 2007, and plans to begin oil production
Libya	No	Libya has the largest oil reserves in Africa and significant oil production, though they have yet to be fully explored. Oil account for ninety-five percent of export Revenue and twenty-five percent GDP. There are numerous foreign companies in Libya, including Eni (Italy), Statoil (Norway), Repsol (Spain), Total (France), and China's National Petroleum Corporation (CNPC). However, as of March–April 2011, oil production has been disrupted given the conflict and the eventual assassination of the Libyan Leader Moammar Gaddafi in October 2011
Liberia	No	Liberia has possible oil reserves and has signed a three-year deal with Chevron (United States) for oil exploration. China's focus is on Liberia's Iron Ore reserves; China's aid projects with Liberia, including a $10 million agreement of debt cancelation and a $25 million agreement for various development projects
Chad	No	Chad oil industry is still nascent. Chad signed an oil pipeline agreement with the World Bank, ExxonMobil, and other oil companies in 2000, but the World Bank canceled this deal in 2008. Sino-Chadian relations improved after Chad established diplomatic relations with China in 2006. China has hoped to gain greater footing in Chad and has supported a controversial pipeline project in Chad
Kenya	Nos	Kenya signed a multi-billion dollar deal on transport infrastructure with China in return for oil, in 2009. However, it remains to be seen whether Kenya will house lucrative oil resources. In 2010, CNOOC halted oil exploration in Kenya

Source: Shelly Zhao, "The Geopolitics of China-African Oil," April 13, 2011. China Briefing, https://www.china-briefing.com/news/2011/04/13/the-geopolitics-of-china-africa-oil.html

and sold across the world. It should be noted here that in 2007 with good Chinese diplomatic relations and African recent growth, African countries provided 30 percent of China's oil needs, with Sudan's oil accounting for ten percent of these.[13]

CHINESE OIL COMPANIES IN AFRICA

Chinese oil companies are gaining the invaluable experience of working in African nations, which will prepare them for larger projects on the far more competitive world market. The efficiency of Chinese assistance, loans, and proposals has generally been praised. Finally, Chinese industry has found in Africa a budding market for its low-cost manufactured goods. Chinese diaspora in Africa has been actively supported by Chinese embassies, continuously building the *Blood Brother* relations between China and Africa as perceived victims of Western imperialism.[14] The modern Chinese version is that the European mercantilism in the so-called age of discovery (in fact it was the age of exploitation-plundering of African resources by the Europeans)[15] aggressively ended Sino-Africa relations. This point of view enforces the rhetoric of the blood brother relations between China and Africa.

African leaders earn legitimacy through Chinese partnerships. They work together with the Chinese to provide Africa with key structural infrastructure such as roads, railways, ports, hydroelectric dams, and refineries, fundamentals which will help Africa avoid the *resource curse*. Success in this endeavor means avoiding the exploitation of their natural wealth and the beginning of fundamental social and economic transformations on the continent.

African countries partnering with China today are signing with a future world superpower. In Africa, this hope shows African elites an example of success which they may take as exemplars—Chinese alliance provides strong psychological consequences. It provides economic prospects of their own future. Harry Broadman pointed out that "if Chinese investments in key sectors of infrastructure, such as in telecommunication, manufacturing, foods, and textiles radically alter the African continent, the main change would have taken place in African minds."[16] With the recent growth and economic improvement, more Africans students are returning to Africa after studies abroad to bring their skills and industry home.

Sharing technology with the former Soviet Union through the mid-1960s and internal reserves such as the Daqing oil field, the People's Republic of China became oil sufficient in 1963.[17] However, Chinese technology and the United States led embargo isolated the Chinese oil industry from 1950 to 1970, preventing their evolution into powerful multinational companies. Chinese oil exports peaked in 1985, but the rapid post-communist economic reforms and an internal increase in oil demand brought China into an oil deficit, becoming a net oil importer in 1993, and a net crude importer in 1996,[18] a trend which is accelerating.[19] Indeed, Chinese reserves, such as the Trim Basin, have proven both difficult to extract and difficult to transport toward Chinese coastal provinces where energy demand is centered. Pipeline construction, as well as processing facilities, lags demand.[20]

Through the end of the twentieth century, China has been working to establish long-term energy security. Achieving this goal has required investment in oil and gas fields abroad, diversifying energy resource providers, and incorporating nontraditional energy sources like nuclear, solar, and other renewable resources. However, the rapid overseas activities by China's energy companies had been driven by the needs of both government and the People's Republic of China's National Oil Companies (NOC), which have worked in an uncommonly close partnership to increase overseas production of oil and gas.[21] Together, they gained access to projects of strategic importance in African nations like Angola, Sudan, and Nigeria in the 1990s, while leaving smaller opportunities to the companies alone.[22]

Chinese actions in these areas have not always been successful. For instance, the 2006 agreement in Rwanda proved unproductive, while Guinean oil technologies were not familiar to Chinese Companies. The expansion has also been limited: altogether, Chinese oil companies produced 257,000 barrels per day in Africa in 2005, just one third of what ExxonMobil alone produced, and just two percent of Africa's total oil reserves.[23] Moreover, China's arrival on the world oil scene has been perturbing for established players. China has been attacked for its increasingly close relationship with rogue states, such as Sudan and Angola, countries known for their human rights abuses, political censorship, and widespread corruption. China's world image has suffered from critiques, leading the nation to move to a more diplomatic approach, avoiding crisis areas, such as Niger Delta in Nigeria.[24] Nevertheless, as a consumer country and budding powerhouse, China has little choice in choosing its source of supply.[25]

Chinese access to international oil markets has satisfied the country's immediate thirst. But despite its large coal-based energy system, China is a key part of the vicious cycle which had led to increasing oil prices worldwide, and to the disadvantage of all industrialized and oil-importing countries, including China itself, but China made a forty percent consummation increase.[26] In 2006, China imported forty-seven percent of its total oil consumption (145 million tons of crude oil, up 14.5 percent).[27] With such high demand, Chinese companies such as State Grid and China National Petroleum (Sinopec), China National Petroleum Company (CNPC), and China National Offshore Oil Corporation (CNOOC) have looked to Africa for oil.

CHINA'S OIL CONSUMPTION

The total worldwide oil consumption is 93 million barrels per day according to the International Energy Agency (IEA). The United States is the largest oil consumer in the world with 19,880,000 barrels per day as of 2017, followed by China as the second largest oil consumer with 13,226,000 barrels per day as of 2017.[28] In 2010, world energy consumption of refined products increased 3.8 percent; which was the first increase since 2004. According to Enerdata, this trend was supported by fast-growing demand for road and air transport, particularly in developing countries. In China, demand for refined products surged by twelve percent due to increasing needs. Asia accounted for more than forty percent of the overall increase in consumption.[29] With China projected to account for twenty-five percent of global energy consumption by 2035; Beijing's investment in Africa is unsurprisingly motivated by resource extraction. For example, in 2016, China was the largest investor in Africa, making up thirty-nine percent of global investment inflows.[30] The three major countries in China's investments in African oil are Angola, Nigeria, and Sudan.

CHINA'S INVESTMENT IN ANGOLAN OIL

The recent Sino-Angolan association is illustrative. When a petroleum-rich country like Angola called for investment and rebuilding, China advanced a $5 billion loan to be repaid in oil. They sent Chinese technicians, fixing a large part of the electrical system, and leading a part of the reconstruction. In the short-term Angola benefits from Chinese built roads, hospitals, schools, hotels, football stadiums, shopping centers and telecommunication projects. In turn, Angola mortgaged future oil production of a valuable, nonrenewable resource. It turned out to be a costly trade for Angola, but their needs for infrastructure were immediate and that was precisely what China provided when no one else was willing to do so. Thus, Angola has become China's leading energy supplier.[31] China also plans to establish five special economic zones in Africa—East, West, North, South, and central zones—where "the Chinese government will create the enabling environment into which Chinese companies can follow."[32]

However, China remained the top destination of Angolan goods and services, and particularly oil in the second and third quarters of 2017, accounting for 52.6 percent of Angolan exports, as reported by the Angolan National Statistics Institute (NSI). In terms of oil exports, Angola overtook Russia as China's biggest oil supplier from September 2016, exporting 1.02 million barrels per day to the Asian country, up 45.8 percent.[33] It should be noted that Sinopec owns fifty percent of Angola BP-operated Greater Plutonio Project in Angola.[34]

CHINA'S INVESTMENT IN NIGERIAN OIL

However, "most, if not all, of Africa's oil-producing nations have been beset at different times by insecurity, corruption or all-out civil war,"[35] said John Prendergast, Senior Adviser at the International Crisis Group in Washington D.C., an organization that is working to prevent conflicts around the world. Adding to the supply uncertainties, the United States faces new competition for oil from an energy-hungry China to feed its economy. In January 2006, China's state-run-National Offshore Oil Corporation (CNOOC) oil firm paid $2.3 billion for forty-five percent stake in Nigeria's offshore oil.[36] In addition to investments in oil and agriculture, China secured a $311 million contract with the Nigerian government in 2004 to build and launch a communications satellite known as NIGCOMSAT-1. Thus, on May 14, 2007, the Chinese-manufactured communications satellite was launched into orbit on behalf of Nigeria. The satellite will provide communications services over Africa and parts of the Middle East and Southern Europe. A Chinese state-owned Aerospace Company, Great Wall Industry Corporation (GWIC), will monitor the satellite from a ground station in northwestern China. It will also train Nigerian engineers to operate a tracking station and manage the satellite from a control station in Nigeria.[37]

During President Buhari's visit to China to attend the Beijing Summit of the Forum on China-Africa Cooperation (FOCAC) held September 3 to 4, 2018, he secured a loan agreement of $328 million with Chinese Exim Bank. This loan amount of $328 million is to finance the National Information and Communication Technology Infrastructure Backbone Phase II (NICTIB II) project. The concessional loan agreement between Galaxy Backbone Limited and Huawei Technologies Limited (HUAWEI) was signed by Nigeria's Minister of Finance, Kemi Adeosun, and the Chinese Director-General, International Development Agency, Wang Xiaotoa, in the presence of President Buhari and President Xi Jinping in Beijing.[38]

Nigeria and China also signed a Memorandum of Understanding for One Belt One Road Initiative (OBORI). The One Belt One Road Initiative of President Xi Jinping focuses on improving connectivity and cooperation among over 70 countries spread across the continents of Asia, Africa, and Europe.[39] President Buhari spoke about the growing relationship between both countries, and thanked China for accepting to support the international efforts to recharge lake Chad. President Buhari said; "The inclusion of Lake Chad project in the Forum on China-Africa Cooperation (FOCAC) Action Plan 2019 to 2021 will go a long way in supporting our efforts to rehabilitate and resettle the conflict-impacted North East region of Nigeria."[40] Before meeting Chinese President Xi Jinping, President Buhari met with Nigerian students and entrepreneurs in China, as well as Chinese students who were learning Nigerian languages.

In addition, Nigeria and China signed currency swap agreements. This agreement will allow Nigerians to use Nigerian Naira (currency) to buy and pay for Chinese goods. President Buhari said; "Another measure that will improve our trade volumes will be to introduce import duty waivers on Nigeria's commodity exports to China. Today, our commodities such as sesame seeds, hibiscus, and cassava amongst others attract import duty in China."[41] And in terms of security and Nigeria's fight against terrorism and the progress that has been made so far, President Xi Jinping "promised China's support in capacity building and intelligence sharing and pledged 50 million Chinese Yuan in support to Nigeria's military."[42]

China's Investment in Sudanese Oil

In 1997, China National Petroleum Company's (CNPC) Great Wall Drilling company agreed to buy a forty percent stake in the $1.7 billion "Greater Nile Petroleum Operating Company (GNPOC), contract renewed and expanded in 2000. China National Petroleum Company owns most of a field in south Darfur and forty-one percent of a field in Melut Basin producing 300,000 barrels per day in 2006; and State Grid and China National Petroleum (Sinopec) is erecting a pipeline, building a tanker terminal in Port-Sudan.[43] Most important, the continuing strife in Sudan's western region of Darfur threatens large-scale Chinese investment in Darfur Region of Sudan. For instance, sixty percent of Sudan's oil output goes to China, and since the 1990s, China has invested $15 billion, mainly in oil infrastructure.[44] Thus, China National Petroleum Company (CNPC) is the largest investor in Sudanese oil industry.

China's Energy/Oil Investments in Africa

Overseas investment offers China an opportunity to not just bolster its own economy but also leverage its economic strength to increase its influence abroad. Driven in part by Beijing's *going global strategy* that encourages investment in foreign markets, Chinese companies have actively expanded their overseas footprint in recent years and explored investment opportunities in a range of sectors.

Chinese investment in Africa fluctuated considerably between 2006 and 2017. There was a small downturn between 2009 and 2010, caused by the global financial crisis, and a spike to $22 billion in 2013. During the 12-year span 2005–2017, West Africa received 28.6 percent of Chinese investment in the African continent, followed by Central Africa with 25.3 percent, and most of these investments are in oil.[45]

According to the 2018 United Nations Conference on Trade and Development (UNCTAD) Investment Report, China held the third largest Foreign Direct Investment stock in Africa in 2016 at $53 billion; if including Hong Kong, behind the United States at $57 billion, the United Kingdom at $55 billion, and France at $49 billion. This is a dramatic improvement from 2011, when China's investment stock in Africa was only $16 billion, placing it at the same level as Singapore and India.[46]

Notably, global investment flows into Africa fell from $59.4 billion in 2016 to $42 billion in 2017. Southern Africa was particularly affected by this drop, with a sixty-six percent decline in investment in 2017. Investment in the African continent from China was no exception. Its input into the continent fell across the board, dropping from the peak of $8.12 billion investment in 2016 to $980 million in 2017. China's Foreign Direct Investment into Central Africa experienced the largest decline, with a year-on-year decrease from $5.04 billion to $250 million.

The International Monetary Fund (IMF) has classified twenty African countries as resource-rich, with energy and mineral resources comprising large portions of their respective exports. With China projected to account for twenty-five percent of global energy consumption by 2035, Beijing's investment in Africa is unsurprisingly motivated by resource extraction. For example, in 2016, China was the largest investor in Africa, making up thirty-nine percent of global investment inflows.[47]

Of the total $83.01 billion China invested in Africa between 2005 and 2017, 40.3 percent of it was invested in metals and 33.4 percent into energy. The Democratic Republic of Congo, South Africa, Nigeria, Egypt,

4 CHINA AND RESOURCE (OIL) DIPLOMACY IN AFRICA

Table 4.3 China foreign direct investment top destinations in Africa 2005–2017

Country	Volume in billion dollars$	Global ranking	Economic development level
Democratic Republic of Congo (DRC)	11.74	26	Lower Middle-income
South Africa	10.83	20	Upper Middle-income
Nigeria	7.64	30	Low Income
Egypt	5.39	38	Lower Middle-income
Niger	5.18	39	Low-income

Source: China Power Team, "Does China Dominate Global Investment?" *China Power*, July 19, 2018. https://chinapower.csis.org/china-foreign-direct-investment

and Niger were the five largest recipients of these investments, making up 49.1 percent of China's total regional Foreign Direct Investment (see Table 4.3). Natural resource contracts made up four out of five largest investment deals—$4.9 and $4.21 billion deals in Niger and Mozambique in 2008 and 2013 by China National Petroleum Company (CNPC); respectively, a $3.1 billion deal in Egypt in 2013 signed by (Sinopec), and a $2.7 billion deal in Tanzania signed by Sichuan Hanlong in 2015.[48]

China's investment in Africa has grown dramatically in comparison to other investor countries. As detailed in the 2018 World Investment Report, China invested a total of $45.1 billion in greenfield projects between 2016 and 2017, a jump of nearly $40 billion from the total between 2013 and 2014. Comparatively, China's investment also surpassed that of the European Union at $34.57 billion and the United States at $7.54 billion over the 2016–2017 period. China's greenfield investments suggest that Chinese companies are diversifying their interests in Africa, as there has been a marked increase in manufacturing projects and construction contracts. The number of private investment projects in Africa registered with the Chinese government increased from 52 in 2005 to 923 in 2012.[49]

In addition to direct investments, China has emerged as one of the world's largest providers of development finance. In order to learn more about the nature of China's developmental assistance, it is important to examine the goals which China seeks to attain. China's development assistance is critical to furthering Beijing's interests, and a considerable portion of China's Exim Bank (Chexim's) operations entail the financing of Chinese projects across Africa. From 2000 to 2014, China funded 2390 projects in Africa. Combined, these projects totaled $121.6 billion and made up 34.3 percent of China's total development finance over that period. Roughly ninety-four percent of this financing was loaned by China's Exim Bank (Chexim), with countries like Angola, Ethiopia, Nigeria, and Sudan having consistently received infrastructure loans since 1994. And by comparison, the total amount of aid offered by the United States to Africa between 2000 and 2014 was roughly $100 billion.[50]

Some Chinese investments are partially funded through infrastructure-for-loan arrangements. In these transactions, Chinese companies offer loans for resource-development projects to prospective African partners in exchange for resources. China has loaned almost $60 billion dollars to Angola since the two countries established diplomatic relations in 1983; much of this debt is serviced with oil. China has also pursued similar financing schemes with Ethiopia, Eritrea, and Tanzania for sugar cane, gold, and iron ore.[51] China needs African resources and particularly oil and this will continue for a long time in this twenty-first century.

NOTES

1. Thomas T. Yager, Omayra Bermudez-Lugo, Philip M. Mobbs, Harold R. Newman, and David R. Wilburn, "The Mineral Industries of Africa," *U.S. Geological Survey. Minerals Year Book*, 2005, p. 1.1.
2. Ibid., p. 1.7.
3. Ibid., p. 1.6.
4. Shelly Zhao, "The Geopolitics of China-African Oil," https://www.china-briefing.com. Retrieved September 13, 2018.
5. Ibid.
6. Ibid.
7. Ibid.
8. *The CIA World Fact-Book 2012*, Oil Exporters, Central Intelligence Agency (CIA), Way back Machine May 12, 2012. https://web.archive.org/web/20120512233445/https://www.cia.gov/library/publications/the-world-factbook/rankorder/2173.html. Retrieved August 13, 2018.
9. Thomas T. Yager, Omayra Bermudez-Lugo, Philip M. Mobbs, Harold R. Newman, and David R. Wilburn, "The Mineral Industries of Africa," *U.S. Geological Survey. Minerals Year Book*, 2005, p. 1.7
10. *The CIA World Fact-Book 2012*, Oil Exporters, Central Intelligence Agency (CIA), Way back Machine May 12, 2012, op. cit.
11. Thomas T. Yager, Omayra Bermudez-Lugo, Philip M. Mobbs, Harold R. Newman, and David R. Wilburn, "The Mineral Industries of Africa," *U.S. Geological Survey. Minerals Year Book*, 2005, p. 1.7.
12. Ibid.

13. Michael Serge, and Monod Fabrice, *Drapeau Rouge sur le Continent Noir, Red Flag on Black Africa*, https://wiki.france5.fr/index.php/DRAPEAU_ROUGE_SUR_LE_CONTINENT_NOIR. France5.fr/A7Media. 52min.; LCApdf: quotes (https://www.lesyeuxrouges.info/archieves/297.html). Retrieved August 13, 2018.
14. Drew Thompson, "Beijing's Participation in United Nations Peacekeeping Operations," *Jamestown Foundation China Brief,* Volume 5, no. 11, pp. 1–4; Information Services, A Division of CBIS, pp. 1–4.
15. For details on neocolonialism and imperialism and exploitation of African resources see Walter Rodney, *How Europe Under-Developed Africa*, Washington, DC: Howard University Press, 1994. Also see Kwame Nkrumah, *Neo-Colonialism: The Last Stage of Imperialism.* New York: International Publishers, 1965.
16. Zha Daojiong, "China's Energy Security and its International Relations," *The China and Eurasia Forum Quarterly, 3 (3)*, November 2005, pp. 39–40.
17. Ibid.
18. Ibid.
19. Ibid., p. 41.
20. Robert Priddle, *China's Worldwide Quest for Energy Security*, The International Energy Agency, Washington, DC: 2000, p. 80.
21. Philip Andrew-Speed, Xin, The Overseas Activities of China's National Oil Companies: Rationale and Outlook, Mineral and Energy – Raw Materials Report, March 2006, pp. 17–30, https://www.worldcat.org/issn/14041040500504343, Retrieved August 12, 2018.
22. Ibid.
23. Africa-China Trade, Special Report, *Financial Times*, January 24, 2008, p. 6.
24. Ibid.
25. Zha Daojiong, "China's Energy Security and its International Relations," *The China and Eurasia Forum Quarterly, 3 (3)*, November 2005, pp. 39–40.
26. Ibid., pp. 44–45.
27. China's Oil Imports Set New Record, *Business Week*, May 22, 2011. Also see China's 2006 Crude Oil Imports 145 million tons, up 14.5 percent.
28. https://web.archive.org/web/20110321034717/http://www.enerdata.net/enerdatauk. Retrieved August 15, 2018.
29. Energy Statistics, https://yearbook.enerdata.net. Retrieved August 15, 2018.
30. The Economist Intelligence Unit, *China Power Project*, "China Going Global Investment Index 2017," 2017.
31. APG-BBC News, China in Angola. https://news.bbc.co.uk/2/shared/sp1hi/picture_gallery/07/africa_china_in_angola/html/1.stm. Retrieved August 9, 2018.

32. Africa-China Trade, Special Report, *Financial Times*, January 24, 2008, p. 31.
33. Tsvetana Paraskova, "Angola was China's Largest Foreign Crude Supplier in September 2017," *Toil Price.com The Number 1 Source for Oil and Energy News*, October 24, 2016.
34. Andrea E. Goldstein, Nicolas Pinaud, and Helmult Reisen, *The rise of China and India: What's in it for Africa?* Organization for Economic Co-operation and Development (OECD), Development Center, 2006, pp. 81–83.
35. Rob Crilly, "Oil from Africa Comes with Political Instability," *USA TODAY*, May 1, 2006.
36. *Nigeria Today Online*, "China Seals $2.3 billion Nigerian Oil Deal," January 10, 2006.
37. Emeka Anuforo, "Nigeria Launches Satellite," *The Guardian*, Lagos, May 13, 2007.
38. Eromosele Ebhomele, "As Buhari Arrives Beijing, Nigeria and China Signs $328 million ICT Deal." September 10, 2018. Also see www.Naija.ng.
39. Nigerian Channels Television, "Buhari Seeks China's Support for Mambila Power Project," September 5, 2018.
40. Ibid.
41. Ibid.
42. Ibid.
43. Andrea E. Goldstein, Nicolas Pinaud, and Helmult Reisen, *The rise of China and India: What's in it for Africa?* Organization for Economic Co-operation and Development (OECD), Development Center, 2006, pp. 81–83.
44. Chris Alden, editor, *China in Africa*, London: International African Institute, Royal African Society, Zed Books, 2007, pp. 11–12.
45. Center for Strategic and International Studies China Power Project, Washington, DC, and United Nations Conference on Trade and Development (UNCTAD). https://unctad.org/en/pages/DIAE/FDI/20Statistics/FDI-Statistics.aspx. Retrieved August 15, 2018.
46. Ibid.
47. The Economist Intelligence Unit, *China Power Project*, "China Going Global Investment Index 2017," 2017.
48. Ibid.
49. Ibid.
50. United Nations Conference on Trade and Development (UNCTAD). https://unctad.org/en/pages/DIAE/FDI/20Statistics/FDI-Statistics. aspx. Retrieved August 15, 2018.
51. Ibid. Also see James Zhan et al. "World Investment Report 2018." *United Nations Conference on Trade and Development*, June 2018.

CHAPTER 5

China's Involvement in Southern African Liberation Struggles

INTRODUCTION

Despite the considerable distance between China and Southern Africa, China was still able to play a critical and sometimes overlooked role in Africa's liberation war struggles. When looking at Southern Africa today, it is almost impossible to ignore China's involvement in the various liberation struggles that occurred decades ago. The rubble which represented the remnants of the fierce fighting between the liberation movements and the colonialist may have been replaced by more modern infrastructure, and the excitement and euphoria that swept through the region at the realization of a free Southern Africa may have faded, but China's mark on the region is still visible to this day and its contribution to the fight for freedom in these African nations cannot be overlooked. It has become common knowledge that China had a hand to play in the liberation struggles in Southern Africa and the African continent at large. China was heavily involved from the very birth of the various liberation movements and the subsequent struggle that ensued within the region that aimed to end white oppression in Zimbabwe, Mozambique, and South Africa. It is important to discuss China's involvement and the impact this had on the outcome of the various liberation struggles. One cannot dispute that without struggle, Africa would not have been liberated and one needs to look closely at the nature of the relationship between China and the liberation movements in Southern Africa. One also needs to pay some level of

© The Author(s) 2020   75
O. Abegunrin, C. Manyeruke, *China's Power in Africa*,
Politics and Development of Contemporary China,
https://doi.org/10.1007/978-3-030-21994-9_5

attention to the forms of support that China provided. China's involvement in Southern Africa's liberation struggle came in the form of China acting as a benefactor to many of the liberation war movements. China provided military, ideological, and financial support to the various Liberation Movements that had aligned themselves to Beijing. However, it is important to highlight that China was not the only nation outside Africa that assisted the liberation war struggles. Russia also played a fierce role through supporting various movements such as ZANU in Zimbabwe and the ANC in South Africa. It has been said that China made the decision to support liberation movements that were not aligned to the Soviet Union to spite the USSR and fight some form of proxy war with the USSR on the African continent through these liberation movements.

This chapter will therefore discuss the form of support that was given to liberation struggles, which include military support, financial aid, and ideological training support. There are factors which came into play when determining the amount and quality of support. For example, the China-Moscow tensions affected the amount of support. It is said that ZANU PF got more support than PAC in their quest for freedom. PAC was largely perceived as ineffective, so China also supported FRELIMO and its breakaway faction, COREMO during the liberation struggle in Mozambique. Beijing supported the Zimbabwe African National Union Patriotic Front (ZANU PF) over Nkomo's Zimbabwe African People's Union, which was supported by Russia. ZANU PF received military training in China. They were provided with material and moral support. They got welfare support such as medical supplies, clothes, food, and various forms of logistical support. This chapter will also discuss the reasons why China chose to support the liberation organizations in Southern Africa.

Concepts, Context, and Theoretical Considerations

A few concepts and arguments have been associated with the topic of liberation struggles in African nations. China's involvement in Africa can be explained from the realist perspective in International Relations. The realist theory most suitably explains China's political standpoint towards Africa. China's involvement fits well within the political realism argument as postulated by Morgenthau. According to Hans Morgenthau, "the main aim of states within the international system is the pursuit of their mutual interests, defined in terms of power."[1] Therefore, getting involved in Africa's liberation struggle was an opportunity for China to present itself as a world power capable of making a contribution that could make a difference in global politics. Assisting liberation movements was one such means of achieving this new status for China, which shared a similar history with most of these colonized nations in the developing world. Zhao notes that "China's external behaviour and foreign policy in this case was interpreted as a response to the changing dynamics in the international environment."[2] More so, the state of the China-USSR relations played a part on both China and the USSR's involvement in Southern Africa. The Cold War also contributed to China and the USSR's involvement in these liberation struggles. However, one should be wary in noting that the Cold War is not the only major reason for the involvement of outside forces in Southern Africa's liberation efforts. Shubin asserts that, the decision to be involved was seen as part of the world *anti-imperialist struggle*, which was waged by the 'socialist community', 'the national liberation movements', and the 'working class of the capitalist countries'.[3] With regard to the Cold War and the part it played in all this, it must be noted that this global struggle was not viewed by many as a battle between the 'superpowers' assisted by their 'satellites" and "proxies" but was, rather, a united fight of the world's progressive forces against imperialism. Hence, the East-West confrontation was undeniably not the only reason for the China and the USSR's involvement in Southern Africa. Shubin further notes that "assistance to nationalists from socialist countries, first and foremost the Soviet Union, then China was a natural reply to their appeal for such help."[4]

On the other hand, the aspect of emancipation from foreign and oppressive rulers was a central and a major driving force of liberation movements. October is of the view that "freedom for the oppressed African nations could only be achieved through the transference of power from the colonisers to a kind of a people's power."[5] Britz points out that "liberation movements have been regarded as a form of social movement that aims to achieve some sort of radical social change through the use of revolutionary tactics and rhetoric so as to attain their objectives."[6] In a bid to come up with an all-inclusive definition of national liberation movements, Clapham states that "liberation movements are the struggle to set free, people and territories from oppressive regimes, be it oligarchy, domestic dictatorships or colonialists."[7] This broader understanding of liberation movements is essential to understanding the liberation struggles waged in Southern Africa, as it allows movements in South Africa to be included, as they are at times often excluded when discussing national liberation movements for the simple reason that the apartheid regime is not regarded universally as a colonial regime.

When looking at liberation struggles within the region, one cannot help but notice that there was a shared perception amongst the liberation movements of a people that were not free and were oppressed by another group of individuals.[8] Wallerstein states that "there are two distinct concepts that are advanced by liberation movements, namely: liberation and nation."[9] In Southern Africa, the tactics that were widely used by such movements include guerrilla warfare, insurrection, and a revolutionary seizure of power. All this was aimed at a social transformation that would result in a people's power. October points out that "for liberation movements to occur, there had to be formation of a mass organisation based on social solidarities and mobilisation of a popular following by the oppressed groups/individuals all aimed at seizing power from the oppressors in order to enable a rule by the people (majority rule)."[10] Although liberation movements often found themselves in different contexts, their aim remained largely the same with focus placed on ensuring the rule of the people, putting an end to oppression, and creating an environment of equality. For countries like Zimbabwe and Mozambique, the idea was to change completely the form of white minority oppressive government and introduce a kind of black majority rule. For South Africa, it was a little different, as the liberation movements there particularly aimed at achieving some form of racial equality. Southall notes that "in the case of Zimbabwe and Mozambique, they waged wars of liberation so as to free their nations from the clutches of oppression at the hands of their respective colonial masters, whereas when looking at South Africa it was more of a struggle for racial equality rather than a struggle for national independence from a colonial power."[11] Liberation movements in Zimbabwe and Mozambique advocated for total black majority rule, whereas the movements in South Africa were focused more on the principle of *one person, one vote* and social equality.

China's Involvement with Africa's Liberation Movements in a Historical Perspective

The relationship between China and African states in modern times has evolved over the last 70 or so years. These relations were conceived during the quest for African nations to attain independence and for China to end the dominance of the West and the Soviet Union. The first official encounter between China and the African nations was at the (Afro-Asian Conference) Bandung conference in Indonesia in April 1955. Botha notes

5 CHINA'S INVOLVEMENT IN SOUTHERN AFRICAN LIBERATION STRUGGLES 79

that the aim of the conference was to promote Afro-Asian solidarity anchored in the belief that the political and economic challenges of states on both continents were not far apart but were similar in more ways than one.[12] This belief, coupled with the events of the Cold War, encouraged China to increase its role within the international system, and hence China began a campaign to present itself as a leader amongst this group of developing world nations.[13]

China's involvement can further be understood along the lines of the process of decolonization in Africa, which presented a golden opportunity for China to play a role in Africa through supporting African liberation and independence. Roy asserts that through this support of liberation movements, China aimed at depriving the capitalist colonial powers of their colonies that were vital to their flourishing economies.[14] As a result, almost, all the different liberation movements in Africa benefited at some point from China's support in terms of food, finances, arms, medical supplies, and military training.

China's involvement with liberation movements in Africa was more pronounced in the period 1949 to 1979, where China was associated with many liberation and independence struggle movements across Africa. This involvement included efforts that largely comprised ideological and political considerations. Relations between China and African states made significant steps toward being more defined and developed around the 1950s. According to de Looy, prior to that time, China did not see Africa as important, but from the 1950s onward, China became embroiled in a quest to gain political allies and be internationally recognized as a major power with the aim of fortifying international alliances against the revisionist Soviet Union and Capitalist West interests.[15]

China and Southern Africa's Liberation Movements

Since the Soviet Union, which at some point had been China's ally had turned into its major political rival—United States in the late 1950s and the 1960s, China made efforts to spread its influence in other regions to counter both the USSR and the United States of America.[16] Matambo notes that China felt that the only way to be recognized as a powerful nation that could rival the Soviet Union and discredit the United States at the same time was to align itself with the global south. In this way, China would be the de facto spokesperson of the marginalized developing world.[17] Wasserman reports that, with that as its driving force, China strongly aimed at supporting revolutions through the barrel of the gun and hence played a major role in Southern Africa's liberation struggles, mostly as a reliable ally and supplier of weapons to colonized African states, amongst them Zimbabwe, Mozambique, Angola, Namibia, and South Africa.[18] On the other hand, because African nations were driven by a dire and desperate need for powerful allies to aid them in overthrowing the imperialists' regimes, it became natural that China would be involved in Southern Africa's liberation struggles. Consequently, a relationship was carved out of this situation with potential mutual benefits which these countries, almost worlds apart, found themselves in. Since Southern African states were amongst the last to be freed from the jaws of colonialism and looking at China's history and struggles with Western nations, it became prudent that China would provide a lending hand to emancipate Southern African nations from colonialism.

China's common history and an equally shared perception of white dominance by the West became one of the major forces that compelled it to get involved in the liberation struggles in Southern Africa. China was more than generous in lending a hand to African nations that sought independence from colonial rule and provided them with economic, technical, and military support, with the aim of curtailing the Western powers' dominance. Silence Masiya highlighted that China's involvement in liberation war struggles in Southern Africa was premised on its communist philosophy of waging a *people's war*, and this essentially took off in Southern Africa.[19] It can be said that China was instrumental and enjoyed considerable success in exporting the flame of the revolution to Southern Africa. China's involvement can also be explained by its approach, which was anchored in a policy of supporting any revolutionary movement that aimed at overthrowing any form of colonial rule that was either feudal or authoritarian and was not based on majority rule. China felt obligated to act and began a quest to assist those countries on the African continent that were still under colonial rule in the last half of the twentieth century to liberate themselves. The reason for this timing has been noted by some scholars as the fact that it is in the latter half of the twentieth century that China had managed to consolidate its revolution.

After the establishment of the Organisation of African Unity (OAU), now African Union in 1963, the United Republic of Tanzania, which had gained its independence in 1961, became the seat of the OAU Liberation Coordination Committee,[20] tasked with obtaining material support and training for Southern African countries seeking liberation from Western imperialist rule. China used its strong ties with the United Republic of Tanzania to provide support to the OAU Liberation Coordination Committee and this support lasted for well over 30 years, until the fall of the apartheid regime in South Africa in 1994. During this period, it has been argued that it is when China played its single most important role in Africa in the twentieth century. China's involvement came through support in the form of arms and military training for the freedom fighters.

CASE STUDIES

China and the Liberation Struggle in Zimbabwe

The People's Republic of China was established in 1949, at a time when there was a subsequent rise of national liberation movements in Asia, Africa, and Latin America. This created an international context that led to the comradeship between Zimbabwe and China, who both had common interests in fighting for national liberation.[21] China played a pivotal role in assisting several African nations such as Zimbabwe attain their independence from colonial rule. Chingono is of the view that China's relationship with Zimbabwe has received widespread attention because it has been regarded by many as a special one.[22] This relationship dates back to the 1960s and 1970s during Zimbabwe's liberation war struggle. Since the Zimbabwe African Peoples Union (ZAPU), the first liberation struggle movement was at the time being supported by the Soviet Union, who belonged to the "revisionist communist" doctrine at the time, China opted to support the Zimbabwe African National Union (ZANU). Alao states that China's support for ZANU in the liberation war struggle enabled a new Zimbabwe to have a take-off advantage upon independence.[23] Alao further argues that China's role in Zimbabwe's liberation war was instrumental in establishing friendship between the two countries, particularly in the early 2000s, when China became fondly known as *Zimbabwe's all-weather friend.*[24]

Forms of Support Provided to Zimbabwe's Liberation Struggle by China
China's assistance to Zimbabwe's liberation war struggle largely came through as military assistance, in the form of military hardware provided to the Zimbabwe National Liberation Army (ZANLA), which was ZANU's military wing. Extensive military training was provided to the ZANLA guerrillas, which saw several ZANLA soldiers receive training in

China to advance ZANLA's insurgency against the enemy. China supported Zimbabwe in the early 1960s by providing unconditional military support at the time. In 1963, the first group of five ZANU recruits received training in military science in China for six months. The second group, which had received some basic training in Ghana in 1964, received some advanced training as instructors in China in 1965. In 1966, the Nanjing Academy in Beijing hosted and trained a group of eleven fighters led by Josiah Tongogara in mass mobilization, strategy, and tactics.[25] This group later returned to Tanzania that year. This is where Tongogara, ZANLA's commander at the time, learnt of the importance of mobilizing the people, an important lesson which proved vital in shaping the future strategy of ZANLA. Chezi Vincent noted that "it is important to highlight that it is not only the ZANLA fighters that travelled to China for training, but the Chinese government also sent instructors to Africa, particularly to Tanzania at ZANLA's Intumbi Camp in 1969."[26] Abiodun Alao states that China sent Comrade Li, an infantry expert to assist in shaping ZANLA's new fighting strategy.[27] It is at Intumbi under Comrade Li that the fighters learnt the meaning of a people's war, a people's army, the objectives of the war, and the basic teachings of Chairman Mao on guerrilla warfare. By 1969, the Chinese already had about 20 instructors at Mgagao who had the sole purpose of instilling the right philosophy in the minds of the recruits. Their teachings were based on the belief that the decisive factor was not the weapons, as one would assume, but rather the people. Zimbabwe's attempts at attaining independence were also given financial backing by the Chinese. Through this, it can be said that the nature and extent of the support that Zimbabwe received from the Chinese was strongly rooted on ideological solidarity that culminated in the above-mentioned forms of assistance rendered by China.

China's Involvement with ZANU

After the breakout of the Zimbabwean (Rhodesian) Bush War in 1965, China made the choice to support ZANU, which had been formed in 1963 out of ZAPU. ZAPU had been, for a considerable amount of time, the major liberation movement that had been fighting against the Rhodesian government with the aid of the USSR. Ernest Takura pointed out that "China unveiled military and strategic support to ZANU after the liberation movement's numerous requests for assistance had been rebuffed by the Soviet Union on a number of occasions."[28] As a result, it has been argued that China gave ZANU all the means through which it was able to

5 CHINA'S INVOLVEMENT IN SOUTHERN AFRICAN LIBERATION STRUGGLES 83

prosecute its struggle. According to John Chirime "China provided training for ZANU's military wing (ZANLA) which emphasized on discipline as well as *nzira dzemasoja*, which was the way of the revolutionary fighter based on Mao's doctrine."[29] Strategic assistance, which was instrumental in transforming ZANLA' military strategy from conventional military tactics into the Maoist model, was also provided.[30] This approach was centered on mass mobilization of the population for it to be effective. Through China's involvement, ZANU was able to turn the war of liberation into a *people's war*. ZANU's victory in the 1980 elections that resulted in an independent Zimbabwe has been attributed to the support offered by China during the liberation struggle to some extent. This support undoubtedly gave some form of advantage to ZANU over other liberation movements, particularly ZAPU. Since the USSR's support of ZAPU fuelled rivalry between the two major liberation movements in Zimbabwe, ZANU and ZAPU, the victory by ZANU was the triumph of the Maoist doctrine of military insurgency over the doctrine of guerrilla warfare, which belonged to Russia.[31]

It should be noted that China's support for ZANU was not only to the benefit of the liberation movement but it also worked immensely to China's advantage as well through giving China the means to propagate its anti-Soviet campaign in Southern Africa. Chun believes "support for ZANU was a vehicle by which Beijing's anti-Sovietism could be pursued in Africa and also for ZANU, the China-USSR split presented an opportunity to maximise its gains in its struggle with ZAPU."[32] The war in Zimbabwe thus became more of a proxy war for China and the Union of Soviet Socialist Republics (USSR).

China and the Fight Against Apartheid in South Africa

China aligned itself with South African liberation movements whose agenda was to put an end to apartheid, especially after the rest of the world had condemned this kind of system as oppressive. This was one of the means China used to fight minority rule and colonialism. At the outset, the South African liberation movements did not favor China and aligned themselves with the USSR instead. In South Africa, China took an approach of aligning itself and supporting any liberation movement that had weak or no ties at all with the USSR. Initially China gave its support to the Pan Africanist Congress (PAC), which was described as a radical organization that had emerged and severed ties with the ANC. The desire to counter Soviet influence in the anti-apartheid era was one of the major reasons why China chose to support the PAC, since the Soviets were already sponsoring the ANC. According to Matambo, China's support of the PAC has also been attributed to utter desperation on the part of PAC, hence it was more than willing to allow China to train its members both politically and militarily.[33] Grimm et al. have pointed out that Beijing's choice to support the PAC can also be explained in terms of the alliance that had been built between the USSR and the ANC, which in turn precluded any ANC-China relations.[34] In the 1950s and 1960s, South African Communist Party (SACP) and ANC officials including Vela Pillay, Yusuf Dadoo, and Walter Sisulu had made visits to China to forge some form of alliance, but these visits failed to yield any meaningful results due to the SACP and ANC's ties with Moscow. Alden and Wu suggest that, at some point, the Chinese even extended a hand and offered some Umkhonto Wesizwe members military training, but this failed to materialize due to the divisions within international socialist movement, particularly the Sino-Soviet dispute, which led to China severing all ties with the SACP.[35] However, in 1982 party-to-party relations were to some degree restored, which allowed China to provide limited financial assistance to the SACP, which set the tone for China's entry into South Africa's main stream struggle against apartheid.[36]

China and the African National Congress (ANC)
In the 1960s, China had initially made promises to the SACP, since the SACP had been the first component of the congress alliance to make the decision after consultations with Mao Zedong to embark on an armed struggle against apartheid.[37] As a result, China managed to provide secret training to senior ANC office holders that even some of the officials in the ANC were not aware of. Alden and Wu postulate that this shows how the ANC had originally been close to China earlier on in the 1950s, but ultimately sided with the Soviets during the Sino-Soviet dispute.[38] The ANC-SACP linkage circumscribed China's involvement in the fight against apartheid in South Africa, and support from the USSR prevented Beijing from having a closer and more defined involvement. Throughout the greater part of South Africa's struggle against apartheid, China's relations with the ANC were hampered by the rift between China and the USSR. Consequently, the Chinese Communist Party managed to maintain strong ties with the PAC. The relationship between China and the ANC seemed to move in a positive trajectory after Oliver Tambo's visit to

China in 1975 and a subsequent meeting between the two parties in Lusaka in 1982. By the mid-1980s, China had succeeded in creating a bond with the ANC, the major movement fighting apartheid in South Africa at the time. Sino-ANC relations further improved after Moscow decided to make a shift in focus to other areas such as its preoccupation with Afghanistan, the events in Poland, events in the Middle East, and the arms race with Washington. This meant that Moscow diverted its attention from Southern Africa and all its troubles and started encouraging the ANC to form coalitions with other liberation movements to ease its burden. It has been argued that by this, Moscow was increasingly becoming reluctant to bear all the costs of liberation movements in Southern Africa. This therefore paved the way for Sino-ANC relations to improve tremendously. After 1983, China made a proclamation to treat all liberation movements in Southern Africa equally and without discrimination. Taylor believes the result was that PAC lost its strong grip on Beijing and China became more drawn to the ANC, the larger and more organized grouping. China now had come to believe that no solution was possible without the ANC.[39] However, even at this point, China's involvement remained one which was rhetorical and symbolic, and China in fact was even more content to play this somewhat inactive role in the actual struggle.

China's Involvement with the Pan Africanist Congress PAC of South Africa

Of interest to note is the fact that, the PAC mostly turned to China because they desperately needed money and even though the OAU helped, it was hardly enough. One of the earliest known significant involvements of China and the PAC was when a seven-member delegation disguised as a "study delegation" from the PAC made a visit to China in October 1964, but, in fact, the actual reason for the visit was military training. Another visit followed in 1967 and then in 1976. The training that was acquired during these visits was said to have had a profound bearing on the PAC in general. Houston et al. note that the structure of the Azanian People's Liberation Army, PAC's military wing, was influenced and based on that of the Chinese People's Liberation Army (PLA).[40] The APLA members that received military training in China were also provided with ideological training. They were trained to carry out revolutionary propaganda and mobilization work amongst the people together with attacks on the enemy. This enabled APLA to elevate its training and ideology, which were essential components of its warfare. More so, the military tactics employed by

APLA were based on the principles of China's revolutionary struggle which emphasized "schematic acceleration of operations."[41] Its operations encompassed raids, which allowed APLA operatives to obtain a supply of arms and ammunition. This had the effect of enhancing the confidence of APLA soldiers. Cadres that were trained in China during the 1970s were also given cultural, political training and lectures on the Chinese revolution and on the work of the CCP. Knowledge was further provided on how to establish an underground and guerrilla army, the use of light and medium weapons, how to make homemade explosives and regimental drill. There was also training in martial arts and some theoretical training that was provided by Chinese trainers at training camps in Tanzania.[42] Taylor notes that the PAC received $10,000 when its secretary general, Potlake Leballo visited Beijing in 1964.[43] It has, however, been argued that the international support which the PAC received in the form of military training, arms, and ammunition was insignificant as compared to the support that the ANC obtained from the USSR. The support given to the PAC by the Chinese has been criticized as lacking strategic direction and PAC's military camps failed to reach the level of development of the main camps used by the ANC.

The Clandestine Relationship Between China and the Apartheid Government

More controversy has been noted in China's involvement in the fight against apartheid in South Africa. It has been argued that at some point China was dishonest and deceiving both sides by supplying the apartheid regime with bombs and guns from as early as 1980 despite being a major ally to the liberation movements. Van Vuuren states that this clandestine relationship lasted for well over a decade.[44] This secret arms trade was conducted directly between the South African military with the assistance of military intelligence and an Armscor front company. A middle man was also used to obscure this trade in the form of Mobuto Sese Seko in (Zaire) Democratic Republic of Congo (DRC), who at the time had become a mutual friend of these two parties. It was only natural that Zaire became the fraudulent destination for these weapons. Van Vuuren further notes that it is believed that in 1985, China shipped about 282,000 kg of weapons valued at about $5 million from Shanghai to Durban via the Zairean port of Matadi to the apartheid regime in Pretoria.[45] By the second half of the 1980s, this secret trade between China and the apartheid government had blossomed to a strategic and comprehensive partnership of a special kind.

China's Role in Mozambique's Liberation Struggle

Mozambique was a beneficiary of China's military and financial assistance in its quest for freedom. China's involvement in Mozambique's liberation struggle can be simplified in terms of China providing aid to Front for the Liberation of Mozambique (FRELIMO) and other subsequent liberation movements in their armed struggle against Portugal. Njal is of the view that FRELIMO has often acknowledged the role China played in Mozambique's liberation war struggle and the China-Mozambique ties predate Mozambique's Independence Day which is June 25, 1975.[46] China, together with other states, particularly the Nordic countries, assisted FRELIMO and the liberation movements in Mozambique with essential military and nonmilitary aid, vital material, and diplomatic assistance for about a decade spanning from 1964 to 1974. Njal further notes that this support was largely driven by China's public condemnation of colonialism in Southern Africa and the developing world.[47] China is one of the few countries in the world that actively encouraged African liberation movements, FRELIMO included, to fight colonialism. China did not only offer encouragement but also provided weapons and training. Most FRELIMO fighters were trained in Tanzania, where also the ZANU (ZANLA) fighters received training. This training offered the much-needed military expertise for Mozambique's liberation movements to fight colonialism.

Fuelled by its rivalry with the USSR, China also provided military assistance to smaller FRELIMO split movements until 1971. In Mozambique, South Africa, Angola, Namibia, and Zimbabwe, the USSR had initially been the main sponsor of the major and "authentic" liberation movements during the different phases of the armed struggles. Chinese assistance also found its way into some of these Soviet aided movements such as FRELIMO. In a sense, it can be argued that China's involvement in Mozambique's liberation struggle through supporting FRELIMO and later other smaller movements was venturing into Soviet territory. This greatly worked to FRELIMO's advantage as FRELIMO managed to balance the two opponents and thus obtained a lot of military benefits from both the PRC and the USSR.[48] One of the major reasons for China getting involved and supporting liberation movements in Mozambique was to expand its influence to counter the United States and its former ally, the USSR. China did this through the adoption of quite an ambitious position of supporting rival anti-imperialist movements.

88   O. ABEGUNRIN AND C. MANYERUKE

China and FRELIMO During the Colonial Period 1962–1975
China's presence in FRELIMO's affairs dates to the very creation of the liberation struggle movement, where FRELIMO managed to establish important and strong ties with China. Chichava asserts that these ties ensured that FRELIMO would be organized as a formidable force and a powerful political-military movement.[49] The relationship with China culminating in strong ties between the two allowed FRELIMO to be highly organized and gave it the ability to lead the liberation war struggle. Zhou states that FRELIMO was provided with a generous amount of both political and military assistance from China.[50] China further provided essential military and guerrilla training to FRELIMO.

The first Mozambicans were trained in China in 1963 and they included Filipe Samuel Magala, FRELIMO's future head of defense and Jose Moiane.[51] Henriksen notes that it is within this same year that FRELIMO's first President, Eduardo Mondlane, visited China and upon his return to Mozambique was convinced that "the historical struggle of the Chinese people had relevance to the present struggle of the people of Africa."[52] Because of this support FRELIMO enjoyed from the Chinese, it is not surprising that FRELIMO ended up employing the Maoist ideology of guerrilla tactics in its fight against the oppressors. The support that Mozambique and FRELIMO received from China was through the African Liberation Committee (LAC). The ties that had been established between Tanzania and China allowed China to easily extend support to FRELIMO in the form of training, military equipment, and financial support, with the military training being conducted in mainland China and in Tanzania. China also took advantage of divisions within FRELIMO to provide military and financial assistance to COREMO, a rival of FRELIMO.

China's Involvement with COREMO and Other Subsequent Movements
COREMO was a military movement conceived out of the divisions within FRELIMO in 1965. It contained FRELIMO's former dissidents and operated mostly from the Tete region in Mozambique. Upon its formation, it essentially became the second most important anti-colonial movement after FRELIMO in Mozambique. More like the leaders of FRELIMO, immediately after its formation, the leaders of COREMO visited China in 1965, where they solicited for and acquired some level of support.

More controversially, China was further involved with Adelimo Gwambe, when he was expelled from COREMO and formed his own separate movement, PAPAMO, even though China was still an ally and the main sponsor of COREMO. Chichava points out that, at the invitation of the Chinese Institute of Foreign Affairs, Gwambe and several members of the PAPAMO leadership paid a visit to Beijing, where they received training for *"revolutionary leaders"* and military enhancement.[53] Through this, the Chinese had started a campaign of supporting their allies' rivals. During this period, COREMO also had almost 30 combatants, who were undergoing military training in China. It has been suggested that the confusion that was reigning in COREMO by 1968 was because of Gwambe's meddling, who had been provided with financial support to destabilize COREMO.[54] However, China's relations with COREMO continued until the 1970s amidst these presuppositions. According to Chichava, PAPAMO, despite all the support it received from China, only existed on paper, unlike COREMO, which was an actual physical organization with functioning structures.[55] At the time, rumors of China supporting other liberation war movements with the aim of destabilizing FRELIMO were not uncommon. There were several reports of China playing a part in the creation of other movements such as the Liberation Portazana of Mozambique (ULIPAMO), which comprised former leaders of FRELIMO and COREMO. China is said to have been the hand behind the creation of the Communist Party of Mozambique, which was a political wing of ULIPAMO. Surprisingly enough, all these other liberation movements never truly saw the light of day when it came to making an actual impact on Mozambique's liberation struggle and were mostly based on rumors and speculation. Either way, as controversial as China's actions were in this regard, it still points to the active involvement of China in colonial Mozambique and its attempts to end colonialism through supporting in various ways the liberation struggle movements in Mozambique and Southern Africa at large.

Even with the existence of all these claims of China playing both sides, relations between China and FRELIMO continued to grow as evidenced by the fact that in 1971, Samora Machel, who was the head of FRELIMO's department of defense, visited Beijing and was given more aid and arms.[56] This relationship continued further until Mozambique attained independence in 1975. Mozambique's independence in turn spelled the end and collapse of COREMO and other political movements as the relationship between China and FRELIMO continued to grow in strength.

Evaluation of China's Involvement in Southern African Liberation Struggles

China's support of ZANU in Zimbabwe can be argued to have been the most significant, as the evidence presented above shows that, of all the liberation movements in Sothern Africa that China was involved with, ZANU is the one it had a constant and unbroken relationship with. This relationship was uninterrupted from ZANU's formation all the way to when Zimbabwe attained its independence in 1980 and beyond. In this regard, Zimbabwe may very well be China's greatest success story when looking at Beijing's involvement with liberation struggles in Southern Africa. China's role in Mozambique raises a lot of eyebrows. It is no surprise that, after her independence in 1975, Mozambique chose to align herself with Moscow through declaring that the country would follow the USSR's form of *revisionist communism* over China's. This was indeed a blow to China as she lost a potential ally, and since then it has been difficult to establish strong ties between the two countries. One wonders if this was not as a direct result of China's controversial involvement with FRELIMO, COREMO, and subsequent breakaway movements and China's sponsorship of these movements to destabilize FRELIMO.[57] China's involvement in the apartheid struggle in South Africa was based on the support for liberation movements fighting the regime in Pretoria. This support was, however, limited because of the Sino-Soviet tensions, which resulted in Beijing failing to play an effective role and supporting the largely ineffective PAC. It has been argued that China, having supported the PAC for a few years and with a small active part to play in the liberation struggle and, at the same time, also secretly trading arms with the apartheid regime, had no real moral claim to Pretoria's recognition. Beijing's secret arms dealings with the Pretoria apartheid regime lead one to question China's exact intentions. It is almost inconceivable that China would support the apartheid regime whilst at the same time sponsoring liberation movements aimed at putting an end to the oppression brought by such regimes.

China's involvement with Southern African liberation struggle movements allowed China to depict itself as a concerned member of the international community through providing aid to the oppressed peoples in Africa. This has been interpreted by some as also a tactical maneuver on the part of China to win African support and vote to be able to replace Taiwan— also known as Republic of China (ROC) in the UN. In Zimbabwe, China enjoyed a lot of success there, in Mozambique China's role was shrouded in controversy and in South Africa China was a marginalized player in the fight against apartheid. Despite her best efforts, China was unable to provide military support extensively throughout the Southern African region and thus could not match Moscow's outlay, which meant that liberation movements would prefer and align themselves with the Soviet Union as their first choice.

CONCLUSION

In conclusion, it is apparent that Southern African nations will forever be indebted to China because of the assistance that Beijing and the CCP provided to their liberation efforts. Evidently, it is almost insurmountable to imagine a decolonized and free Southern Africa without the involvement of China. The military, ideological, and financial support that China rendered to various liberation movements was instrumental in attaining the goal of freedom and emancipation in Zimbabwe, South Africa, and Mozambique. Although Russia also played a critical role in the support of the major liberation movements, China's involvement does not go unnoticed. Countries like Zimbabwe owe a huge debt of gratitude and even up to this day China enjoys good relations with them because of the ties that were conceived during the war of liberation struggle. China was undoubtedly one of the biggest benefactors of the oppressed nations in Southern Africa who yearned for freedom.

However, it is difficult to ascertain China's exact intentions when it comes to its involvement in Southern African liberation struggles. On the one hand, it seems as if China had a genuine desire to lend a helping hand to the various liberation movements to ward off colonial rule and ensure some form of freedom for the peoples of Southern Africa. On the other hand, China's involvement is shrouded in controversy as Beijing seemed to not only fuel division through supporting breakaway factions from the liberation movements she was aligned with, as was the case in Mozambique, but was also engaged in underhand dealings through providing weapons to the enemy, as was the case with China's secret arms dealings with the South African apartheid regime.[58] China thus played both sides. In more instances than one, China showed herself to be an unreliable ally through supporting both sides in the conflict. This has led some to believe that Beijing's involvement was not because of the desire to spread freedom as initially thought but was largely based on her own selfish interests, particularly to take over Taipei's seat in the UN, her strong desire to thwart any form of Soviet expansion, and to keep in check the United States' dominance. In the end, it is apparent that China managed to reap a few benefits from its meddling in Southern Africa, as she won the seat in the UN's Security Council in 1971 and managed to create lasting ties with Zimbabwe and South Africa, with South Africa now being one of China's largest trading partners on the African continent. All the same, China's involvement managed to benefit both sides, as Southern African nations are free from colonialism and oppression and their freedom can be attributed to China's support to a considerable extent.

NOTES

1. Hans Morgenthau. *Politics Among Nations the Struggle for Power and Peace*, 5th edition. New York: Alfred A. Knopf, 1973, 5.
2. Quansheng Zhao. "Interpreting Chinese Foreign Policy," *The China Review*, 1 (1), (1996): 16.
3. Vladimir Shubin. *The Hot "Cold War": The USSR in Southern Africa.* London: Pluto Press, 2008, 3.
4. Ibid.
5. Lauren Sue October. *Liberation Movements as Governments: Understanding the ANC's Quality of Government.* Johannesburg: Stellenbosch University, 2015, 26.
6. Anna Christina Britz. *The Struggle for Liberation and the Fight for Democracy: The impact of liberation movement governance on democratic consolidation in Zimbabwe and South Africa.* Johannesburg: University of Stellenbosch, 2011.
7. Christopher Clapham. *From Liberation Movement to Government Past Legacies and the Challenge of transition in Africa.* Johannesburg: The Brenthurst Foundation, 2012, 4.
8. October, *Liberation Movements as Governments: Understanding the ANC's Quality of Government*, 25.
9. Immanuel Wallerstein. "The ANC and South Africa: Past and Future of Liberation Movements in World-System," *Economic and Political Weekly*, 31, no. 39 (1996): 2695–2699.
10. October, *Liberation Movements as Governments: Understanding the ANC's Quality of Government*, 25.
11. Roger Southall. *Liberation Movements in Power: Party and State in Southern Africa.* London: Boydell and Brewer, 2013, 2.
12. Ilana Botha. *China in Africa: Friend or Foe? China's Contemporary Political and Economic Relations with Africa*, 2006, 6.

5 CHINA'S INVOLVEMENT IN SOUTHERN AFRICAN LIBERATION STRUGGLES   93

13. Ibid.
14. Roy, D. *China's Foreign Relations*. Basingstoke: Macmillan, 1998, 25.
15. Judith van de Looy. *Africa and China: A Strategic Partnership*. Leiden: African Studies Centre, 2006, 2.
16. Sergio Chichava. "Mozambique and China: From Politics to Business," *Institute of Social and Economic Studies Discussion Paper*, no. 5 (2008): 3.
17. Emmanuel Matambo. *The Evolution of China-South Africa Relations: A Constructivist Interpretation*. Pietermaritzburg: University of KwaZulu-Natal, 2014, 1.
18. Herman Wasserman. China in South Africa: The Media's Response to a Developing Relationship (2011): 2.
19. Silence Masiya, *Interview with Charity Manyeruke*, November 13, 2018.
20. See Abegunrin, Olayiwola, *Africa in Global Politics in the Twenty-First Century: A Pan-African Perspective*, New York: Palgrave Macmillan, 2009, 147–148.
21. Zhang Chun. "China–Zimbabwe Relations: A Model of China – Africa Relations?" *Occasional Paper 205, Global Powers and Africa Programme* (2014): 6.
22. Hebert Chingono. Revolutionary *Warfare and the Zimbabwe War of Liberation: A Strategic Analysis*. Washington, DC: National War College, 1999, 4.
23. Abiodun Alao. "China and Zimbabwe: The Context and Contents of a Complex Relationship," *Occasional Paper 202; Global Powers and Africa Programme* (2014): 3.
24. Ibid.
25. Ibid., 6.
26. Chezi Vincent, *Interview with Charity Manyeruke*, November 14, 2018.
27. Alao, China and Zimbabwe: The Context and Contents of a Complex Relationship, 7.
28. Ernest Takura, *Interview with Charity Manyeruke*, November 15, 2018.
29. John Chirime, *Interview with Charity Manyeruke*, November 15, 2018.
30. Chun, *China–Zimbabwe Relations: A Model of China – Africa Relations?* 6.
31. Alao, China and Zimbabwe: The Context and Contents of a Complex Relationship, 7.
32. Chun, *China–Zimbabwe Relations: A Model of China – Africa Relations?* 6.
33. Matambo, *The Evolution of China-South Africa Relations: A Constructivist Interpretation*, 27.
34. Sven Grimm, Yejoo Kim, Ross Anthony, Robert Attwell and Xin Xiao. *South African Relations with China and Taiwan – Economic Realism and the 'One-China' Doctrine*. Johannesburg: Centre for Chinese Studies, Stellenbosch University, 2013, 15.

35. Chris Alden and Yu-Shan Wu. "South Africa and China: The Making of a Partnership," *Occasional Paper 199, Global powers and Africa Programme* (2014): 6.
36. Ibid.
37. Stephen Ellis. The *Genesis of the ANC's Armed Struggle in South Africa-1961.* Oxford: Oxford University Press, 2011, 1.
38. Chris Alden and Yu-Shan Wu. South African Foreign Policy and China: Converging Visions, Competing Interests, Contested Identities. *Common Wealth and Comparative Politics,* 54, 2 (2016): 203–231.
39. Ian Taylor. "The Ambiguous Commitment: The People's Republic of China and the Anti-Apartheid Struggle in South Africa," *Journal of Contemporary African Studies,* 18 no. 1 (2000): 91–106.
40. Gregory Houston, Thami ka Plaatjie and Thozama April." Military training and camps of the Pan Africanist Congress of South Africa, 1961–1981" *Historia,* 60, no. 2 (2015): 1.
41. Ibid.
42. Ibid., 2.
43. Taylor, *The Ambiguous Commitment: The People's Republic of China and the Anti-Apartheid Struggle in South Africa,* 94.
44. Hennie van Vuuren. *Apartheid Guns and Money: A Tale of Profit.* Johannesburg: Vacana Media, 2017, 1.
45. Ibid.
46. Joege Njal. The "Chinese Connection" in Mozambique Hosting the 2011 Maputo All Africa Games," *African East Asian Affairs* (2012): 2.
47. Ibid., 5.
48. Ibid., 6.
49. Chichava, *Mozambique and China: From Politics to Business,* 3.
50. Zhou Jinyan and He Wenping Chinese Cooperation in Mozambique and Angola: A Focus on Agriculture and Health, *BPC Papers − V. 2 N. 03* (2014): 6.
51. Chichava, *Mozambique and China: From Politics to Business,* 4.
52. Thomas Henriksen. "Marxism and Mozambique," *African Affairs,* Vol. 77, No. 309 (1978): 443.
53. Chichava, *Mozambique and China: From Politics to Business Chichava,* 5.
54. Ibid.
55. Ibid.
56. Ibid., 6.
57. Ibid.
58. Hennie van Vuuren. *Apartheid Guns and Money: A Tale of Profit.* Johannesburg: Vacana Media, 2017, 1.

CHAPTER 6

China-Zimbabwe Relations: A Strategic Partnership?

INTRODUCTION

The all-encompassing nature of the China-Zimbabwe relations has led some scholars to classify this partnership as strategic. The two nations have become partners in almost every sector ranging from economic, social, and even the military. This relationship has been characterized by a rapid increase in the amount of trade between the two nations. Zimbabwe has come to rely on China's investment, loans, aid, and grants. China, on the other hand, sees Zimbabwe as a source of raw materials that China desperately needs to expand its empire. Mutuality has become a central feature of the relationship between these two countries. Both countries seem to be gaining from the other what they cannot obtain on their own. China now also plays an important political role on the international arena, particularly as one of Zimbabwe's defenders from the Western nations' aggression. More often than can be counted, China has blocked several moves by some Western powers to invoke sanctions on Zimbabwe from the United Nations Security Council. Notably in 2008, the year of heated presidential elections, China vetoed the United Nations Security Council (UNSC) draft resolution calling for sanctions on Zimbabwe.[1] The relationship between China and Zimbabwe has been woven around three developments, namely, the West's decision to ostracize Zimbabwe after the land reform program, former President Mugabe's desire to shift the country's focus from the West (where the sun sets) to the east (where the

© The Author(s) 2020
O. Abegunrin, C. Manyeruke, *China's Power in Africa,*
Politics and Development of Contemporary China,
https://doi.org/10.1007/978-3-030-21994-9_6

95

96   O. ABEGUNRIN AND C. MANYERUKE

sun rises), and the change in China's policy toward economic expansion particularly in Africa. Zimbabwe's *Look East Policy* has resulted in China now being Zimbabwe's economic and political strategic partner. The *Look East Policy* is thus essential to the trade links and Chinese investments with Zimbabwe.

This chapter therefore seeks to examine the China-Zimbabwe relations with a view to understanding if this relationship is a strategic partnership or not. Various sectors of interest for both nations make up the areas of interaction and where ties have been established. It is worth examining whether Zimbabwe has benefited economically from her relationship with China since her fallout with the Western nations. The amount of trade between the two nations, which has grown exponentially over the past few years, will be analyzed. China has also heavily invested in a number of developmental projects in Zimbabwe. The various trade agreements entered into have often been scrutinized by a number of scholars. The chapter also questions if the mining concessions awarded to China in exchange for trade facilities and investment have truly been to the benefit of both countries or if they have benefited only the Chinese. It has been argued that this relationship between China and Zimbabwe represents a new wave of neocolonialism, where China is siphoning off resources of poor African nations in exchange for international support for its own benefit. The mutually reinforcing political relationship of the two countries in question will also take center stage together with the military ties between China and Zimbabwe, which have been regarded by some, particularly the Western nations, as controversial.

Historical Background

Zimbabwe's friendship with China began during the period leading up to the struggle for independence, where China gave support to Zimbabwe's independence efforts through providing weapons and military training. Xing and Shaw argue that the relationship between China and Africa is premised on the grounds of ideological similarity and similar historical accounts as the Chinese just like Zimbabwe suffered under the ruthless British rule during the Opium Wars in 1841–1843.[2] This created a bond and sharing of the victim mentality between the two and hence resulted in China's involvement in the fight against imperialism in Africa. Alao is of the view that China's relationship with ZANU was a strong gamble for both sides during the time of the liberation war struggle.[3] It is, however, this history upon which the relationship between the two states is premised. This placed China at a great advantage upon Zimbabwe's independence. China has been Zimbabwe's ally since the liberation war struggle, and Zimbabwe's policies were influenced by Communist China until the 1990s, when Zimbabwe briefly adopted a Western-oriented developmental model. The land reform program and the presidential elections of 2002 that were deemed by Western nations as fraudulent led to the suspension of Zimbabwe from accessing most developmental facilities. The subsequent *Look East Policy* arose from the Zimbabwean government's need to look elsewhere for material and financial support for its land reform program. It has been noted that, during this time, China presented a series of features that attracted Zimbabwe. As a result, China has become an important provider of foreign direct investment because of its economic success.[4] Zimbabwe's relationship with China gained much prominence after the year 2003, when Zimbabwe's standoff with the European Union resulted in capital flight and economic depression. Zimbabwe's further isolation by the Western countries deepened her relationship with China as she offered her a crying pad at a difficult time. This supports the view that China and Zimbabwe's relationship has been constant and solid from as far back as before Zimbabwe's independence.[5]

CONCEPTUAL AND CONTEXTUAL CONSIDERATIONS

Strategic partnerships are a new component in International Relations and they comprise one of many types of cooperative interstate behavior.[6] Wilkins notes that "strategic partnership involves closer ties between states through normal *ad hoc* bilateral relations and they adhere to a 'goal driven' rationale of alignment."[7] What differentiates strategic partnerships from any other form of partnerships is that they extend beyond security alignments. With strategic partnerships, there is the desire to commonly pursue joint interests and mutual goals. With the Chinese form of partnerships, all forms of disagreements are muted for the benefit of both parties. With that in mind, the establishment and maintenance of ongoing relations between Zimbabwe and China can be explained in terms of the achievement of immediate and tangible results or rule-based cooperation. This explains why the China-Zimbabwe relations have lasted for so long and, hence can be seen as a strategic partnership.

China's African policy best describes the China-Zimbabwe relationship. Youde is of the view that "the relationship between China and Zimbabwe offers an ideal venue for exploring the interests of African nations in pursuing closer ties with China."[8] China adopted its Africa Policy in 2006 and held the Forum on China-Africa Cooperation (FOCAC) Summit that same year as the first step in seeking external support for its developmental initiative. It has been noted that, at the beginning of the twenty-first century, China developed a dynamic and futuristic outlook and this had its roots in the mid-twentieth century, where China's Africa Policy had undergone a rapid revolutionary process. Although China initially shunned Africa in the 1980s for its lack of economic development, the realization of the role Africa could play toward the attainment of China's goals and the shared history between the two changed China's attitude in the mid-1990s. The establishment of FOCAC represented China's reengagement drive with Africa after it had shifted its attention to the developed and industrialized nations in the West because they had a huge abundance of capital and development experience. Youde further notes that "the result was that both parties began to enthusiastically embrace each other as bulwarks against Western hegemony."[9] Initially, China's interests in Africa were more ideological than anything else and aimed at building ideological solidarity with other underdeveloped nations. Brooks and Shin note that this was done with the "intention of advancing the Chinese style of communism and at the same time repelling Western imperialism."[10] According to de Villiers, "China's first breakthrough was the assistance she gave in the construction of the Tanzam railway line between Tanzania and Zambia from 1970 to 1975."[11] At the same time, the pulling out of Africa by the Cold War powers worked to China's advantage, as it allowed her to maintain her foothold on Africa, as she, instead, kept up her contacts.

China's current proactive foreign policy can be attributed to its economic growth and sophisticated leadership.[12] Hilsum points out that "since investing in Africa is relatively cheaper, China sees it as a good environment for investment."[13] China's relations with Zimbabwe can also be understood in terms of Wallerstein's World systems theory. According to Wallerstein, "a lasting division of the world in core, semi-periphery and periphery is an inherent feature of the world system."[14] The periphery plays a role of supplying raw materials, agricultural output and cheap labor for the growing core which is characterized by a higher level of technological development and produces complex manufactured products. Thus the economic exchange that occurs between the two is on equal terms. In this regard, China is the core and Africa (Zimbabwe to be specific for our case) is the periphery. This is a crucial element of the China-Africa-West trade triangle, which is now clearly under the control of China as she now sits at the apex of all trade. Through this arrangement, China is able to obtain cheap raw materials from Africa and profits from them through selling manufactured products to the West, her biggest and evidently more lucrative market. At the same time that China is profiteering from this, she is also strategically weakening the link between Africa and the West and strengthening her grip on Africa's raw materials.

It has been argued that African nations that have been depicted as being pariah states by the West are guaranteed of China's support against any form of drastic action or resolutions by the United Nations Security Council.[15] More so, some scholars believe the relativist approach taken by the Chinese government regarding human rights and democracy has offered an opportunity for Zimbabwean African National Union Patriotic Front's (ZANU PF's) government to end its isolation and form an ideological alliance with one of the permanent members of the United Nations Security Council (UNSC). Also, there are prospects of export opportunities for Zimbabwe's raw materials that have come into consideration. There is a mix of interests on the part of the Chinese government that act as a motivation for the Chinese authorities. These are specific to Zimbabwe and others are within China's broader strategy toward the region and Africa. Zweig and Jianhai contend that "China's foreign policy with Africa is anchored on China's interests in Africa's natural resources especially oil in countries such as Angola, Nigeria and Sudan as well as a plethora of other natural resources on the continent."[16] Since China's economic development is dependent upon China's ability to import raw materials in the form of minerals, energy products, and agricultural commodities, Zimbabwe comes into the fray, as she can provide exports in some of these categories. However, Friedrich-Ebert-Stiftung argues that "Zimbabwe is not key to China's economic interests and there are other countries that top this list namely Nigeria, Angola, Sudan and South Africa."[17] China has interests mainly in Zimbabwe's tobacco and platinum.

Look East Policy

Zimbabwe's look east policy was officially declared in 2003 with the central focus being to cultivate stronger ties with China. This has led to numerous trade and cooperation agreements being concluded over the years. The *Look East Policy* is premised on the idea that Zimbabwe and Asia (China) share a common colonial history. The idea is that Zimbabwe's economic future and progress can follow the same pattern of Asian countries, who are now seen as economic powerhouses, particularly China. The reason for turning to the East and China under the *Look East Policy* is that the Chinese and other Asian countries will aid Zimbabwe without meddling in her internal affairs. The "Look East Policy" has enabled Zimbabwe to establish stronger ties with Asian countries, especially China. According to Youde "this policy was necessitated by Zimbabwe's isolation by Western nations on the grounds of perceived electoral fraud, government's land reform programme, economic mismanagement and widespread violations of human and political rights."[18]

Zimbabwe turned east to China and Asian countries because they sympathized with her plight and were willing to offer a shoulder to lean on, particularly because of the shared history of exploitation at the hands of the Westerns nations, particularly the British.[19] This policy to focus eastward was thus interpreted as the government's efforts toward taking some form of corrective action toward these historical imbalances. Today the *Look East Policy* has spread to include every sector of Zimbabwe's society. The aid that Zimbabwe obtains from China has been described by some as the complete package, particularly because it includes areas that the Western nations had previously neglected such as healthcare and infrastructure development. On top of providing finances and technological knowledge, the Chinese have also been protecting Zimbabwe from the passage of sanctions by Western powers in international organizations such as the UNSC. Zimbabwe's *Look East Policy* has further enabled it to access loans and aid with no conditionalities in terms of political or economic reform. This has allowed Zimbabwe to access foreign direct investment without any form of burden to go along with it. This is in line with China's policy of "no string attached aid." Chingono notes that the policy has further heightened the dealings between China and Zimbabwe and has also yielded an equal share of both tangible and intangible benefits and challenges.[20] However, it has been argued that, despite all this economic infusion, the look east policy has not been ratified by parliament and no official policy document exists on it yet. The ideas of the *Look East Policy* still have a strong influence on Zimbabwe's official foreign policy and have acted as some form of a guide.

China and Zimbabwe Relations Today

The relationship between China and Zimbabwe today is an extension of the ties that were established during Zimbabwe's liberation struggle. China-Zimbabwe relations have been described as among the closest on the continent. Alao is of the view that Zimbabwe's relationship with China draws a great deal of attention, particularly due to the controversies associated with the contents and multidimensional nature of the relationship.[21] China is strongly opposed to the sanctions imposed on Zimbabwe by the Western nations because it curtails the sovereignty of Zimbabwe. There is, however, a need to examine the disadvantages associated with the *Look East Policy*, especially the presumed negative impact the increased Chinese presence has had on Zimbabwe's domestic production. A number of scholars have raised further doubt on the level of direct investments that are being promised. The international press and media have in the past reported on several irregularities on the evolution of the relationship between China and Zimbabwe, arguing that 'the relationship has been used for propaganda purposes to favor the ruling party and against the Western powers.[22] However, all this has not been substantiated by any concrete evidence.

When looking at the China-Zimbabwe relationship, it is apparent that a commonality of interests exists between the two countries. China's relationship with Zimbabwe has often at times been described as the best thing that has ever happened to Zimbabwe and the friendship has been dubbed *all weather friends*. This has resulted in comprehensive agreements being concluded between the two nations in various core sectors. The relationship between China and Zimbabwe today is characterized by sectorial corporation. This cooperation has been in place since independence and it has been described by some as lopsided, with Zimbabwe seeking support from China. China in turn has assisted Zimbabwe in a number of sectors, such as in the construction of sports facilities, hospitals, schools, and the development of Zimbabwe's textile industry. Sachikonye states that "China has also had a hand to play in the development of Zimbabwe's steel industry through the provision of finances in the acquisition of equipment for Zimbabwean Iron and Steel Company (ZISCO)."[23] Different infrastructure development projects have been provided with free loans and grants by China. Corporation notably goes beyond construction and has also been established in the energy and mining sectors.

The magnitude of the links between the two countries makes Zimbabwe one of the countries experiencing the most extensive Chinese influence, ranging from mining, investment, and trade to energy.[24] The relationship has been characterized by Chinese development in exchange of Zimbabwe's raw materials and natural resources. The Forum on China and Africa Cooperation and Zimbabwe's *Look east Policy* have resulted in the rapid development of the economic pillar of the relationship between China and

Zimbabwe. This economic relationship has, however, remained only a small aspect of China's overall foreign economic engagement. It has, however, been noted that there is a difference when it comes to the relative importance each of the two sides attaches to this relationship.

ECONOMIC TIES

Sino-Zimbabwe deals are all-embracing, covering the economic and political aspects amongst other elements. It is worth examining whether Zimbabwe has benefited economically from her relationship with China since her fallout with the Western nations. FOCAC and Zimbabwe's *Look East Policy* have resulted in the rapid development of the economic pillar of the relationship between China and Zimbabwe. This economic relationship, however, remains only a small aspect of China's overall foreign economic engagement. This has seen Zimbabwe being provided with new significant revenue streams. According to Youde, trade has also increased by over 147 percent between the two nations, for instance, China is now the largest buyer of Zimbabwe's tobacco and has become an important player in cell phones, television, radio, and power generation.[25] As a result of this increased trade, China has received various mineral concessions that Zimbabwe cannot develop on its own. Zimbabwe's development of stronger ties with China has been interpreted by some as evidence of the country's resourcefulness in the face of condemnation and sanctions from the West. The close relationship between Zimbabwe and China can be interpreted in terms of China's longing to establish a relationship with nations that are willing to turn a blind eye to its questionable human rights record, its need to secure resources and food security, and its desire to deny Taiwan a seat at the international table.[26] More so, Africa has presented itself as a market for low-quality mass produced goods, a situation which greatly benefits China economically. China mostly trades with countries that the Western states refuse to trade with on the African continent. Therefore, China and these countries (Zimbabwe included) are important economic lifelines for each other.

Questions have been raised over what an African country like Zimbabwe benefits economically from developing a stronger relationship with China. Many have argued that Zimbabwe's *Look East Policy* provides an opportunity for Zimbabwe to reassert its role on the international stage and gain some form of prestige and legitimacy both at home and abroad. Through Beijing's strong economic interests in Zimbabwe, China has been able to secure contracts to develop Zimbabwe's mineral and hydroelectric resources. China also supports small to medium enterprises (SMEs) through providing lines of credit from Chinese banks. Eisenman notes that the industries receiving these funds include the textile, soap, tile, and fiberglass manufacturers and these funds were to the tune of $12 billion on the onset.[27] Large firms such as ZISCO have also received some form of funding. Between the years 2003 and 2013, China's economic and commercial interests in Zimbabwe had become so extensive and diversified that hardly any aspect of Zimbabwean life was spared from this impact.

Trade

The trade relationship between China-Zimbabwe has been augmented since the early 2000s. The high-level visits by government officials between the two countries have strengthened the trade relations between these two. Most notably, the 2018 visit by President Emmerson Mnangagwa to China as his first overseas visit, where his government signed a comprehensive strategic partnership with China in April 2018, demonstrates the importance of the trade relationship between the two countries. Chun notes that, in 2004, the two countries signed an economic and technical agreement aimed at strengthening trade relations between them.[28] With this agreement, China would assist Zimbabwe improve its tobacco production through providing the required resources to revamp the sector, which had been negatively affected by the land reform program. This would in turn yield mutual benefits for both parties as China essentially became one of the largest importers of Zimbabwe's tobacco. As a result, by 2014, China had become Zimbabwe's third largest trading partner, after South Africa and the European Union, respectively.[29] Trade between China and Zimbabwe has thus increased significantly over the years. According to China's National Bureau of Statistics (CNBS) there has been a steady increase over the years from US$52.2 million in 1996 to about US$1.1 billion by 2013.[30] Main exports to China include tobacco, asbestos, iron and steel, chrome, and platinum. Zimbabwe imports manufactured products, that is, machinery, electrical items, engine and motor parts, plastics, and telecommunications equipment, amongst others items. This trade between these two nations embodies the trade between developing and developed economies. What can be gleaned from this is that there is some form of two-way trade relationship between the two, with China gaining a source of raw materials and a market for its industrial goods and Zimbabwe also gaining a market for its raw materials, particularly agricultural produce and minerals at a time the West has isolated the southern African country. Thus, there has been an increase in the amount of Chinese imports on Zimbabwe's local market. However, locals have raised concerns over this, citing that the local market has now been flooded with low-quality goods in the form of food, clothing, textiles, and electrical gadgets. It has also been noted that this trade is particularly driven by China's insatiable thirst for raw materials and mineral resources, which Zimbabwe has in abundance.

Investment

The increase in the number of Chinese locals in Zimbabwe reflects the significant increase in the amount of Chinese investment in the country. Chinese investment in Zimbabwe can be traced as far back as 1994 and, since the launch of the *Look East Policy*, this investment has grown exponentially from three companies in 1994 to about sixty-two companies by 2014.[31] This has resulted in Zimbabwe being one of the African countries receiving the most FDI from China. According to Edinger and Burke, Chinese investment has seemingly occupied gaps which were deemed as risk laden by other investors[32] Initially, Chinese investments were more concentrated on the extractive sector as a result of China's rapid demand for raw materials and mineral ores, but have now expanded to include companies in sectors such as manufacturing, agriculture, retail, transport, and infrastructure development (the construction of the National Sports Stadium in the 1980s falls into this category).

Mining

China has shown a keen interest in Zimbabwe's mining sector, particularly in iron, steel, chrome, and platinum. Several cooperation agreements have been signed over time with regard to the mining sector.[33] The mineral concessions offer a windfall for both countries, particularly on Zimbabwe's platinum and copper deposits, which had remained undeveloped for a significant amount of time. At a time of growing demand for natural resources, the China-Zimbabwe relationship offers China secure access to these natural resources, which are critical to its economy. This has been to China's advantage, as its economy needs these raw materials to support its growth in terms of industry and infrastructure. It has been noted that the increase in the need for these resources by China has fueled the increase of world prices. Chingono is of the view that the China-Zimbabwe relationship has benefited Zimbabwe's mining sector through the provision of inputs and transfer of technical expertise.[34]

Energy

China has been playing an active role in Zimbabwe's energy sector. China has, over the years, been supplying Zimbabwe with equipment for the utilization of solar energy. In 2005, an agreement was made for the Chinese to rehabilitate the national power grid in exchange for chrome resources. More so, China has been involved in Zimbabwe's electricity generation through the supply of equipment, mostly transformers. Eisenman notes that through its efforts, China has secured the contracts to develop Zimbabwe's electricity resources.[35] In 2004, ZESA received equipment worth $110 million from China. That same year, ZESA Holdings also signed a cooperation agreement with CATIC, a Chinese company for the supply of more equipment valued at about $2.4 billion.[36] This agreement included Hwange Thermal Power Plant's expansion and the creation of two new production units. This was aimed at reducing Zimbabwe's dependency and overreliance on electricity imports from Mozambique and South Africa. There has been a $1.3 billion deal with China Machine-Building International Corporation to allow the Chinese to mine coal and build thermal power generators in Zimbabwe to reduce electricity shortages. With that, China now holds a seventy percent stake in Zimbabwe's electricity generation facilities at Hwange and Kariba. According to Alao, China also assisted through the Sino-Hydro Company the installation of two generators at Kariba South worth $4 billion.[37] CATIC China also played a significant part in Zimbabwe's Rural Electrification Agency through providing equipment worth over $6 billion.[38]

POLITICAL TIES

The political ties between Zimbabwe and China can be described as strategic government ties. According to Chun, there is evidently mutual support between China and Zimbabwe both in the international arena and mutual respect in domestic affairs.[39] Zimbabwe has stood by China's side especially on China's *One China policy*, where China has sought external support to finish her reunification. Zimbabwe has been unwaveringly consistent in its support of "One China" and other core political interests of China. Zimbabwe has enjoyed the benefit of China's veto power in the UNSC, where China has continued to support and protect Zimbabwe. Both China and Russia have been the only super powers that have given credibility to Zimbabwe's government over the years. China, along with Russia, vetoed a resolution to impose targeted sanctions on Zimbabwe's government.

It has been argued that China could more conceivably and willingly be involved with the affairs of African states if the two were linked through political ties.[40] From the outset, in an attempt to create and improve the political relations between China and Zimbabwe, Mugabe declared himself "a Marxist-Leninist of a Maoist thought," which showed his commitment toward waging "a people's war."[41] Zimbabwe has also taken advantage of the split between China and the USSR to gain support from the Chinese. From this, Zimbabwe has gained an important patron in the form of China, and at the same time China has been able to bolster its image as a friend of the developing world. The political benefits China and Zimbabwe have both enjoyed have been mutually shared on both sides. A turning point in this relationship was when Zimbabwe's former President, Mugabe, made statements in support of China's actions in the Tiananmen Square incident of 1989. To reward Zimbabwe's support, China increased its trade with Zimbabwe significantly together with other African countries that had come to China's defense.[42] According to Alden and Wu, as a result, aid from China to African states was also significantly increased in the years after the Tiananmen Square incident, as noted by the fact that before the incident in 1988, China had managed to give just $60.4 million worth of aid to only 13 countries, but by 1990, the amount of aid availed had significantly increased to $374.6 million and the number of countries had also increased to 43 African states.[43] The political basis of engagement between China and Africa, Zimbabwe included, became centered on the Five Points Proposal for relations with Africa, which were reliable friendship, sovereignty, equality, nonintervention, mutually beneficial development, and infrastructural development.[44]

MILITARY TIES

The military ties between China and Zimbabwe are amongst the strongest China has in Africa. The military exchanges have been the most controversial aspect of the relationship between China and Zimbabwe. According to

Chun, these military relations have been simplified in terms of arms trade mainly because Zimbabwe has been under arms embargoes from the West.[45] De Looy states that it has often been argued by some scholars that selling arms to some African leaders improves bilateral relationships and can augment Chinese access to natural resources.[46] This military relationship between China and Zimbabwe is, however, not a new one, as it was forged during the days of Zimbabwe's liberation struggle, where China supplied Zimbabwean African National Liberation Army (ZANLA) members with weapons and military training. In terms of military support, Zimbabwe has benefited a great deal from China over a number of years. This support dates back to the pre-independence era and it has even intensified in recent times. Zimbabwe relies on China to replace its old artillery and for the supply of arms. China has not only sent military personnel to Zimbabwe, there have also been several arms procurement agreements that have been entered by the two countries.[47] Eisenman notes that Zimbabwe, in the past, has been supplied with 8 fighter jets and other military equipment worth more than $200 million by their Chinese counterparts.[48] This deal has, however, been constantly denied by the Chinese as not having taken place. It also raised a lot of eyebrows as it was said to have taken place outside the regulations as it did not go through the State Procurement Board as required by law. The major arms exchanges between the two countries include: 2 fighter jets and 1000 military vehicles valued at an estimated $240 million that were supplied to Zimbabwe in 2004, and 6 trainer/combat aircraft acquired by Zimbabwe from China in 2005, 6 more obtained in 2006, and 20,000 AK-47 rifles, 21,000 pairs of handcuffs, and 12–15 military trucks in 2011.[49] It has been reported that, between 2000 and 2009, China accounted for thirty-nine percent of Zimbabwe's imports of major conventional weapons. There is also personnel exchange and training between the two countries mostly through the Zimbabwe National Defence College.

China has received widespread criticism from Western nations for supporting the military in Zimbabwe, especially in 2008, when China is said to have sold a ship full of arms to Zimbabwe which caused a lot of uproar, since these arms were sold at the time when Zimbabwe was going through one of its worst ever political crises. The infamous An Yue Jiang incident of March 2009 was seen as the most unpopular and controversial Chinese military link between China and Zimbabwe. Chingono is of the view that the sale of these arms had happened long before the controversial elections of 2008, and hence the criticism was unjustified.[50]

AID

It has been said that the aid that China extends to Zimbabwe and other African nations is better than the one offered by the Western states, which is often accompanied by harsh conditions. To create a more favorable perception, China often makes press and public statements that make African leaders believe that this aid has no strings attached to it. This has been argued to be a misleading assumption, as some scholars are of the view that aid is an effective but subtle method of maintaining a position of influence and control. China has strategically used aid to ensure that African countries do not fall into the hands of Taiwan and the United States. Hayter is of the view that aid is thus "merely the smooth face of imperialism."[51] Some have noted that it seems the new China does not want the collapse of capitalism but rather intends on wrestling capitalism away from the hands of the Western powers. Aid is a concession by the imperialist powers to enable them to continue their exploitation of the semicolonial powers.[52]

Even though China provides aid to more than twenty countries on the African continent, it is its relationship with Zimbabwe which has drawn a great deal of attention. Chun is of the view that China's focus in Zimbabwe is centered more on business partnership with the country instead of simply providing aid.[53] However, Zimbabwe has received developmental aid amounting to $103 billion between 2005 and 2013, through grants, concessional loans, and contributions to the World Food Programmes.[54] Loans have also been restructured by the China Export Bank (China Exim Bank) in ways that are more favorable to Zimbabwe with the reduction of the interest rate from four percent and three percent, respectively, to about two percent on two of the loans availed by Zimbabwe amounting to $17.9 million.[55] China has provided the Zimbabwean government with considerable aid, grants, export credits, and concessional loans, together with technical and economic assistance.

CRITICISM OF CHINA-ZIMBABWE RELATIONS

China's relationship with Zimbabwe has been criticized by some as a representation of neocolonialism. Although the China-Africa dealings are supposed to be on a win-win basis, it has been argued that the principle of mutual benefit, which the Chinese stick to, has failed Kwame Nkrumah's test, who had the view that "the methods of neo-colonialism are subtle and varied."[56] Kwame Nkrumah was of the belief that neocolonialists have conjured up a number of means to achieve the aims previously accomplished through naked colonialism. Through this, China is now said to be perpetrating a new wave of colonialism and, at the same time, preaching about freedom, noninterference in the affairs of weaker developing nations, and supporting the sovereignty of these nations. All this has been argued to be part of Chinese imperialism, only more subtle. China's relationship with Zimbabwe offers critical support in international forums such as the UN, since Africa has the single largest bloc of votes in the UN and WTO. As a result, Beijing is now beginning to have a more defined and active presence and is thus creating a paradigm of globalization that favors China that would eventually lead to China staking a claim as one of the great powers in the world.

CONCLUSION

As stated above, there are contradictory views of the China–Zimbabwe relations that stimulate a lot of debate. The relationship has largely been emphasized on the economic and political dimensions. It is apparent that this relationship arose from the strong historical ties that the two nations share, particularly the bond they created during Zimbabwe's liberation war struggle. The result of these historical ties has been a strategic partnership with a somewhat structured framework for collaboration between the two countries. Due to the lack of a policy document or formal structures to oversee the running of this collaboration between these two countries, especially on the part of Zimbabwe, this partnership has been characterized as organized in a loose and nonbinding way, with the aim of enabling the pursuit of shared interests and solving common challenges. The subsequent political and economic pillars of the China-Zimbabwe relationship and the historical ties, emotional or ideological, between China and Zimbabwe seem to be even superior to the relations China has with the rest of the other African nations in general. Combining the economic, political, and military ties between the two countries and taking into account the emotional history, this chapter concludes that the relationship between China and Zimbabwe is indeed strategic, with mutual benefits for both parties.

Not only are the China-Zimbabwe relations strategic, they are also unique, as shown by that China has a totally different momentum from relations between China and other African countries with the relations it shares with Zimbabwe. It can thus be said that Zimbabwe holds a special place in China's foreign affairs, particularly with regard to Africa. The momentum of the China-Zimbabwe relationship comes from two directions, specifically the sanctions imposed on Zimbabwe by Western countries and China's reengagement policy. The land reform program in the early 2000s led to Zimbabwe's isolation and souring of relations with the Western nations, which resulted in sanctions being imposed on Zimbabwe by the United States and some European countries. These sanctions were varied and included a number of restrictions, amongst them trade restrictions, which have been detrimental to Zimbabwe's economy. This compelled Zimbabwe to look east to China as an attempt to replace the United States and European Union as its major trading and political partners. Based on China's history with Zimbabwe during the liberation war struggle, China responded positively to Zimbabwe's call, which culminated in Zimbabwe launching its "Look East Policy" in 2003.

The relationship between China and Zimbabwe is a bit unusual due to the relatively balanced development of the different pillars that make up this partnership, particularly the political and economic aspects. As noted earlier, China-Zimbabwe relations were not particularly vibrant between 1980 and 2000, as Zimbabwe was aligned to the Western model of development, and to date Zimbabwe's biggest trading partners are South Africa and the European Union, with China only coming in third. This shows that a lot still needs to be done before this relationship becomes fully fledged and realizes its full potential. The significant strides this relationship has made in the twenty-first century can be attributed to the political and strategic considerations which have become the main driving forces behind Zimbabwe's desire to develop and expand relations with China. This makes the China-Zimbabwe relationship a relatively balanced and strategic development for both nations. The political, economic, and military dimensions of this bilateral relationship have developed steadily and in tandem, and it is this balance and simultaneous development that has the Western nations worried and distrustful of this partnership. These relations between China and Zimbabwe have become more strategic at the same time as the China-Africa relations in general have morphed from a monocycle (political and/or ideological links from the 1950s to mid-1990s) to a bicycle (with an economic dimension added since the mid-1990s). Thus, it can be stated that the China–Zimbabwe relationship, in contrast to general China-Africa relations, established its internal balance from the very first day. There seems to be a great deal of potential for the growth of this relationship in the near future.

Notes

1. Olayiwola Abegunrin, "Zimbabwe," in David Levi and Karen Christensen, editors, *Global Perspectives on the United States: A Nation by Nation Survey, Volume 2*, Great Barrington, MA: Berkshire Publishing Group, 2007, 685.
2. Li Xing and Timothy Shaw, The Political Economy of Chinese State Capitalism, *Journal of International Relations*, 1, No. 1 (2013): 23.
3. Abiodun Alao, "China and Zimbabwe: The Context and Contents of a Complex Relationship", *Occasional Paper 202; Global Powers and Africa Programme* (2014): 6.
4. Friedrich-Ebert-Stiftung. *The 'Look East Policy' of Zimbabwe now focuses on China*. Harare: Friedrich-Ebert-Stiftung, 2004, 10.
5. Ibid., 2.
6. Thomas Wilkins, "Alignment", not 'Alliance' – the Shifting Paradigm of International Security Cooperation: Toward a Conceptual Taxonomy of Alignment." *Review of International Studies*, 38. No. 1 (2012): 53–76.
7. Ibid., 61.
8. Jeremy Youde, "Why Look East? Zimbabwean Foreign Policy and China." *Africa Today*, 53, No. 53 (2007): 4.
9. Ibid., 9.
10. Peter Brooks and Ji Hye Shinson, China's Influence in Africa: Implications for the United States, *The Heritage Foundation*, no. 1916 (2006): 5.
11. Cas de Villiers. *African Problems and Challenges: Selected Essays on Contemporary African Affairs*. Sandton: Valiant Publishers (Pty) Ltd., 1976, 28.
12. Joshua Eisenman and Joshua Kurlantzick, "China's Africa Strategy," *Current History* (2006): 14.
13. Lindsey Hilsum, "Re-enter the Dragon: China's New Mission in Africa," *Review of African Political Economy*, 32, no. 104/105 (2005): 7.
14. Immanuel Wallerstein. "The ANC and South Africa: Past and Future of Liberation Movements in World-System", *Economic and Political Weekly*, 31, no. 39 (1996): 2695–2699.
15. Talent Mguni, *An Assessment of The Chinese Geopolitical Interests in Africa: A Case of Zimbabwe-China Bilateral Engagements From 2003–2015*, (2016): 5.
16. David Zweig and Bi Jianhai, China's Global Hunt for Energy. *Foreign Affairs*, 85, No. 5 (2005): 14.
17. Friedrich-Ebert-Stiftung. *The 'Look East Policy' of Zimbabwe now focuses on China*, 10.
18. Youde, *Why Look East? Zimbabwean Foreign Policy and China*, 9.
19. Xing and Shaw, *The Political Economy of Chinese State Capitalism*, 23.

20. Heather Chingono, "Zimbabwe's Look East Policy", *The China Monitor: Centre for Chinese studies*, 10 (2010): 7.
21. Alao, *China and Zimbabwe: The Context and Contents of a Complex Relationship*, 5.
22. Friedrich-Ebert-Stiftung. *The 'Look East Policy' of Zimbabwe now focuses on China*, 3.
23. Lloyd Sachikonye. Crouching Tiger, Hidden Agenda: Zimbabwe-China Relations. South Africa: University of KwaZulu-Natal Press, 2008, 59.
24. Alao, *China and Zimbabwe: The Context and Contents of a Complex Relationship*, 8.
25. Youde, *Why Look East? Zimbabwean Foreign Policy and China*, 11.
26. Ibid., 4.
27. Joshua Eisenman, "Zimbabwe: China's African Ally." *China Brief*, 5 (2011): 9–11.
28. Zhang Chun, "China-Zimbabwe Relations: A Model of China – Africa Relations?" *Global Powers and Africa Programme, Occasional Paper 205* (2014): 4.
29. Ibid., 14.
30. Friedrich-Ebert-Stiftung. *The 'Look East Policy' of Zimbabwe now focuses on China*, 3.
31. Mguni, *An Assessment Of The Chinese Geopolitical Interests In Africa: A Case Of Zimbabwe-China Bilateral Engagements From 2003–2015*, 5.
32. Hannah Edinger and Christopher Burke. *China-Africa Relations: A Research Report on Zimbabwe*, Stellenbosch: Centre for Chinese Studies, University of Stellenbosch, 2008, 11.
33. Friedrich-Ebert-Stiftung. *The 'Look East Policy' of Zimbabwe now focuses on China*, 5.
34. Chingono, *Zimbabwe's Look East Policy*, 7.
35. Eisenman, *Zimbabwe: China's African Ally*, 2.
36. Ibid.
37. Alao, *China and Zimbabwe: The Context and Contents of a Complex Relationship*, 12.
38. Ibid.
39. Chun, *China-Zimbabwe Relations: A Model of China – Africa Relations?* 11.
40. Youde, *Why Look East? Zimbabwean Foreign Policy and China*, 7.
41. Ibid., 8.
42. Ibid., 9.
43. Chris Alden and Yu-Shan Wu. "South African Foreign Policy and China: Converging Visions, Competing Interests, Contested Identities," *Common Wealth and Comparative Politics*, 54, no. 2 (2016): 147.
44. Ibid.
45. Chun, *China-Zimbabwe Relations: A Model of China – Africa Relations?* 13.

6 CHINA-ZIMBABWE RELATIONS: A STRATEGIC PARTNERSHIP? 113

46. Judith van de Looy. *Africa and China: A Strategic Partnership*. Leiden: African Studies Centre, 2006, 25.
47. Friedrich-Ebert-Stiftung. *The 'Look East Policy' of Zimbabwe now focuses on China*, 7.
48. Eisenman, *Zimbabwe: China's African Ally*, 3.
49. Ibid.
50. Chingono, *Zimbabwe's Look East Policy*, 7.
51. Teresa Hayter. *Aid as Imperialism*. Middlesex: Penguin Books, 1971, 7.
52. Ibid., 9.
53. Chun, *China-Zimbabwe Relations: A Model of China – Africa Relations?* 19.
54. Ibid.
55. Ibid.
56. Kwame Nkrumah, *Neo-Colonialism: The Last Stage of Imperialism*. New York: International Publishers, 1965.

CHAPTER 7

Zambia's Bilateral Relations with China

INTRODUCTION

China has risen to become a global economic powerhouse and force to reckon with. Its economic growth has come to reshape the global economy. This is especially true for countries such as Zambia, where China has come to influence the political, economic, and social setup. Regardless of the commonly held views and perceptions concerning Zambia's bilateral relations with China, it cannot be denied that the ties between Lusaka and Beijing are possibly the most pragmatic example of an all-weather friendship on the African continent. At a glance, Zambia and China seem to be outstandingly dissimilar in many aspects. However, these two, when looked at closely enough, offer a revelation that they have striking similarities, which include a shared and common long history of close relations and development cooperation. The increase in the Chinese-Zambian bilateral relations has stimulated a lot of debate, with people holding several perspectives regarding the nature of implications this might have on Zambia's bilateral relations with other nations or what these relations mean for the country moving forward. For decades, Zambia has received significant support from China in several sectors, such as infrastructure development trade and investment amongst others. The Tazara railway line, constructed in the 1970s to link Zambia and Tanzania, is still one of the most illustrious icons of China-Zambia relations to date. The current China-Zambia relations are characterized by an increased amount of trade

© The Author(s) 2020
O. Abegunrin, C. Manyeruke, *China's Power in Africa*,
Politics and Development of Contemporary China,
https://doi.org/10.1007/978-3-030-21994-9_7

115

between the two nations and increased investment inflows coming into Zambia from China. Although these investments cover several sectors, the lion's share has been diverted to the mining sector. It cannot be argued that Chinese FDI coming into Zambia clearly has the potential to bring about both positive and negative implications. There have been arguments that China's ties with Zambia epitomize a new wave of oppression. This chapter, therefore, seeks to analyze the bilateral relations that exist between China and Zambia, with a view to offering unique perspectives and an understanding on the nature of these relations. This chapter will also assess whether the relationship is mutually beneficial.

Historical Background of Sino-Zambia Relations

Economic ties between China and Africa can be traced as far back as five centuries ago, however, the era before the latest economic ties dates to the 1950s.[1] Over the past few years, these ties have been extended to include financial investment, trade, developmental aid, and infrastructure development. The starting point of the modern Sino-Zambia relations is the Bandung Summit (1955) and the China Communist Party's policy as directed by Mao's theory of the developing world.[2] Alves believes the diplomatic ties that exist between China and Zambia are perhaps one of the richest historical records on China's cooperation with Africa.[3] The historical ties that exist between Zambia and China can also be traced back to the pre-independence era, a time when Zambia was under the colonial rule of Britain. During this period, China provided financial and material assistance to Zambia's opposition parties. Mwanawamina holds the view that the historical ties between Zambia and China are based on a shared and similar historical experience in the form of the struggle for national liberation and independence.[4] The period between 1949 and 1979 was characterized by China rendering support and aid to Zambia in its efforts at attaining independence and China established diplomatic missions, economic reconstruction, and consolidation of independence.[5] In return, during this period, African countries, Zambia included, offered support to China with her diplomatic endeavors on the international stage. After attaining its independence, Zambia became the first Southern African country to establish diplomatic relations with China.

In recent times, the bilateral relations between the two countries have gradually increased and spread to encompass political, trade relations, economic and technical cooperation. The Tanzania Zambia Railway (Tazara), which was a monumental feat achieved with the assistance of China, serves as the keystone of Sino-Zambia relations. Wu believes this railway construction, although it was undertaken in the 1960s and 1970s, is notably the most significant Chinese project in Africa to date.[6] This monumental project is of great significance to the relations between the two nations, as it signaled the level of commitment China had in its efforts to build strong and lasting bilateral relations with Zambia. It is from this point going forward that the relations between the two nations blossomed and have gained momentum ever since.

CONTEXTUAL CONSIDERATIONS

The relationship that exists between Zambia and China today, just like the relationship between China and a host of other African countries, can be best explained by the Forum on China and Africa Cooperation (FOCAC) initiated in 2000 as the basis of a new friendship between China and Africa. FOCAC became a platform for collective dialogue, consultation, and coordination based on the principles of mutual trust, political equality, cultural exchange, and an economic "win-win" scenario for both parties. Mwanawamina holds the view that "over the years FOCAC has occasionally been reviewed and it is this forum that has been responsible for China's increased interests not only in Africa but in Zambia as well."[7]

China is on a renewed drive for unification with Taiwan and has thus sought to establish relations with countries that support this vision. The China-Africa policy thus comes in to address China's economic, political, and developmental cooperation, paying attention to trade-related issues. More so, Zafar opines that "China's insatiable thirst for natural resources to feed is booming industrialisation has led it to Sub-Saharan Africa's doorstep."[8] Sata supports this view and asserts that "China's recent march into Africa can be owed to China's search for natural resources particularly timber, base metals and oil to guarantee the survival of her people."[9] Because of China's interests in this regard, bilateral relationships that are mutually beneficial for both parties have emerged. These relationships have come in different forms, such as exchange visits and signed agreements. To that end, Chileshe points out that "China came up with its policy on Africa which underscores the need for mutual trust, political equality, cultural exchange and mutual 'win-win' cooperation."[10] To achieve this, in 2006, China crafted its African Policy Paper, which set the tone for China-Africa bilateral relations. According to Mubita, "there are five pillars upon which the China-African policy is anchored, and these include mutual benefit, common prosperity and reciprocity; equality and friendship; sincerity; mutual support and close coordination and the One China principle."[11] Through this policy, China seeks to promote and assist Africa's development. It is upon this framework that the China-Zambia relations are premised.

On the other hand, Zambia's foreign policy best explains its relations with China. Zambia has a foreign policy in place which seeks to maximize global economic integration and economic benefits through peaceful coexistence with its neighbors.[12] This vision is essentially crucial to Zambia's relations with other states in the international system, as it clearly articulates Zambia's strategic interests. Through its foreign policy, Zambia is devoted to promoting investment and trade, economic growth and development through attracting foreign direct investment into the country. It is also within this context that Zambia and China's bilateral relations have flourished.

Bilateral Ties between Zambia and China

Over the years, the relations between China and Zambia have shifted focus from a mere political alliance into an economic cooperation anchored on mutual economic benefits aimed at achieving common development. Wu opines that "Zambia enjoys a unique position as the show piece of the success of Sino-African relations as well as the 'experimental region' of new Chinese diplomatic policies in Africa."[13] Zambia is one of the African countries with the longest standing diplomatic relations with China. Alden states that the China-Zambia relations have been known to be based on "reliable friendship, non-interference and sovereign equality."[14]

China's relations with Zambia are part of a broader framework of China-Africa relations, which are based on "win-win" cooperation. This current impetus held by China in her engagement with Zambia and Africa at large is directed by the desire to gain access to Africa's vast markets, natural resources and build strong and lasting diplomatic ties, as proven by the long history of political engagements between the two.[15] China has anchored these engagements on the need for "*South-South Cooperation.*" Africa views this engagement to gaining unconditional aid, FDI, and infrastructure development in a manner that is much more tenable as compared to the one offered by Western nations. This accordingly shows the China-Zambia relations as dynamic.

However, over the past few years, China's relations with Zambia and other African nations have been demonized and depicted as "China's new colonialism of Africa". Li argues that this perception has been designed to depict the ethical and moral supremacy of Western approaches and hence China's activities in African countries have been depicted as nothing short of being completely negative.[16] This has been because China's activities in Africa are overscrutinized, yet they are poorly understood. Fortunately, there has been an awakening on the part of many scholars who have become cognizant of this propensity and have thus avoided the reductionist conclusions that characterize such a perspective.[17]

CHINESE INVESTMENTS IN ZAMBIA

The impressive economic growth that China has achieved over the past few decades has turned China into a notable economic powerhouse and development icon for Zambia and Africa at large. It has been argued that FOCAC is responsible for creating new opportunities in Zambia's development efforts. Mwanawamina notes that "through FOCAC, China has gained a platform to utilise its advanced technology and robust financial resources to scale up Zambia's efforts aimed at development."[18] Chinese investments have been through a combination of loans, grants, joint ventures, and aid. Zambia has further benefited from being a recipient of favorable investments and loans that do not have any conditionalities attached, which is quite dissimilar from the Western investments, loans, and aid. It is estimated that Chinese investments in Zambia amount to approximately US$4 billion and she owes approximately US$5 billion to China.[19] On the other hand, Zambia has been shown to present extensive investment opportunities which China can exploit. Haggai states that "the Zambia Development Agency offers some attractive incentives for investors who wish to invest in certain key priority areas such as manufacturing, mining and infrastructure development."[20] When looking at Chinese FDI coming into Africa, Zambia presents an example par excellence, and this is largely owed to the country's historical ties with China and the two countries' ever-increasing economic ties.[21]

Zambia's strategic importance to China's current foreign policy has been highlighted by China's establishment of the first five African Preferential Investment and Trade Special Economic Zones in Zambia. Consequently, Lubinda notes that, in 2018, Chinese FDI into Zambia amounted to US$2.2 billion, which was a significant increase from a mere

US$144 million in 2003.[22] Such impressive amounts of FDI coming into Zambia have resulted in the creation of thousands of jobs for the locals. Most importantly, Chinese capital has facilitated the construction of vital infrastructure in Zambia such as schools, roads, bridges, and hospitals. Haggai states that, in 2015 alone, US$1 billion was invested in Zambia in a manufacturing hub dubbed "One Belt and One Road Industrial Park" which will span over 700 hectares of land and will be host to over 20 high-tech firms specializing in different sectors.[23] According to Lubinda, "China has further made notable investments totalling an excess of US$3 billion in 2014 in Zambia's mining sector within the past few years."[24] To that effect, by 2014, there were over 550 Chinese businesses operating in Zambia.[25] It should be noted that such a colossal investment undertaking depicts huge confidence Chinese investors have in Zambia's economy. It has further been argued that Chinese investments and donor aid has assisted both small private and large state-owned entities to expand their market opportunities.

However, such investments have been criticized by several individuals. One common issue that has been criticized a lot is the alleged ill-treatment of Zambian workers by their Chinese employers. There have also been accusations that the Chinese business owners have a disregard for local labor and safety procedures and have further been accused of paying very low wages. Others have deemed China's actions in Africa as like the colonial tendencies by the Europeans. Wu notes that the "past depiction of the Sino-Zambian brotherhood as being healthy and the position Zambia holds in China's African policy, questions the anti-Chinese political campaign that has arisen since 2006."[26] More so, Haglund argues that "the overreliance on the state as a broker by Chinese investors undermines the stability of investments in the long term, as their prospects essentially became intertwined with the political fortunes of the current governments."[27]

Infrastructure Development

Closely linked to Chinese investments in Zambia are the massive infrastructure projects being spearheaded by the Chinese in the country? Poor and inadequate infrastructure has been one of the main challenges to Zambia's economic development and poverty alleviation drive. China has been playing an active role in funding governments and paying for infrastructure projects in developing countries. Evidence suggests that China has been playing a dominant role in Zambia's infrastructure development projects. Some of these notable projects include roads, hospitals, and power generation. As a sign of a good gesture, it has been noted that some bilateral donors in Zambia have partnered with hospital projects financed by the Chinese. Chinese FDI coming into Zambia's energy sector, which is one of the key infrastructure projects for the country, witnessed a significant increase after FOCAC was initiated. According to Lubinda, China has been investing in several of Zambia's energy projects, particularly in hydro and coal power.[28] These projects have been aimed at improving Zambia's national energy output to reduce the country's energy shortfall. Although China is leading the financing and construction aspects of this initiative, it is Zambia Electricity Supply Corporation (ZESCO) which will be the owners of this new power generation capacity.

With regard to the transportation infrastructure, China has been actively involved in reviving this sector. Zambia has, over the years, been plagued by poor road networks. China has actively been involved in Zambia's road infrastructure projects. China has provided nearly eighty-five percent of funds utilized in Zambia's road rehabilitation projects and, from the twenty-three contracts availed to undertake the Accelerated National Roads Construction Programme, sixteen were contracted to Chinese firms.[29] Chinese companies have further been awarded numerous other contracts to revamp Zambia's road infrastructure. These include a $108 million contract awarded in 2013 to Sino-Hydro to construct a 45.5 km dual carriageway linking Kitwe and Chingola.[30] Also, in 2005, a US$207 million contract was awarded to China Henan International Corporation by the Zambian Road Development Agency (RDA) to design and construct the Mansa-Luwingu Road.[31] These projects will clearly develop Zambia's road infrastructure upon completion.

Furthermore, with regard to Zambia's railway system, the initial Tazara rail project that China sponsored the construction of between 1968 and 1976 has been facing several challenges. According to Chileshe, if China's initial role in the construction of Tazara was not enough, she has been investing more funds in the form of billions of dollars (US$2.2 billion in 2009, to be precise) in Zambia's rail lines as part of a much bigger investment initiative in Africa's infrastructure.[32] Through a firm named Chinastruck, China is assisting Zambia construct railway lines that will connect Zambia to neighboring countries such as Malawi and Mozambique to enhance regional trade. China has also chipped in by providing US$5 million in the rehabilitation of ninety wagons.[33] Chileshe further points out that, "although Chinese firms now have a lion's share of all construction projects in Zambia, questions have arisen with regards to authenticity of the tenders and contracts which have been awarded to Chinese firms."[34]

TRADE

The amount of trade between China and Zambia has witnessed a sharp increase over the last few years. Lubinda states that in 2013 alone, Chinese direct trade with Zambia amounted to a staggering US$3.1 billion, up from just US$10 million in 2003.[35] Lubinda further notes that "the Zambia-China relations have become a sight to marvel at due to the increased trade volumes between the two nations which has exponentially increased from US$100 million at the start of the 21st century to well over US$3 billion in recent years."[36] This increased amount of trade has been described as nothing short of dramatic. Under the FOCAC initiative, Zambia has been awarded special trading arrangements by China to promote Zambia's exports to China. Ambassador Tian XueJian states that "China exempted the tariff on 97 percent of the commodities exported to China from 31 least developed African countries, with Zambia being among these countries."[37] Because of this, China has risen to become Zambia's second largest trading partner.

Such impressive trade volumes ideally should be to Zambia's advantage, but, unfortunately for Africa, just like other developed nations that had a notable presence in Africa before her, China is also deeply engrossed in the extraction business.[38] The trade and investment deals between China, Zambia, and other African countries are opaque and are based on "barter" terms essentially dictated by the Chinese government. The trade between China and Zambia is, for the most part, characterized by natural resources from Zambia to China and finished goods from China to Zambia and is, in this regard, not any different than Africa's past experiences with the West. On the other hand, China offers an opportunity for Zambia to take full advantage of China's huge and rapidly increasing export market for finished products, especially considering that China has put in place a zero-tariff provision for trade with African countries, which Zambia is a part of. This has enabled Zambia within the past few years to increase the number of zero-tariff exports into China. This offers a huge advantage for Zambia and fellow African countries, as it is happening at a time where there has been a notable decrease in the demand for Africa's exports into Western countries. China's increasing demand for Africa's natural resources has been instrumental in reinstating Zambia as a cradle for some of the most prized commodities for the world market. China further seems to be gaining an improved interest in trade and investment in Africa. To that end, Zambia has witnessed an increase in the number of Chinese technical experts and business people. Although the government has viewed this as positive steps, several Zambians have viewed these occurrences with suspicion.

The Zambia-China Cooperation Zone (ZCCZ)

The Zambia-China Cooperation Zone is known as the first economic and trade cooperation zone established by China in Africa. The origins of this initiative were the converging interests of the two countries. Alves notes that "there was a need for Zambia to develop a manufacturing base around its mining sector at the same time that China was gaining an increased interest in Zambia's copper reserves."[39] This initiative originally surfaced in 2004, spearheaded by a Zambian subsidiary of China Non-Ferrous Metal Group Company (CNMC) known as Non-Ferrous Metals Corporation of Africa (NFCA).[40] The NFCA's advances to the Zambian government, with the aim of setting up an industrial park for copper processing in Chambishi, were well received; however, the project was delayed by the legal framework that existed in Zambia at the time. Nevertheless, the Zambian Development Agency Act No 11 of 2006 paved the way for the commencement of this project. Because of this Act, China was able to set up more economic and trade cooperation zones (ETCZs) in Zambia within the framework of FOCAC as well. Consequently, the ZCCZ thus became the first Multi-Facility Economic Zones (MFEZ) for Zambia and the first Economic and Trade Co-operation Zones (ETCZ) for China as well in Africa.[41] To show the importance of this initiative for both countries, Zambia's late former President Levy Mwanawasa and China's President officially initiated the ZCCZ in February 2007.

MINING

The importance that Zambia has to China can be attributed to Zambia's plentiful mineral resources. Li states that "since the start of copper mining in Zambia during the 1920s, copper has played a significant role in the country's economy, with mining activities alone constituting close to 8 percent of the country's earnings from foreign exchange."[42] Zambia's mining sector has thus been attractive to China, since access to natural resources, copper for example, is of the utmost importance to China's economic endeavors. China has over the years grown into the largest consumer of copper and, consequently, Chinese investments into the mining sector make up eighty-eight percent of its total investments in Zambia.[43] The largest copper mining firm in Zambia, Chambishi Copper Mine, is owned by NFCA, which is a subsidiary of CNMC, a Chinese state-owned entity. Another large Chinese company conducting mining activities in Zambia is Jinchuan, which accounts for ninety percent of the total production of platinum and nickel.[44] On top of these larger firms, there are also smaller mining companies active in Zambia's mining sector but keeping a very low profile, which makes it difficult to pinpoint with accuracy their numbers and scale of operations.

Be that as it may, FDI coming in from China has boosted the development of Zambia's copper industry. Taylor is of the view that this Chinese FDI "rejuvenated an industry that had been dead and on its feet in the 1990s."[45] To that end, Chinese FDI was also instrumental in bolstering Zambia's mining sector during the financial crisis that occurred between 2008 and 2010, a time which saw Zambia's economy feeling the full force of this economic decline, particularly the extractive sector. Li points out that "during 2008 and 2009, a number of Western owned mining companies scaled down and some even halted production, which had a devastating effect on Zambian employees as an estimated 85 000 workers lost their jobs."[46] It is at the realization of this devastation that Chinese mining firms took on the mantle and augmented their investments in Zambia's mining industry. Despite a difficult business climate resulting from the global financial crisis, Chinese state-owned companies in the mining sector such as CNMC weathered the storm and did not scale down operations. Chinese firms at the time became increasingly involved in the acquisition of other struggling mining firms in Zambia at a time when Western owned companies were choosing to pull out of Zambia's mining sector. In this regard, Chinese firms have been depicted as picking up the scraps where Western firms lack the courage to invest. It is evident that Zambia's mining sector will remain a key driver of the country's economic growth. However, Chinese investments in Zambia's mining sector should not be overestimated and only viewed from one side, which paints them as completely having a positive impact. It should be noted that Chinese FDI can either be good or bad and this largely depends on the structure and quality of the economy of the host nation as well as the strategies and policies the host government has in place to manage the FDI.

Implications of China's Involvement in Zambia

It has been argued that Zambia has the most dependent relation with China. More so, the current China-Zambia trade relation has prolonged Zambia's dependence on natural resources and raw materials. Zambia has been recording some trade imbalances in its dealing with China. According to Haggai, Zambia's trade balance only grew by a mere 0.6 percent from 2012, amounting to US$ 927,683.[47] The current pattern of trade clearly favors China. There have been other challenges experienced in the form of low returns for the Zambian government during the initial stages of Chinese projects in Zambia. This has been coupled with difficulties experienced by the Zambian government in bringing on board new investors.

More so, the demand for raw materials has been reduced by the decline of the performance of China's GDP, which makes uncertain the performance of Zambia's exports to China at a time when Zambia is heavily reliant on China for her exports. Romei notes that "a general sluggish global economic growth has resulted in reduced external demand for most commodities, which in turn has caused a steep contraction in the amount of Chinese imports."[48] Consequently, this has had a negative effect on Zambia and other African countries, such as Congo and Equatorial Guinea."[49]

Another challenge noted is the absence of a cohesive absorbent regulatory framework to guarantee the essential domestic spill-overs, which include the transfer of skills and technology and the integration of Zambia's domestic private sector into these large-scale investment programs.[50] The investment threshold, which is too high, has made local entrepreneurs feel left out, with local authorities also expressing their fears of missed opportunities. Zambian suppliers have been missing out due to the overreliance on Chinese supply chains by the Chinese investors. This has been owed to the language and culture barriers and evidently the cheaper options back home in China. The cultural differences and language barriers have resulted in several misunderstandings. This has had the negative effect of changing Zambian perceptions of Chinese workers and investors and the relations between Zambian communities and Chinese expatriates. Furthermore, there are weaknesses in Zambia's regulatory framework that have been taken advantage of by the Chinese firms. These firms have been exploiting weaknesses in this regard, such as poor land allocation, labor protection, and quality control, and these bad practices have been exported into Zambia along with the Chinese investments.

These bad practices have further fuelled the debate on the issue of cheap, low-quality products being dumped into Zambia by the Chinese. Chinese cheap products have chocked many Zambian small-scale traders, a situation which has led to a great deal of uneasiness. Some local Zambian firms have even been pushed into shutting down operations, which has resulted in job losses for many Zambians and a wastage of infrastructure, which, in most cases, is left to lie idle. A case in point is the Mulungushi Textiles factory, which was once the largest textile factory in Zambia, but, in 2007, was forced to shut down its operations due to its failure to keep up with competitive Chinese imports.

The activities of Chinese firms conducting mining activities in Zambia's Copper belt have aroused a great deal of attention. Li points out that the NFCA and other Chinese firms have been known to have a terrible reputation when it comes to labor and environmental practices.[51] These firms have further been accused of paying Zambian employees lower wages than what is expected. More so, Chinese firms have been accused of failing to adhere to Zambia's occupational and safety regulations. The poor labor practices, however, cannot be blamed on the Chinese firms alone. The Zambian government has played its equal part, as it has failed to implement adequate labor laws and laws to govern the terms of investment.

Recommendations and Policy Direction

Both Zambia and China must find a common solution to concerns raised over the labor issues. The AU and individual African countries like Zambia with strong bilateral ties with China should come up with policies that will guide the relations between these parties and match China's policy on Africa.

The Zambian authorities need to examine their regulations and their enforcement as well. Quality control issues, environmental impact analysis, land tenure processes, tendering and labor standards must be reinforced to thwart any efforts by the Chinese investors that may be aimed at exploiting the Zambian people and their resources. There is a need to acquire suitable rent from China's exploitation of Zambia's natural resources and ensure that this revenue is utilized in long-term development projects.

The Zambian government should further ensure that bilateral cooperation is reformulated in a manner that promotes joint and sub-contracting arrangements, to enhance the transfer of skills, knowledge, and capacity building. Zambia's private sector should also make efforts to fully exploit the zero-tariff export provision that China provides to African countries. These local Zambian industries can achieve this by adding value to the products they intend to export. The Zambian government needs to shift its focus as well and ensure that the raw materials that are exported have added value and, at the same time, penalize the export of these raw materials in their natural state through punitive export tax.

Furthermore, there is need for Zambia to reshape its bilateral cooperation with China in terms of joint and subcontracting arrangements to ensure the transfer of skills and capacitate local industry.

Because of the increased trade volumes and the trade potential Zambia has with China, Zambia ought to exploit the preferential trade treatment from China through expanding its export portfolio and, at the same time, also offer tax incentives on the importation of industrial equipment to improve the diversification of her products and scale up the industrialization process.

To deal with the challenges presented by language and cultural barriers between African countries, such as Zambia and China, African and Chinese linguistic and social centers must be brought into the fray under the FOCAC initiative and commissioned to conduct research and development on the subject matter. More so, the recent establishment of the Confucius Institute in Zambia can be used to further cement Zambia-China relations through adding extra resources to the University of Zambia to improve its research in Chinese language and culture. It has been noted that, since its establishment in 2010, the Confucius Institute at the University of Zambia has been instrumental in improving engagement with China through Chinese learning, education exchange, and the promotion of contemporary China. It has become the center for Chinese language learning and a core center for Chinese culture in Zambia. In that regard, the institute must therefore do more work so that it reaches out to the ordinary people who get more work and jobs in Chinese companies and projects. This is instrumental in dealing with the language and cultural barriers which act as a hindrance to China-Zambia bilateral relations.

CONCLUSION

The past few years have seen a monumental and historic shift in the way China relates with African countries. Moving forward, it is evident that the ties between China and its African partners such as Zambia have become a solid foundation for the continued growth of their future relationship aimed at attaining shared goals and driven by mutual interests. It remains to be seen if China's increasing role in Zambia and other African countries through bilateral relations will act as a catalyst for the development of such African countries or it will turn out to be just another episode of powerful global actors pursuing their narrow self-interests. China's bilateral relations with Zambia confirm that Chinese engagement with African nations offers some exciting opportunities for several countries on the continent to focus more on their development, divorced from the neoliberal and aid-focused approaches traditionally favored by Western nations. Zambia's case is a clear testament that investment focused Chinese engagement with Africa is more pragmatic.

It is apparent that the impact China has had on the Zambian economy because of the bilateral relations that exist between the two, has been varied over time and in different sectors. Whereas the trade opportunities and investment coming in from China is certainly welcome, the challenges associated with the Chinese activities in Zambia are a reminder of unanticipated consequences and should be given due attention to be adequately dealt with. To achieve full benefits, Zambia should significantly alter the way it engages with China. Since China has a policy on Africa, it only makes sense that, in the very least, Zambia also devises its own policy on China as a starting point.

NOTES

1. The African Development Bank (AfDB) Group Chief Economist Complex, "Policy Brief," *Chinese Trade and Investment Activities in Africa*, 1, no 4 (2010): 15.
2. Mulundano Comfort Lubinda. "China-Zambia Economic Relations: Current Developments, Challenges and Future Prospects for Regional Integrations." *International Journal of Economics, Commerce and Management*, Vol. VI, Issue 1 (2018): 207.
3. Anna Cristina Alves. The Zambia–China Cooperation Zone at a Crossroads: What Now? *SAIIA Policy Briefing 41* (2011): 1.
4. Inyambo Mwanawina. *China-Africa Economic Relations: The Case of Zambia*. African Economic Research Consortium (AERC), 2008, 1.
5. Mubita Oliver Mubita. *Increased Economic Relations Between China and Zambia In the Last Decade: Implications on Zambia's Existing Bilateral Relations with the United States*. Fort Leavenworth: U.S. Army Command and General Staff College, 2013, 3.

7 ZAMBIA'S BILATERAL RELATIONS WITH CHINA   129

6. Wu, D. *Every Day Life of Chinese Migrants in Zambia: Emotion, Sociality and Moral Interaction*, 2014.
7. Mwanawima, *China-Africa Economic Relations: The Case of Zambia*, 2.
8. Zafar, A. *The Gravity Relationship Between China and Sub-Saharan Africa: Macroeconomics, Trade, Investment and Aid Links*. Oxford: Oxford University Press, 2007.
9. Michael Sata. *Chinese Investment in Africa and Implications for International Relations, Consolidation of Democracy and Respect for Human Rights: The Case of Zambia*. Cambridge: Harvard University, 2007.
10. Chilufya Chileshe. Chinese Debt, Aid and Trade: Opportunity or Threat for Zambia. *SAIIA Occasional Paper No 72* (2010): 5.
11. Mubita, *Increased Economic Relations Between China and Zambia In the Last Decade: Implications on Zambia's Existing Bilateral Relations with the United States*, 15.
12. Ibid., 28.
13. Wu, *Every Day Life of Chinese Migrants in Zambia: Emotion, Sociality and Moral Interaction*.
14. Chris Alden. China in Africa: Survival. *Global Politics and Strategy 47:3* (2005):147–164.
15. Kanenga Haggai. "Understanding Sino-Zambia Trade Relations: Trends, Determinants and Policy Implications." *World Journal of Social Sciences and Humanities* (2016): Vol. 2, No. 2, 52–77.
16. Pengatao Li. The Myth and Reality of Chinese Investors: A Case Study of Chinese Investment in Zambia's Copper Industry. *SAIIA Occasional Paper No 2* (2010): 5.
17. Ibid.
18. Mwanawamina, *China-Africa Economic Relations: The Case of Zambia*, 3.
19. Lungu, *Chinese Investment Brims Over.*
20. Haggai, *Understanding Sino-Zambia Trade Relations: Trends, Determinants and Policy Implications*, 61.
21. Li, *The Myth and Reality of Chinese Investors: A Case Study of Chinese Investment in Zambia's Copper Industry*, 3.
22. Lubinda, *China-Zambia Economic Relations: Current Developments, Challenges and Future Prospects for Regional Integrations*, 206.
23. Haggai, *Understanding Sino-Zambia Trade Relations: Trends, Determinants and Policy Implications*, 62.
24. Ibid., 209.
25. Haggai, *Understanding Sino-Zambia Trade Relations: Trends, Determinants and Policy Implications*, 62.
26. Wu, *Every Day Life of Chinese Migrants in Zambia: Emotion, Sociality and Moral Interaction*.

27. Dan Haglund. Chinese Investors in Zambia; Is it for a Long Term? Chinese Investorsin Zambia; Is it for a Long Term? Cambridge, UK: Cambridge University Press, 2007, 1.
28. Lubinda, *China-Zambia Economic Relations: Current Developments, Challenges and Future Prospects for Regional Integrations*, 210.
29. Ibid., 213.
30. Lusaka times.com, 16 April 2010, quoting minister of Finance and National planning, Situmbeko Musokotwane's response to questions about the real Benefit of Chinese Investments to Zambia.
31. Ibid.
32. Chileshe, *Chinese Debt, Aid and Trade: Opportunity or Threat for Zambia*, 11.
33. Lubinda, *China-Zambia Economic Relations: Current Developments, Challenges and Future Prospects for Regional Integrations*, 211.
34. Chileshe, *Chinese Debt, Aid and Trade: Opportunity or Threat for Zambia*, 11.
35. Lubinda, *China-Zambia Economic Relations: Current Developments, Challenges and Future Prospects for Regional Integrations*, 206.
36. Ibid.
37. Tian XueJian. *A new Era for China-Africa Relations*. The Thinker. 2016.
38. Chileshe, *Chinese Debt, Aid and Trade: Opportunity or Threat for Zambia*, 9.
39. Alves, *The Zambia–China Cooperation Zone at a Crossroads: What Now?* 1.
40. Ibid.
41. Ibid.
42. Li, *The Myth and Reality of Chinese Investors: A Case Study of Chinese Investment in Zambia's Copper Industry*, 5.
43. Ibid.
44. Ibid.
45. Taylor I, *China and Africa: Engagement and Compromise*. London: Routledge, 2006, 179.
46. Li, *The Myth and Reality of Chinese Investors: A Case Study of Chinese Investment in Zambia's Copper Industry*, 8.
47. Haggai, *Understanding Sino-Zambia Trade Relations: Trends, Determinants and Policy Implications*, 53.
48. Romei, V. *China and Africa: Trade Relationship Evolves*. Financial Times, 2015.
49. Ibid.
50. Alves, *The Zambia–China Cooperation Zone at a Crossroads: What Now?* 4.
51. Li, *The Myth and Reality of Chinese Investors: A Case Study of Chinese Investment in Zambia's Copper Industry*, 11.

CHAPTER 8

Ethiopia-China Relations: A Focus on Factors Driving Investment Inflows and the Socioeconomic Impact

INTRODUCTION

A look at the way China-Ethiopia political and economic relations have gained momentum during the past few years shows that this momentum will only increase. China's rise to become the world's second largest economy has strategically positioned her in such a way that she is now able to play an influential role in the global economy. China's new found position at the apex of global trade and economics has worked to the advantage of a number of developing countries, especially those in Africa, over the past decade. Having realized that she cannot achieve her objectives in isolation, China has been at the forefront of promoting South-South Cooperation, which is a development cooperation aimed at the exchange of resources, technology, and knowledge for sustainable development and the eradication of poverty within developing countries. Since Ethiopia aims at becoming a middle income country by 2025, it has closely been working with China over the past few years to achieve this goal, since their interests seem to be aligned.

The fact that Ethiopia is not particularly rich in natural resources makes the Ethio-China relations unique and, at the same time, quite fascinating, as the basis for this relationship is dissimilar to what China has with other African nations. It has been argued by some that Ethiopia's lack of a significant amount of natural resources and minerals makes China's interests in Ethiopia different from its interest in other African countries, where

© The Author(s) 2020
O. Abegunrin, C. Manyeruke, *China's Power in Africa*,
Politics and Development of Contemporary China,
https://doi.org/10.1007/978-3-030-21994-9_8

131

natural resources have tended to be the primary objective. The current relationship between the two nations has also been as a result of China's interests in investing in sectors such as infrastructure, energy, and telecommunications, where large-scale funding is needed for Ethiopia to meet its objective of becoming a middle-income country, as highlighted in its "Growth and Transformation Plan."[1] The economic cooperation that exists between China and Ethiopia is largely anchored on strong political facilitation from the governments of the two nations. The various agreements entered into by the two nations have allowed for increased trade and investment between these nations. This has been used by the Ethiopian government as the basis for ushering Ethiopia into a new economic era with the aim of improving the socioeconomic status of Ethiopians. This chapter seeks to analyze whether the relationship between these two nations has translated to socioeconomic development for Ethiopians. Since it is common in Africa that most of the time those huge investments inflows may be eliticized or corrupted so that the generality of the people will not benefit from them, the ensuing argument will analyze the Ethio-China relations with the aim of gaining an insight as to whether the relations between Ethiopia and China have improved Ethiopia's socioeconomic status.

Historical Background of Ethiopia-China Relations

The interaction and friendship between the Ethiopian and Chinese people can be traced back to ancient times from about 100 B.C., when the Han dynasty of China and the Axumite Empire of Ethiopia had trade exchanges. Mohane and Kale note that the economic and political ties between China and Africa have been said to date as far back as 500 years ago.[2] From the outset, with the establishment of the People's Republic of China and the subsequent Cold War, China and Africa's relations were largely political. The cornerstone for these China-Africa relations was the (Afro-Asian Conference) Bandung conference of 1955, where China started building ties and offered economic, technical, and military support to African countries and liberation movements to unite with them against the imperialist powers.[3]

Although in 1972 relations between China and Ethiopia were formalized with the establishment of embassies in their respective capitals, in the period between 1970 and 1980, Ethiopia's foreign policy was aligned with that of the USSR. However, from the period starting in 1991, there was a shift in tide and attitudes started to change with the fall of the previous military regime, which had been led by Colonel Mengitstu Hailemariam. It is after the fall of this military regime that Ethio-China relations began to surge, with the new Prime Minister in 1991, Menes Zanawi, putting a greater emphasis on the importance of securing policy space suitable for alternative development.[4] This policy space could be attained from partnering with East Asian countries such as China that had undergone the same developmental trajectory which Ethiopia sought to emulate. The successful transformation that had occurred in several East Asian countries from agrarian to industrial based economies fascinated Ethiopia's new leadership at the time, and they sought to achieve something similar for themselves. As a result, Ethiopia started strongly leaning toward Eastern Asia and building ties with nations from that part of the world. Since then, there has notably been movement of Chinese companies into Ethiopia and other African countries, especially in the fields of mining, construction, oil extraction, and this has brought along with it a significant amount of FDI into Africa. Damtew and Tsegay assert that the Chinese government has been actively encouraging such efforts. Brautignam is of the view that there has been a notable increase in the level of cooperation between China and Africa within the past two decades owing to the changes in the global economy, geopolitical competition, and some notable modifications to China's foreign policy.[5] Consequently, China has become one of the top economic partners of Ethiopia, balancing the economic ties of Ethiopia with Western nations.[6] Since the beginning of the Comprehensive Cooperative Partnership (CCP) in 2003, the relations between the two countries have developed at an alarming pace, resulting in the two countries entering into further agreements on socioeconomic, political, and technical cooperation.

CONCEPTUAL CONSIDERATIONS

Chinese Model of Investment

The "*Chinese model*" of investment and infrastructure loans, also known as the "Beijing Consensus," makes China's relationship with Ethiopia and other African nations distinctive. Wenping notes that this model has been "commended for its emphasis on valuing the political and international relations concept of multilateralism, consensus and peaceful co-existence."[7] Ramos is of the view that "the Beijing Consensus is a new attitude towards politics, development and global balance of power."[8] The Chinese model of investment has been said to usher in "no strings attached" financial and technical assistance aimed at achieving economic growth through guiding trade and investment decisions in Africa.[9] This approach is evidently in contrast with the Washington consensus, which some scholars have pitted as a neoliberal paradigm which has its focus on democracy, poverty reduction, and good governance. The conditions set forth by the Washington consensus have been seen by many African countries as unnecessary and harsh conditions for them to access developmental aid and FDI from the United States and its allies. Ramos further states that "in their approach to investment based on their model, the Chinese take on an approach where they bid competitively for infrastructure development and resource projects using loans for infrastructure and investment."[10] These loans are often advanced at zero or near-zero percent interest or their repayment is at times done using natural resources.[11] This has, however, been a bone of contention and has stimulated a lot of debate, with some arguing that the Chinese gain more in terms of resources as compared to what they would have invested in Africa. Consequently, a number of individuals have expressed concerns over China's approach to investment in Africa, arguing that China has been cleverly exploiting Africa's natural resources for its gain. Adisu et al. note that "all the same, Chinese investment on the continent is viewed differently by Africans, from the type of investment and developmental aid that is offered by the western nations mainly because the Chinese do not impose the neo-liberal package of reform that is a prerequisite of western institutions such as the World Bank under its conditionality provisions."[12] According to Sautman and Hairong, "Chinese aid has 'no strings attached' as compared to the western aid and is thus viewed as an initiative which supports African nations in their attempts aimed at addressing developmental issues where Western investment seems to fall short."[13] The Chinese model of development thus promotes a win-win situation and is designed to promote partnerships instead of dependency.

DRIVING FORCES BEHIND CHINESE ENGAGEMENT IN ETHIOPIA

The economic cooperation between China and Ethiopia has some historical roots and is about half a century old. Ethiopia's location on the horn of Africa between Somalia and Sudan makes it one of the most strategic countries in Africa, both politically and economically. China's engagement in Ethiopia can be attributed to a number of factors. These include China's increasing demand for raw materials and natural resources and its need to guarantee food security for its growing population. With the unprecedented growth of China's economy, Chinese presence in Africa is increasingly becoming an obvious sight and this scene is similar in Ethiopia. Carmody states that China has also been driven by its desire to *"rule from a distance"* by building robust diplomatic and economic ties with strategically chosen African nations.[14] This desire will be achieved through China's One Belt One Road (OBOR) initiative. Bataineh et al. point out that the OBOR initiative is predicted to have the capability to "further shift the global strategic landscape in China's favour, with infrastructure lending as its primary lever for global influence."[15] China is also driven by trade and industrial production and is economically motivated to gain access to lucrative markets. Ethiopia offers extremely favorable markets for Chinese products. The rising wages in coastal China have also acted as a push factor. Ethiopia has relatively stable policies which have acted as an important pull factor for a number of Chinese firms who have been attracted by the efforts made by the Ethiopian government to offer space and meet the needs of foreign investors. Ethiopia also offers comparative advantage in form of cheap labor and cheap electricity. Although some have criticized Chinese firms for employing Chinese professionals at the expense of local workers, some evidence presented by the World Bank shows that Chinese firms have created extensive job opportunities for Ethiopians and increased employment by nineteen percent since 2008.[16] The World Bank also notes that sixty-nine percent of Chinese firms operating in Ethiopia had provided some form of training exclusively for Ethiopian workers.[17] It is apparent that a combination of global markets, Asian manufacturing knowledge, and Ethiopian comparative advantage create a *triangle of collaboration.*

China's Investments in Ethiopia

Chinese aid, investment, and trade are on the rise in Ethiopia. One of the major reasons for Chinese investments in Africa is that, Africa offers the highest return on FDI.[18] As a result, China is now having a significant impact on African economies with this increasing expansion being particularly evident in Sub-Saharan Africa, especially in Ethiopia. The amount of Chinese investment in Ethiopia is relatively higher compared to other

African countries such as Kenya, Angola, Uganda, and Rwanda. Nicola postulates that, even though the Ethiopian government has time and again made utterances that all investors are welcome, the close political ties between Ethiopia and China have played a significant part in cementing China's position as Ethiopia's primary economic partner and virtually shutting everyone else out.[19]

Since the European Union has classified Ethiopia as mainly an aid recipient, China has been taking a different approach through establishing a mutual economic partnership with the Ethiopian government by combining aid with official financial flows, FDI, and bilateral trade.[20] To promote Chinese investments in Ethiopia, a joint Ethiopia-China Commission (JECC) was established in 1998 between Ethiopia's "Ministry of Finance and Economic Development" (MOFED) and China's "*Ministry of Finance and Commerce.*" Cheru states that the JECC was established to act as a coordination platform for economic and technical cooperation.[21] Geda and Meskel are of the view that Ethiopia-China economic relations comprise "*market seeking,*" with Chinese investment being largely fixated and dominant in the manufacturing, real estate, telecommunications, and road construction sectors.[22] The economic linkages between Ethiopia and China have been strengthened by both trade and investment and Chinese FDI in Ethiopia for the past few years. The amount of Chinese investment into Ethiopia has been on the rise since 2000 and has taken the form of two modalities of investments, namely, joint ventures and Chinese owned investments.

As part of their investment drive, Chinese companies are building a network of trade, aid, and investment with a host of African countries, Ethiopia included, where they have been on a drive to build and develop the country's roads. Chinese firms have, over the years, signed deals to purchase refineries and explore oil and gas in Ethiopia and other African nations. As of 2016, there were more than a thousand Chinese projects either being undertaken or registered in Ethiopia, with most of these projects being medium-sized investments of amounts ranging from US$5 million to US$20 million, and most being undertaken by private firms.[23] However, Jalata raises some concerns over the financial assistance being offered by China and argues that the use of Chinese companies, employees, and material in Chinese investment projects has some undesirable effects, as it leads to dependency on the part of Ethiopia.[24] More so, China's loans to Ethiopia have been said to be highly commercial and this has the potential effect of forcing Ethiopia into a debt trap.

Foreign Direct Investment (FDI)

Attracting FDI is central to Ethiopia's strategy for industrialization, which has compelled the government to initiate reforms to the country's investment policy to increasingly entice more FDI inflows.[25] Although Ethiopia is by and large an agriculture-based economy, it has, over the years, been able to attract significant amounts of FDI. China's investments in stocks have been on the rise significantly over the past few years. It has been noted that a significant amount of Chinese investments in Ethiopia are not state-owned, as Chinese private investors have come to claim a stake in the manufacturing sector. Chinese FDI in Ethiopia has been on the rise as shown by the fact that it reached US$58.5 million in 2010, from being almost nonexistent in 2004.[26] This has made Ethiopia one of the top destinations of Chinese FDI coming into Africa. Nicola states that FDI from China and India has allowed Ethiopia to undertake the development of technological sophistication of its leather industry. Chinese investments in the manufacturing sector amount to sixty percent.[27] More so, Chinese investment has some additions, which include generous loans, debt cancellation, infrastructure development, and no interference in Ethiopia's politics.

It is worth noting that planned Chinese FDI in Ethiopia will significantly stimulate Ethiopia's industrial infrastructure as it will result in the establishment of a planned Chinese industrial zone. The zone will be constructed 37 km south of Addis Ababa by a Chinese Investment group, Jiangsu Qiyuan. The industrial zone will be named Ethiopian Eastern Industrial Zone (EEIZ) and so far more than 20 Chinese firms have already shown their interest in investing in this project. Additionally, 80 investment projects will be undertaken at a cost of about US$500 million and they will cover the shoe, textile and garment, leather and leather products, electrical materials, steel manufacturing, and food sectors.[28] Upon completion of the construction of this private industrial zone, 20,000 jobs for the locals will have been created. This will notably launch Chinese FDI into Ethiopia to a whole new spectrum that has yet to be experienced. Chinese FDI coming into Ethiopia will most likely strengthen the production chains and specialization, technology spill over, substituting Chinese exports to Ethiopia by local production in the long term. However, the location of the zone has been described as far from ideal, given its distance from the capital and the limited transport links to international transport routes.[29] This situation may potentially be improved by the construction of the Addis-Djibouti railway line.

Infrastructure

Chinese funds have allowed Chinese firms to be extremely active in several infrastructure development initiatives. The Organization of Economic Cooperation and Development (OECD) notes that, estimates indicate that China has surpassed the World Bank as the leader in funding Africa's infrastructure projects.[30] The Chinese have been actively involved and taking a lead role in building infrastructure for African nations, particularly Ethiopia, such as railways, roads, and telecommunications. Although these investment projects are not referred to as FDI as such, since they are basically conducted by or on behalf of the Ethiopian government, it is, however, important to note that these projects would not have been successful without Chinese funding and engagement. When it comes to the infrastructure projects being undertaken by the Chinese in Ethiopia, it was agreed that these projects should be backed by concessional loans and must be carried out by Chinese contractors with a significant amount of goods and services to be used in these projects being obtained from China.[31] Since infrastructure is a panacea to economic development, these projects will significantly play a positive role toward Ethiopia's economic development. It is worth noting that before China itself was able to achieve any meaningful economic development, she first had to undertake massive infrastructural and industrial development initiatives.

It should further be noted that although these projects are of crucial importance to Ethiopia, they also favor Chinese interests. There is a notable presence of Chinese firms that are active as developers of industrial zones. More so, Chinese firms have been dominant in the construction of Ethiopia's railway lines and roads. According to Shinn, a number of these firms are currently undertaking the construction of roads across Ethiopia with funding provided by Chinese banks.[32] Nicolas notes that China's Exim Bank has been a key player in financing projects such as the Addis Ababa light rail system, the 733 km Djibouti-Addis Ababa railway line which was subsequently built by the China Railway Engineering Corporation (CREC).[33] After emphasizing on greater cooperation in energy and natural resources at the FOCAC summit in 2015, Chinese firms are also becoming actively involved in the development of Ethiopia's power sector through the construction of hydroelectric power plants, wind farms, and also biomass plants, all aimed at improving Ethiopia's energy supply for the benefit of its citizens.

TRADE

Since the start of 2000, Ethiopia has undergone significant economic growth as compared to its African counterparts. This has been attributed to the growth of Ethiopia's economic relations with China, which is currently Ethiopia's most important partner in terms of bilateral trade for both imports and exports.[34] It has been reported that, in 2009 alone, the volume of trade between China and Ethiopia amounted to US$1.5 billion.[35] There has been a notable increase in the amount of Ethio-China bilateral trade, which has increased by more than 13 times between 2003 and 2013.[36]

China's pursuit for lucrative markets makes Ethiopia a strategic trading partner since it has a large population and market potential, which makes it attractive to the Chinese. However, Verdonk argues that Ethiopia-China relations have been said to be unequal, with a growing imbalance in trade, where cheap Chinese manufactured products such as textile and plastic find themselves on the Ethiopian market, which negatively affects domestic production.[37] Despite all these concerns, it seems Ethiopia has benefited a great deal through higher export rates to China, facilitated through China's Duty-Free Preference (DFTP) for least developed countries.[38] Tables 8.1 and 8.2 show the number of Chinese exports to Ethiopia (1995–2015) and Chinese imports from Ethiopia (2005–2015) respectively.

Table 8.1 Chinese Exports to Ethiopia (1995–2015)

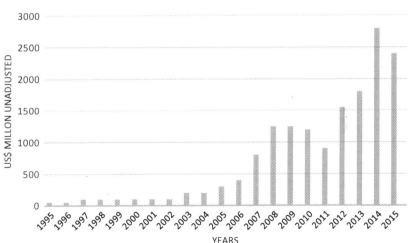

Source: Adapted from Fudan SIRPA (2017).[39] SIRPA—School of International Relations and Public Affairs (China Fudan University)

140   O. ABEGUNRIN AND C. MANYERUKE

Table 8.2   Chinese Imports from Ethiopia (2005–2015)

Source: Adapted from Fudan SIRPA (2017)[40]

Over the past decade, the amount of trade between China and Ethiopia has grown exponentially, with China becoming Ethiopia's most important trading partner ahead of Saudi Arabia, the European Union, and the United States. Ethiopia imports Chinese manufactured goods and equipment, which provides inputs necessary for infrastructure and manufacturing, while China mostly imports primary commodities and basic foodstuffs from Ethiopia. In 2017, Ethiopia exported 27,000 tons of coffee to Guangdong Province in China, which covers a quarter of coffee exports to China. According to the European Commission, there is, however, still a significant difference in terms of the trade quantity between import and export value, which has resulted in a trade deficit.[41] The trade balance between the two countries has been noted to be highly inclined in China's favor. To promote increased imports from African countries, China has implemented a zero-tariff policy for least developed nations, even though it maintains a trade surplus.[42] Ethiopia's exports to China are largely dominated by agricultural products, leather, and spices. Chakrabarty notes that, in recent years, Ethiopia's agricultural exports have grown rapidly and there has been a shift toward higher value products such as sesame seeds, cut flowers, and dried beans.[43] There has also been a notable importance in manufactured leather products through the Ethiopian government's drive for industrialization of the leather value chain through the promotion of FDI into the leather tanneries.

In terms of imports, China has increasingly become a crucial source of imported goods coming into Ethiopia since 2002. China accounted for about 24.6 percent of Ethiopia's total imports in 2017.[44] Consequently, China has grown to be the major source of manufactured goods, machinery, and transport equipment coming into Ethiopia. However, the increase of Chinese manufactured products being imported into Ethiopia has had a negative impact on domestic production. Some local manufacturers have thus been forced to scale down operations as a result. This impact on domestic production has, on the other hand, been deemed by some to be minimal, since Ethiopia has a limited industrial base. It has been argued that the sharp increase of imports from China can be attributed to Chinese development assistance, due to aid being tied in this input.

CHINA'S DEVELOPMENT ASSISTANCE TO ETHIOPIA

Ethiopia's economy has traditionally relied on the inflow of foreign aid. Ethiopia has been an attractive destination for foreign aid due to its strategic location on the Horn of Africa between Somalia and Sudan. More so, Alemu and Scoones note that Ethiopia has a significant number of people living in abject poverty and a government that has a track record of notable successes in aid being implemented.[45] Ethiopia has been a recipient of Chinese developmental assistance since the signing of the Agreement of Economic, Technical, Scientific and Trade Cooperation between the two countries in 1971.[46] China's development assistance to Ethiopia has increasingly become important to the Ethiopian economy. Ethiopia was the third largest recipient of Chinese aid commitments between 2000 and 2014. This undoubtedly shows Ethiopia's crucial position in China's Africa strategy and also reflects the close ties between Chinese aid and Chinese investment. Table 8.3 shows the top 10 recipients of Chinese developmental assistance.

Chinese developmental assistance has brought some notable benefits to Ethiopia's rural populace, especially considering that Ethiopia has one of the highest rates in terms of people living in the rural areas (eighty-one percent). The Wereta-Woldeya road was the first project that was completed with developmental assistance from China, which managed to link two remote parts of Ethiopia and greatly benefited Ethiopia's rural community. Most importantly, the kind of aid China renders to Ethiopia is

Table 8.3 Top 10 Recipients of Chinese Developmental Assistance (2000–2014)

Recipient	Amount (billion US$)
Cuba	6.7
Côte D'Ivoire	4.0
Ethiopia	3.7
Zimbabwe	3.6
Cameroon	3.4
Nigeria	3.1
Tanzania	3.0
Cambodia	3.0
Sri Lanka	2.8
Ghana	2.5

Source: AidData.org/China Fudan SIRPA (2017)[47]

significantly different from the one offered by the Western nations, and it focuses on debt relief, subsidized loans, grants, and aid in kind. According to Fantu Cheru, the Chinese aid thus focuses on solidarity, a mutual win-win relationship and equal benefits.[48] Chinese development aid has been described by some as having a commercial nature and closely associated with investment and trade initiatives. Unlike the Western aid, the Chinese development aid through being demand-driven has been able to align itself with the Ethiopian government's priorities. China's position as Ethiopia's largest bilateral donor within the last decade has strengthened Ethiopia's international bargaining power toward traditional donors. China's funding and engagement in Ethiopia's infrastructure development has been extensive.[49] Chakrabarty notes that China's aid flows are largely concentrated in infrastructure development, particularly the energy and transport sectors, which account for 68.3 percent of the total inflows of Chinese finances into Ethiopia.[50] The source of this funding is mostly the Chinese government, China Development Bank, and the Export-Import Bank of China. It should be noted that China's development assistance plays an important part in Ethiopia's economy especially in terms of infrastructure development. However, a lot of concern has been raised over the number of Chinese projects in infrastructure which are considered to have been funded through "*tied*" Chinese aid, which can be problematic for Ethiopia.[51] These projects are frequently being won through unfair competition, with the Chinese firms being criticized for using imported Chinese materials and professionals, with locals being employed in low paid positions. This prevents skills and technology from being transferred for the benefit of the local workforce.

CHALLENGES

There are several challenges that have arisen from the Ethio-China relations. These challenges can generally be classified under Ethiopia's lack of competitive industries and institutional capacity. As a result, Ethiopia seems to be gaining less from the current arrangement. This can be attributed to the agriculture-based export of Ethiopia and China. A number of scholars have argued that this is affecting the supposed win-win situation between the two countries, and hence China's aid and loan programs are an attempt to compensate Ethiopia. The main challenge has notably arisen from Ethiopia's failure to produce competitive and a sufficient amount of products that can be exported to China. Ethiopia notably lacks strong technological and industrial capacity to manufacture finished goods that could compete with the Chinese products. Ethiopia's lack of a strong economic base which could be used to build competitive industries and turn the relationship into a possible win-win situation has largely been deemed as the cause of this lack of capacity on the part of the Ethiopian industries. More so, the Chinese technologies are challenging Ethiopia's domestic products. The Chinese are using their superior technology and capital advantage and, as a result, Chinese exports and investment are now undermining the locally made products for both export and home use. There is also lack of infrastructure, technology, and awareness by Ethiopian investors in terms of producing large volumes of higher quality goods. The World Bank notes that the Chinese firms in the construction and manufacturing sectors lack well-trained Ethiopian professionals to allow for skill and technology transfer and this could be the reason Chinese firms prefer employing professionals from China.[52] Despite the positive forward momentum, Ethiopia's increased economic growth has not been accompanied by structural transformation, as the country's manufacturing structure is still struggling to make a significant contribution to the Gross Domestic Product (GDP).

BENEFITS

Despite the belief that China is reaping more benefits and dominating this relationship, it has been acknowledged that Ethiopia is also benefitting from this arrangement. The country's economic growth in recent years can be attributed to Chinese investment. Chinese investment is stimulating Ethiopia's economic growth and promoting its exports to other countries. Ethiopia has benefited from China's cancellation of a debt worth US$10 billion for African nations. China has also sent doctors to treat Ethiopians and has hosted a significant number of Ethiopian workers and students in Chinese training centers and universities. Chinese professionals have been coming into Ethiopia to offer a number of capacity-building services in terms of Ethiopia's limited technology, resource management, and agricultural development. China is further promoting Ethiopia's human capacity through various means. Each year the Chinese government offers Ethiopians government scholarships to further their studies in China. China has been assisting Ethiopia in the construction of schools and in the development of the country's human and material resources in its education institutions. The infrastructure development projects in the form of the construction of roads, dams, and bridges by the Chinese have been important contributors to the development of Ethiopia's infrastructure. Gerda and Meskel are of the view that the Chinese are making a notable contribution in the construction of much needed roads, electric power stations, are actively engaged in the exploration of oil, and a host of other productive ventures, all of which stand to greatly benefit Ethiopia and its citizens.[53]

DISCUSSION OF SOCIOECONOMIC EFFECTS OF ETHIO-CHINA RELATIONS

It is quite difficult to accurately assess the advantages and disadvantages of Chinese involvement in Ethiopia. It has been argued that there have been a host of controversial effects in terms of the relationship between China and Ethiopia. Trade has been impacted in terms of competition in domestic markets for locally-oriented manufacturers and competition in external markets from export-oriented industry.[54] According to Alden, the balance of trade between the two nations favors China, as local industries and merchants have been negatively affected by the huge influx of cheap Chinese goods on the market, which cost less and are of better quality than the locally produced ones.[55] Also, the Ethiopian producers clearly do not have the capacity to compete with Chinese companies, since these Chinese manufacturers have a distinct advantage in that they incur low costs of production and market prices. De Lorenzo is of the view that the most worrisome aspect is the impact that Chinese competition has on African enterprises and exports.[56] As a result, some local Ethiopian firms have been forced to close shop, as they can no longer keep up with the competition from the Chinese firms, mainly caused by the unchecked and unlimited Chinese imports. With the influx of Chinese goods on the Ethiopian local market, there has been a notable increase in conflict over labor practices and market strategies.

The use of Chinese labor in Ethiopia instead of local Ethiopian employees in Chinese funded projects has been heavily criticized. This inclination to employ Chinese nationals and the long working hours expected by Chinese managers have been a source of conflict with the local culture and labor laws. The practices by Chinese companies have further resulted in a lot of discontent in local Ethiopian communities, who feel that these companies are not making a meaningful contribution toward increasing local employment and strengthening the local economy. There has been outcry by the public over the quality of Chinese products and infrastructure and the increased number of Chinese nationals present in Ethiopia who have been accused of limiting employment opportunities for the locals. The most serious issue has been accusations of poorly compensated land-expropriation, which has fueled a lot of social unrest to the extent that a state of emergency had to be declared in 2016 due to the fast expansion of industrial zones into the territory of locals who felt that this was happening at their expense and was resulting in a loss of land, which is the major means of production for them.

CONCLUSION

It is evident that there has been a notable growth in the relationship between Africa and China, mostly driven by the Chinese model of development. The strategy adopted by the Chinese has clearly been working in the favor of both parties involved. This is particularly extraordinary, especially considering the very different cultures and agendas of these two countries. The result of the Ethio-China ties has been increased investment and trade, foreign aid and debt forgiveness. The relationship China has with Ethiopia and other African nations has been described as different from the exploitative one that the Western nations have with Africa. China seems to be offering a partnership-oriented relationship, one based on mutual goals and respect. It has been dubbed as a win-win situation with both parties gaining substantially from the arrangement.

The prevailing conditions in Ethiopia have led to China adding value to Ethiopia's manufactured products and improvement of the country's industrial production particularly leather products. This is a critical step for Ethiopia in its efforts toward diversifying its economy in order to achieve its goal of attaining middle income status. Although Chinese investment has not yet been able to match Western investment, it is clearly making notable strides and having a lasting impact on the economies of African countries such as Ethiopia and, if this momentum is maintained, then this relationship is bound to reach new heights. It is apparent that from an Ethiopian viewpoint, Chinese investment has brought in a host of positive benefits. However, Chinese investments have also come with a substantial price and undesirable connotations such as dominance of local culture and considerations. There has also been a somewhat negative effect on local trade and commerce. Ethiopian labor has not fully benefited from Chinese investment as the Chinese have a habit of bringing in with them their own Chinese professionals. Nevertheless, it is evident that the Chinese have a sturdy track record of investing in Africa and supporting its continued development, with Ethiopia being one of the nations that have realized considerable benefits from ties with China.

NOTES

1. Ministry of Finance and Economic Development (MOFED). *Growth and Transformation Plan II.* Addis Ababa: MOFED, 2016.
2. Mohan, G. and Kale, D. *The invisible hand of South-South globalization: Chinese migrants in Africa. A Report for the Rockefeller Foundation prepared by The Development Policy and Practice Department.* Milton Keynes: The Open University, 2007.
3. Kinfu Adisu, Thomas Sharkey and Sam C. Okoroafo, "The Impact of Chinese Investment in Africa," *International Journal of Business and Management*, Vol. 5, No. 9 (2010): 3.
4. Tilda Verdonk, *South-South Cooperation-A case study of Ethiopia's political and economic relations with China and Turkey*, Sweden: Linnaeus University, 2017, 14.
5. Deborah Brautigam, "Close encounters: Chinese business networks as industrial catalysts in Sub-Saharan Africa." *African Affairs*. 102 (2002): 447–467.
6. Rabia Yimam Damtew and Samson Maekele Tsegay, "Developing south-south cooperation: The case of Ethio-China economic relationship," *International Journal of Research Studies in Management*, Vol. 6, No. 1 (2017): 75–89.
7. Wenping, H., The balancing act of China's African Policy. *China Security*, 3 (2007): 23–40.

8 ETHIOPIA-CHINA RELATIONS: A FOCUS ON FACTORS DRIVING...   147

8. Ramos, J. C., *The Beijing Consensus*. The World Bank Research Observer Advance Access, 2004.
9. Jens Stilhoff Sörensen, *Challenging the aid paradigm: Western currents and Asian alternatives*. Basingstoke: Palgrave Macmillan, 2010.
10. Ramos, *The Beijing Consensus*.
11. Ibid.
12. Adisu et al., *The Impact of Chinese Investment in Africa*, 4.
13. Barry Sautman and Yan Hairong, "Friends and Interests: China's distinctive links with Africa." *African Studies Review*, 50(3) (2007): 75–114.
14. Carmody, P., *The New Scramble for Africa*. Cambridge, UK, and Maiden, MA: Polity Press, 2011.
15. Bataineh, B., Bennon, M., and Fukuyama, F. "Beijing's Building Boom." *Foreign Affairs* (2018).
16. World Bank. *Chinese FDI in Ethiopia: A World Bank survey*, 2012. Retrieved from http://wwwwds.worldbank.org/external/default/WDSContentServer/WDSP/IB/2012/12/14/000386194_20121214024800/Rendered/PDF/NonAsciiFileName0.pdf (Accessed on 29/01/2019).
17. Ibid.
18. Adisu et al., *The Impact of Chinese Investment in Africa*, 4.
19. Francoise Nicolas, *Chinese Investors in Ethiopia: The Perfect Match*. Paris: Center for Asian Studies, 2017, 17.
20. Verdonk, *South-South Cooperation-A case study of Ethiopia's political and economic relations with China and Turkey*, 17.
21. Cheru, F., Obi, C., *The rise of China and India in Africa: challenges, opportunities and critical interventions*, London: Zed, 2016.
22. Alemayehu Geda and Atnafu G. Meskel, *Impact of China-Africa Investment Relations: Case Study of Ethiopia. Final Draft Prepared for AERC Collaborative Research on the Impact of China on Africa*. Mombasa: AERC, 2010.
23. Nicolas, *Chinese Investors in Ethiopia: The Perfect Match*, 17.
24. Jalata, G. G., "Development Assistance from the South: Comparative Analysis of Chinese and Indian to Ethiopia." *Chinese Studies* 3 (1) (2014): 24–39.
25. Nicolas, *Chinese Investors in Ethiopia: The Perfect Match*, 13.
26. Damtew and Tsegay, *Developing south-south cooperation: The case of Ethio-China economic relationship*, 83.
27. Nicolas, *Chinese Investors in Ethiopia: The Perfect Match*, 13.
28. Alemayehu Geda and Atnafu G. Meskel, "Impact of China-Africa Investment Relations: Case Study of Ethiopia," *Institute of African Economic Studies, IAES Working Paper Serious No. A04* (2011), 6.

29. United Nations Development Programme (UNDP), *Comparative Study on Special Economic Zones in Africa and China*. Working Paper series, No. 06, 2015.
30. OECD. Unlocking the potential of South-South Cooperation: Policy recommendations from the Task Team on South-South Cooperation, 2011. Retrieved from http://www.oecd.org/dac/effectiveness/TT-SSC%20 Policy%20Recommendations.pdf (accessed on 29/01/2019).
31. David Dollar, *China's Engagement with Africa – from Natural Resources to Human Resources*. New York: Brookings, 2016.
32. David, H. Shinn, Ethiopia and China: How Two Former Empires Connected? *International Policy Digest*, 2014.
33. Nicolas, *Chinese Investors in Ethiopia: The Perfect Match*, 25.
34. Chakrabarty, M., "Ethiopia-China economic relations a classic win-win situation?" *World review of political economy: journal of the World Association for Political Economy*, 7(2) (2016): 226–248.
35. Damtew and Tsegay, *Developing south-south cooperation: The case of Ethio-China economic relationship*, 76.
36. Ibid.
37. Verdonk, *South-South Cooperation-A case study of Ethiopia's political and economic relations with China and Turkey*, 17.
38. Jalata, *Development Assistance from the South: Comparative Analysis of Chinese and Indian to Ethiopia*.
39. Fudan SIRPA, "Development and Industrialization in Ethiopia: Reflections from China's Experience," *Fudan SIRPA Think Tank Report Series*, School of International Relations and Public Affairs Fudan University, 2017.
40. Ibid.
41. European Commission. European Union: *Trade in Goods with Ethiopia*. Brussels: Directorate General for Trade, 2017.
42. Forum on China-Africa Cooperation (FOCAC). *The largest private shoe-manufacturing enterprise in Dongguan makes investment in Ethiopia*. Addis Ababa: FOCAC. Retrieved from http://www.fmprc.gov.cn/zflt/chn/zfgx/zfgxjmhz/t886616.htm (accessed on 02/07/2019).
43. Chakrabarty, *Ethiopia-China economic relations a classic win-win situation*.
44. European Commission, *Trade in Goods with Ethiopia*.
45. Alemu, D., and Scoones, I., "Negotiating New Relationships: How the Ethiopian State Is Involving China and Brazil in Agriculture and Rural Development." *IDS Bulletin 44* (4) (2013): 91–100.
46. Zemene, *An Overview of the Bilateral Relations between the Federal Democratic Republic of Ethiopia and the People's Republic of China*. Addis Ababa: Asia Australasia and the Middle East General Directorate Ministry of Foreign Affairs, Ethiopia, 2006, 5.
47. Fudan SIRPA, *Development and Industrialization in Ethiopia: Reflections from China's Experience*.

48. Fantu Cheru, *The rise of China and India in Africa: challenges, opportunities and critical interventions.*
49. Ibid.
50. Chakrabarty, *Ethiopia-China economic relations a classic win-win situation.*
51. Verdonk, *South-South Cooperation-A case study of Ethiopia's political and economic relations with China and Turkey*, 17.
52. World Bank, *Chinese FDI in Ethiopia: A World Bank survey.*
53. Geda and Meskel, *Impact of China-Africa Investment Relations: Case Study of Ethiopia*, 22.
54. Adisu et al., *The Impact of Chinese Investment in Africa*, 5.
55. Alden, C., China and Africa. *Survival*, 47(3) (2005): 147–164
56. De Lorenzo, M., African Perspective on China. *American Enterprise Institute for Public Policy Research*, 2007.

CHAPTER 9

China and Regional Integration in Africa

INTRODUCTION

The concept of regional integration has drawn much attention and has been preached by several countries over the past few years, both regionally and internationally. Regional integration has been idolized as the key to promoting regional growth and development through the adoption and implementation of policies that will yield mutual benefits for all parties involved. Following the emergence of the euro, there has been a renewed and an increasing global interest to promote economic and regional integration as a means of facilitating economic growth and regional development. With African nations attaining their independence, regional integration has come to be viewed as crucial for facilitating the continent's development. Regional Economic Communities (RECs) have emerged as the building blocks in advancing Africa's sustainable development agenda. Of late, regional integration has become a central figure in the African Union's Vision 2063, which seeks to achieve an integrated continent with free movement of people, goods, capital and services, and infrastructure connections. In recent years, regional integration has become a priority for African policy makers and their governments alike have come to embrace regional integration as a vital component of their strategies for development, especially their engagement with foreign partners such as China. With China's increased presence and activities on the continent, there has arisen a pertinent need for a coordinated and united African voice. China

© The Author(s) 2020
O. Abegunrin, C. Manyeruke, *China's Power in Africa*,
Politics and Development of Contemporary China,
https://doi.org/10.1007/978-3-030-21994-9_9

151

has participated in numerous areas regarding Africa's integration and has also received an active response from Africa. Despite all this, the question remains if China can be considered, directly or indirectly, as a stumbling block or an enabler of regional integration in Africa. Regional integration in Africa will allow for economic growth and participation in a global economy. This chapter thus seeks to explore if African states can utilize a regional approach to economic development whilst still engaging and benefitting from external benefactors such as China, or such global powerhouses in the world economy have been manipulating Africa's efforts at regional integration for their own benefit and gain preferential treatment to Africa's vast resources and markets. African groups such as the AU, which interact with China will be the focus for this chapter and will be used as examples.

Historical Background

China and Africa's economic and political exchanges can be traced to the Han Dynasty as far back as 138 BC.[1] The ancient Silk Road enabled the transportation of silk fabrics from China to Alexandria in Egypt, which at the time was a major economic and trading center for the West. China further established trade links with other ancient African kingdoms, such as the Kingdom of the Kush and the Kingdom of Aksum.[2] This trade was characterized by goods, such as ivory, rhino horns, and spices from East Africa, with silk and porcelain coming in from China during the mid-eighth century to the mid-ninth century.

In the post-independence era of Africa, the similar historical experiences acted as a bridge that connected the two sides and brought them together. There was the existence of mutually beneficial ties, most notably in the support that Africa gave to China in voting for her to gain a permanent seat in the United Nations Security Council in 1971, and China also making considerable efforts through supporting the development initiatives of African nations. Historically, China has always sought to leave lasting footprints on Africa's affairs. To achieve this, China released its official policy on Africa in January 2006. Jin notes that, in recent years, China has been engaged in an initiative to "support the integration of Africa and help Africa improve its overall capacity for development."[3] Africa's obsession with regional integration can be traced as far back as the pre-independence period in the twentieth century. The oldest functioning manifestation of regional integration in Africa remains the Southern

African Customs Union, which was established in 1910. The establishment of the Organisation of African Unity (OAU) in 1963 remains a key symbol, achievement, and stepping stone in efforts aimed at integrating Africa.

The establishment of the Forum on China-Africa Cooperation (FOCAC) in 2000 serves as the focal point for multilateral cooperation between China and African countries and represents a further development of the traditional model of bilateral cooperation.[4] FOCAC acts as a representation of the contemporary China-Africa economic cooperation, which has a long and notable illustrious history. FOCAC has further been a symbol of the development of the traditional model of bilateral cooperation, and the epicenter of China's multilateral cooperation with African countries. As a result, in recent years, China-Africa economic cooperation has been addressing new situations. Most notably, under its initiative to "support the integration of Africa and help Africa improve its overall capacity for development," China has participated in a variety of areas concerning the economic integration of Africa, and it has received an active response from Africa.

Conceptual and Theoretical Considerations

Regional integration is described by Mlambo and Mlambo as the coming together of countries in a bid to share, contribute to knowledge, policy development and growth, peace and security, trade and educational development.[5] The World Bank describes regional integration as "the integration of factor and goods market and coordination of policy across sovereign jurisdictions within a region and can range in depth and scope."[6] Grobbelaar and Meyer state that "according to the international trade theory and the new economic geography, regional integration enables augmented returns and increased consumption which can result in a wide range of effects beneficial to member countries."[7] Such effects include reduced costs of production and consumer prices. Factors such as an improved market size, productivity, and availability of production will ensure larger markets to be served, which will have a positive effect in increasing the attractiveness of regions to foreign firms that will come into these markets. Mlambo and Mlambo point out that "regional integration thus enables coordination and collective bargaining power emanating from regional agreements, improved management of shared natural resources and a decrease in the threat of conflict between countries."[8]

With enough substitutes, there may be an increase in demand in the region, which will in turn result in greater competition in the trade zone.

The theory of regionalism best describes China and regional integration in Africa. Regional integration through the creation of regional groupings has been depicted as a pathway to regional growth and development. Zeb is of the view that:

> When viewed from a political science and international relations perspective, regionalism can be described as the expression of common sense (by people, organisations or nations) of purpose and identity combined the creation and implementation of institutions that express a identify and shape collective action within a geographical region, with the aim of advancing the economic growth of that region through cooperation.[9]

Soderbaum notes that "the theory of regionalism is anchored on the belief that governments and other stakeholders should be able to make an effective contribution to the development of a particular region through for instance, increased trade, regional investments and the crafting of policies that strengthen regional cooperation and integration."[10] The theory suggests that the ideologies of regions are interconnected hence regional countries must harness these ideas and work together to contribute to the overall development of the region as a collective. China has, over the past few years, identified with this and has come in to play a part in forwarding Africa's development. The theory further asserts that national governments have a crucial part to play in this regard. Mlambo and Mlambo hold the view that "it is apparent that African nations have in the face of constant challenges advocated for the strengthening of regional integration in order to spur economic growth and development,"[11] hence the role China now plays in this regard.

It can be argued that China's support of regional integration in Africa is aimed at promoting cooperation and economic development. This support can be explained as an expression of regionalism, as China shares similar developmental traits with African countries that make up Africa's regional integration blocs. The cooperation that exists between China and Africa can thus be studied and understood from a regionalist standpoint, also taking into consideration the various bilateral agreements and protocols that have been established to ensure the consolidation of regional cooperation, and hence this theory is relevant in explaining China's role in Africa's regional integration.

REGIONAL INTEGRATION IN AFRICA

Although a number of African leaders were at the forefront of advocating for regional economic integration in Africa immediately after gaining independence, regional integration institutions only came to life in the 1970s and 1980s. Grobbelaar and Meyer note that during this period, there arose an inward focus and realization that political unity could be used as the impetus for achieving market integration so as to reach economies of scale.[12] Over the years, there have been numerous regional integration experiments on the continent, which include the Southern African Customs Union, the Central African Federation (CAF), and the East African Community (EAC). The most noticeable regional blocs to surface after Africa's independence include the Economic Community on West African States (ECOWAS) created in 1975, the West African Economic Community (WAEC), first launched in 1966 and later remodeled to be the West African Economic and Monetary Union (WAEMU) in 1994. The Southern African Development Coordination Conference (SADCC) created in 1980 and replaced by Southern African Development Community (SADC) in 1992 and the Common Market for Eastern and Southern African States (COMESA).

It cannot be argued that regional integration in Africa is essential if nations on the continent are to reap benefits from economies of scale and strengthen their position in international negotiations, especially in today's globalized world.[13] Africa's population is projected to reach almost the two billion mark by 2050, which makes the need for regional integration even more pressing to address the current economic, social, political, and security challenges that seem to have little prospect for resolution in the prevailing *sovereignty framework*.[14] Regional integration in Africa has as its primary aim the promotion of development amongst African nations and, at the same time, reducing indebtedness and dependence on Western nations. The very idea of regional integration has been seen as a way through which African nations can "pool together their economic sovereignty" so as to improve the living conditions of their people and extend the struggle for political decolonization into one of economic decolonization.

African integration has, in the past few years, been modeled on China's decentralization and central planning policy, which establishes consistent coordination and linkages between the central government and regional and provincial representatives.[15] The African Union (AU) and Regional Economic Communities (RECs) now have similar relations as defined in the 2007 Protocol on Relations between the AU and RECs, which guides the AU in facilitating and implementing regional integration.[16] Given China's new position on the global map as an economic and political powerhouse, the extent to which Africa can engage China in regional integration is thus crucial. It has been argued that China's rise as a global economic powerhouse has created additional opportunities and challenges for African integration. Schiere and Rugamba note that "on one hand, Chinese investment in infrastructure is easing key supply side bottlenecks for further integration and on the other, China's bilateral approach with individual African countries is restricting the prospect of addressing regional issues."[17] Some view Chinese infrastructure investment as supporting intra-Africa trade to alleviate blockages to African integration. The success of the Asian Tigers for example, underlines the importance of promoting and encouraging the growth and strengthening of various regional trading blocs on the continent. Vhumbunu is of the view that the recent lack of progress in the multilateral trade negotiations has further increased emphasis on regional trade blocs.[18] This has also encouraged the growth of nonreciprocal free trade agreements such as the African Growth and Opportunity Act (AGOA) and the European Union's Everything but Arms Agreement. The European Union and Africa also have a reciprocal trade agreement under the Economic Partnership Agreements (EPA) which succeeded the Lomé accord. These agreements offer certain advantages to Africa, as they provide poor exporting nations with temporary price advantages to assist them to develop their export industries and this can be helpful in promoting export-led growth.

However, there have been challenges noted in Africa's efforts at regional integration involving the acceptance of the Economic Partnerships agreements (EPAs) with the European Union by African countries and further challenges associated with harmonizing the South African economy within the Southern African Customs Union (SACU) as agents of regional integration.[19] These bodies evidently do not possess the institutional capacity, implementation, and program development required. Institutional capacity is of the utmost importance, bearing in mind that China will be looking to these bodies and other regional economic communities (REC) to offer the road-map for African integration.

Ties between China and Africa's Regional Organizations

In today's world, regional organizations have come to occupy an important part as agents for development, with different forms of regional cooperation mechanisms in Africa also being constantly improved. The emergence of new players in Africa's economic setting, specifically China, has presented African leaders and development practitioners with an opportunity to consider how the prospects of deepening regional integration can be improved.[20] Bertollo et al. postulate that China's intention to play a role in Africa's regional integration efforts is clearly expressed in its New Asian-African Strategic Partnership.[21] China acknowledges the need for the African Union and subregional organizations to be a dominant force as African actors.[22]

According to Yang, China and Africa's multilevel cooperation, which encompasses bilateral, subregional, and transregional cooperation, has developed into both a crucial part of the South-South cooperation and a vital component of cross-regional cooperation in today's world.[23] One notable example which cannot be ignored is the rapid development of the ties between China and the African Union, which is Africa's largest and principal regional organization. These relations are visibly not a new phenomenon, but, rather, they stretch over 40 years from the interaction between China and the Organisation of African Unity (OAU). Jin asserts that, on the one hand, the AU has shown itself as a consistent partner through its firm support for China and, on the other hand, China has been viewing its influence and role in Africa of conducting regional and international affairs as crucial.[24] China has remained steadfast in its support of the AU in international multilateral meetings, by opposing attempts by Western nations to meddle into Africa's affairs through sanctions and military interventions. China is evidently supportive of Africa's integration in terms of economics, politics, and a response to peace and security issues.[25] So important are the ties between China and Africa that China has been sending its high-level officials as envoys from the Ministry of Foreign Affairs to attend AU summits since 2002, and it was one of the first non-African nations to appoint a representative to the AU. China's "no strings attached" model has notably contributed to African integration, as it has initiated a new debate on African integration and development and is thus a "wake-up call" for traditional actors.[26] Through FOCAC, China has pledged support to the AU in its endeavor to maintain regional peace and stability and the promotion of Africa's unity and development. Important to note is that China has been contributing over US$ 1 million annually as part of efforts aimed at supporting the AU's capacity-building and peace-keeping operations in Somalia and Sudan.[27] In 2011, China completed one of its largest aid projects in Africa to date, through the construction of the AU Conference Centre at an estimated cost of 800 million RMB.

Trade, China, and Africa's RECs

In its efforts to promote regional integration in Africa, China further cooperates with several subregional organizations in Africa such as the Southern African Development Community (SADC), the Economic Community of West African States (ECOWAS), and the East African Community (EAC), all of which form vital components of the AU. In this regard, China has over the past few years been engaged in Free Trade Area negotiations with the Southern African Customs Union (2004), has established the China-SADC dialogue mechanism (2007), and, most significantly, signed the Framework Agreement on economy, investment, trade, and technical cooperation between China and the East African Community in 2011. China has signed important economic and trade agreements with African RECs, such as the EAC and ECOWAS. In 2012, China and the Economic Community of West African States together established an economic and trade cooperation mechanism aimed at achieving improved progress and prosperity for social and economic development. These agreements have the primary objective of promoting trade, direct investment, construction of cross-border infrastructure, amongst other objectives.[28] Moumouni notes that there have been initiatives undertaken to include Africa's business community such as the first China-ECOWAS Economic Trade Forum in Beijing hosted in 2007 by China's Council for the Promotion of International Trade (CCPIT).[29] It is at this forum that China and ECOWAS signed a Memorandum of Understanding to establish an economic cooperation partnership anchored on the provision of capital for infrastructure development and trade facilitation.[30] From this, one notes that RECs have been instrumental in the establishment of transparent and stable regional frameworks to attract greater investment. Economic regionalism has, in this case, been anchored on initiatives and the commitment of key African regional organizations together with China's willingness to lend a hand. RECs have been instrumental in enabling better trade negotiations with China, which has enhanced

Sino-African trade. With the strengthening of the cooperation between the AU, African regional organizations, and China, there has arisen a new road-map for multilateral engagement between the AU and African subregional organizations with China. For instance, Bertollo et al. are of the view that, with the launch of the New Asian-African Strategic Partnership, China has expressed its intention to play a pivotal role in the integration of ECOWAS.[31] This will bring together entrepreneurs from Chinese firms and African RECs to explore further trade and business opportunities. It is evident that China has now expanded its ties with Africa from bilateral and trade cooperation into improved relations with African RECs. However, it has been argued that instruments such as the Rules of Origin, Common External Tariff (CET), and reduction in tariffs may have been compromised on application and purpose because of China's intense bilateral relations with African countries. Alden further argues that the balance of trade between Africa and China is clearly tipped in China's favor.[32] Also, the influx of Chinese products on the continent has consequently influenced intraregional trade.

INFRASTRUCTURE DEVELOPMENT AND REGIONAL INTEGRATION

For several years now, Africa's infrastructure gap has been an impediment for the continent's development and integration. To achieve infrastructure development to fuel its economic growth, catch up with the rest of the world, and achieve region integration, there is need for huge investments from Regional Economic Communities (RECs), together with traditional and emerging partners such as China.[33] According to Kandiero, achieving this and closing Africa's infrastructure gap will need an estimated US$80 billion worth of investment each year.[34] As part of the regional integration plan, African regional organizations, such as the African union (AU), African Development Bank (AfDB), New Partnership for African Development (NEPAD), and RECs have designed regional policies to finance and facilitate infrastructure projects. China has been offering support to the New Partnership for African Development (NEPAD) as a positive force for African development and has, over the years, provided financial aid to NEPAD as part of the concerted efforts aimed at promoting regional integration and structural transformation through addressing Africa's infrastructure gap.[35] Schiere and Rugamba state that, to that end,

160   O. ABEGUNRIN AND C. MANYERUKE

the Africa50fund was established to increase the number of bankable infrastructure projects and direct project finance.[36] China has thus, notably, been playing an increasing role in financing infrastructure development in sub-Saharan Africa,[37] to the extent that it has now become the largest player and largest financier of infrastructure projects in Africa.

Although other nations such as India and Brazil are investing in Africa, they have been unable to match China's level of investment on the continent. It has been argued that these investments are ideal and perfectly timed, since Africa's lack of infrastructure coincides with China's keen interest in the infrastructure projects of African countries. Schiere and Rugamba further state that, the setting up of RECs to harmonize infrastructure development strategies motivates China to promote Africa's regional integration through financing and constructing rail networks, roads, ports, power plants, and information technology infrastructure.[38] Although most of the negotiations between China and African countries are bilateral, China has, at the same time, expressed interest in supporting Africa's regional integration efforts mainly through financing and constructing regional infrastructure projects in Africa.[39] China's contribution to Africa's regional integration efforts is particularly seen through her involvement in port, road, and railway projects aimed at linking several African countries. These infrastructure projects are financed through China's Export and Import Bank (China EXIMBANK) and China Development Bank, who both cooperate with the AfDB, the Development Bank of Southern Africa, and the West African Development Bank to come up with policies that enhance Africa's infrastructure development. Furthermore, the emergence of BRICS economies presents opportunities for the creation of investment linkages and partnerships in Africa's infrastructure development prospects. It is apparent that sustainable infrastructure development in Africa will positively aid regional integration.

China's Role in the Programme for Infrastructure Development in Africa (PIDA)

Africa has determined infrastructure development as one of the development areas it has prioritized, and infrastructure is coincidentally one of China's areas of comparative advantage. Africa has, over the past few years, been embroiled in a bid to industrialize, urbanize, and integrate the region through infrastructure development. As a result, the African Union, in

2012, initiated the Programme for Infrastructure Development in Africa (PIDA) as a calculated agenda for the period up to 2040.[40] Through the PIDA initiative, the African Union has the objective of attaining interconnection throughout the entire continent, particularly in the energy, transport, and information communication sectors.[41] This initiative, which is worth hundreds of billions of U.S. dollars, has drawn the interest of several investors from the international community as well. It is interesting to note that the PIDA initiative essentially covers areas, which are not only of international and comparative advantage to China, but also are of shared interest between Africa and China. This has undoubtedly resulted in a huge potential for cooperation between the two parties. Jin notes that this cooperation has further led to the establishment of the China-Africa partnership on transnational and transregional infrastructure construction in 2012, indicating that the cooperation between the two is part of China's determination to shape a new kind of China-Africa strategic partnership.[42] Through this initiative, Chinese firms and financial institutions will render support to African nations in their attempts to improve trade facilitation. These areas of cooperation comprise preliminary work in the form of consulting, planning, feasibility studies, and scheme design regarding interconnection projects and resource surveys; to train and nurture 300 management and technical aptitudes in several areas relating to infrastructure development through the US$ 20 billion loan advanced to Africa for the construction of infrastructure.[43]

The Impact of China's Involvement in Africa's Regional Integration Efforts

China seems to be pragmatic in its approach, as she has taken a leaf from the positive aspects of the capitalist open economy and fused them with the somewhat positive traits of socialism and has applied this to her own situation.[44] Vhumbunu is of the view that, as a result, the philosophy behind Chinese development is thus neither socialist nor capitalist but is somewhat situated somewhere in between a centrally planned model and a liberal open economy.[45] The model adopted by the Chinese government is quite dissimilar to the "Washington Consensus" and the Africa Growth and Opportunity Act in the sense that the Beijing Consensus (i.e. socialism with Chinese characteristics), "utilizes all the fruits of capitalist civilization."[46]

China has been playing an active role in effecting Africa's regional integration. This has seen cooperation between China, the AU, and various African regional integration organizations deepening their ties and cooperation in several sectors. As a result, there has been an emergence of a new road-map for the AU's and African subregional organizations' multilateral engagement with China. China's engagement in various regional integration projects is strategic, particularly in relation to its resource exploitation and search for new markets for its construction companies in Africa, who are embroiled in projects mostly aimed at connecting African landlocked countries with the coast. All of this has paved the way for China to have easy access into Africa, transport resources out of the continent, and, at the same time, increase the amount of trade and investment between the two and achieve some level of infrastructure development for African nations. The advancement of wide-ranging cooperation between China and Africa in different spheres has turned into one of the most significant driving forces of Africa's development. According to Jin, other views suggest that discussions between China and the Western nations regarding the critical issues of global development concerning Africa, such as economic development, sustainability of growth, and the relationship between economic development, political democracy, and human rights, have had a positive effect on improving the status of Africa in the current global hierarchy.[47]

However, the negative impact of Chinese involvement in Africa's regional integration efforts may include a reduction in tariff revenues, which will result in loss of revenue for national governments. There are further indirect effects in the form of brain drain or capital flight, and these have on occasion become impediments to economic integration, particularly in circumstances where the impact is at national level and not regional level.[48] There may be trade diversion if partners maintain high tariffs for nonmembers, which might result in low-cost products from nonmembers to be replaced by higher cost products from countries with a trade agreement.[49] China's presence in Africa's construction sector has been argued to result in massive infrastructure projects that, at times, fall short of meeting international standards, with cases where the infrastructure rapidly deteriorates shortly after delivery and a notable lack of transparency in the financing of these projects.[50] In most cases, the Chinese firms who provide funding for the construction projects do not carry out impact assessments. Grimm et al. assert that almost nothing is disclosed in terms of the success rates or impact of the projects.[51] The lack of transparency in loan deals and contract bidding of Chinese funded projects in Africa results in increased financial burdens for African countries.[52]

BARRIERS TO REGIONAL INTEGRATION IN AFRICA

Although African nations have been making efforts designed to promote regional integration, there are several challenges and difficulties that have been experienced. African nations in general suffer from too many structural realities to allow for smooth integration. The process of regional integration in Africa has been hampered by inherent internal weaknesses in Africa's social, political, and economic milieu. Kuhnhardt is of the view that, historically, African integration has enjoyed significant political support, but implementation has been hampered by the desire of individual countries to safeguard their national sovereignty.[53] Regional agreements such as the African, Caribbean and Pacific (ACP) group of states that offer preferential market access to developed nations, have certainly not helped the situation either. One crucial inhibition to coordination across the various regional organizations is that African countries are members to more than one regional organization. United Nations Economic Commission for Africa (UNECA) notes that, of the fifty-three African countries, twenty-six are members of two regional economic communities and twenty are members of three regional groups, with only six countries maintaining membership in just one regional economic community.[54] This results in a wastage of the limited financial and administrative resources and further complicates the negotiation of bilateral trade treaties with China.

Regional integration is further hindered by the different trade policies that exist between African countries, coupled with trade barriers in the form of tariffs, import and export bans, and the absence of enough financial and physical infrastructure across the continent.[55] According to the World Bank, although there is the existence of huge opportunities for African nations to be engaged in trade amongst themselves, the current African market is still fragmented, which is a hindrance to cross border trade and investments.[56] The proliferation of regional organizations also affects African regional integration. Although it is easier at times to achieve trade integration agreements within the smaller regional organizations than with the larger blocs, these small organizations can become a stumbling block to African integration. This is particularly the case in instances where each one of them seeks to attain the interests of its members, sometimes at the expense of promoting trade liberalization at the continental level. It has also been argued that, because of the differences in language, culture, and regulatory systems, Chinese investors in Africa encounter a host of challenges concerning matters related to corporate social responsibility, labor relations and environmental protection.

Whereas several nations the world over have managed to set aside their differences and come up with policies designed to be regionally beneficial, African countries have not been able to realize such benefits that come with regional integration as compared to Asian and European countries, owing to a plethora of challenges bedeviling the region. According to Mlambo and Mlambo, political instability, disagreements amongst member states, and trust issues have been the major factors which have inhibited the ability of regional groupings in Africa to realize their full potential and associated benefits.[57] Peace and security challenges have also been identified as one of the largest obstacles to Africa's regional integration. Qobo notes that, in some instances, progress has further been retarded by political conflict and instability, especially in countries such as Somalia, Sudan, and the Democratic Republic of Congo.[58] The conflict and unrest caused by Boko Haram in the West and Central African region is a clear indication that conflicts rapidly spill over across borders and hinder regional integration.[59] These conflicts come at tremendous economic, environmental, social, and human costs. For instance, estimates show that the Boko Haram crisis has come at a huge economic cost of nearly US$9 billion in North East Nigeria alone.[60]

China's Role, Stumbling Block or Enabler?

It is of the utmost importance to highlight whether China has been a stumbling block or an enabler of Africa's efforts at fully attaining regional integration, as per the objective of this chapter. Based on the evidence presented throughout the entire chapter, there are numerous examples that show China as having truly been an enabler of African integration. China has shown to be supporting several projects and initiatives that are crucial to the advancement of regionalism on the continent. China's efforts and investments on the continent cannot be ignored as evidenced by the increased amount of FDI coming into many African countries. Infrastructure development initiatives spearheaded by China have been a chief proponent of Africa's integration. China's support to the efforts of the AU and other regional organizations in peacekeeping initiatives is a step toward unifying Africa by eliminating conflict, which is a source of division. Based on these factors, it is evident that China is clearly enabling Africa to "Solve African problems by African solutions," which is undoubtedly enabling regional integration on the continent.

However, China's efforts have to some degree been acting as a stumbling block to Africa's regional integration efforts as well. One of the crucial aspects has been the identity of African nations, which has a colonial dimension. China's adherence to colonial borders drawn in European capitals in its dealing with individual African nations has certainly hindered the progress of regional integration on the continent. According to Jian, the geographic makeup and the large degree of importance placed upon economic integration across Africa's subregions have evidently led to a flawed implementation of regionalism.[61] Regionalism initiatives supported by China are further making attempts to work against fundamentally flawed geography, overambitious targets, and overoptimistic goals in relation to achieving comprehensive integration. Even though China uses its own model of development (the Beijing Consensus), its support in terms of developing infrastructure and identities of African nations depicts the European legacy and has clearly been a stumbling block to Africa's integration. The political and geostrategic context within African countries evidently has a noticeable impact on the progress of regionalism on the continent.[62] Mistry opines that China is blindly supporting Africa's attempts "to remain politically separate while being convinced of the need to attain economic fusion at arm length, which is confused means and ends."[63] China's focus on Africa's raw materials and natural resources especially depicts it as "the new colonizer on the block," which is also an impediment to regional integration on the continent.

RECOMMENDATIONS

For Africa to be able to reap substantial benefits from regional integration, there is an urgent need to address the structural challenges, such as improving trade facilitation, establishing an appropriate environment for private sector development, and improving the skills of the labor force.[64] Increased investment in infrastructure is vital to alleviating the impediments to African integration. Through regional integration, infrastructure projects can be instrumental in addressing the continent's current infrastructure requirements.

Considering that the EU integration took decades to be attained despite a common vision, African integration will most likely be an even lengthier process unless Africa's moves toward regional integration come from within.[65] There is a need for African governments to be wary of the advantages and benefits that can be attained through regional integration and thus be able to move beyond the bilateral agreements with China, which limit any benefits to surrounding countries. African countries must find ways to unite at government level to pursue common goals at a regional level.

African integration can be accelerated through effective policy planning, implementation, and coordination in the same manner that China did. Africa should emulate China's coordination of various regions and provinces and aggregation of conflicting demands and interests across the width and breadth of such a populous and expansive territory. It is apparent that the accelerated development experienced by China since 1978 is a result of effective policy planning and coordination over a complex and diverse polity. The success and development achieved by China should serve as a reminder and a source of inspiration for Africa and the realization that long-term visions are attainable when leaders of the process share common visions and are united in their efforts. China can offer a crucial development opportunity for Africa and can assist Africa's integration drive through alleviating infrastructure bottlenecks and expanding trade.

China's engagement with Africa should be utilized in a manner which is mutually beneficial. Since China is currently in Africa *to help and not to teach*, it is recommended that China's efforts be redirected by Africans in terms of how the continent can benefit from this.[66] African governments must be strategic with China in terms of fostering intraregional trade on the continent. It is suggested that the so-called *Angola model* of exchanging resources, which results in an exchange of resources at prices below the international market, be done away with.[67]

Regional integration requires sustainable peace, good governance, minimization of trade barriers, equitable benefits from wider markets, and economic policy harmonization among other factors.[68] In terms of China's cooperation with African regional organizations, there is need to fully utilize FOCAC and the channels of African regional organizations to establish transnational and cross-regional partnerships on African infrastructure development. There should be efforts made to offer support to preparatory work such as consulting, planning, feasibility studies, and scheme design relating to interconnection projects, as well as training and developing management and technical talents in various areas concerning African infrastructure construction.

CONCLUSION

From the above-presented argument, it is ostensive that China has certainly been an enabler of regional integration in Africa. China has been making considerable efforts in different sectors, which will facilitate Africa's integration. The process of China's bilateral engagement with

African countries is likely to continue until regional voices are strengthened toward common needs and goals. It is evident that China has a deep longing to be engaged in Africa's regional integration institutions and will rely on Africans to initiate and lead this process. Through funding and the construction of regional infrastructure, China has committed to regional integration in Africa. China's emerging role as a financier for regional infrastructure development, which is a panacea for regional integration in Africa, could be described as positive. The infrastructure projects being financed by China could enhance the movement of people and goods across countries and regions and, at the same time, promote intraregional trade. While China has made immense contributions to the rehabilitation of Africa's road and railway networks, it should also be acknowledged that Chinese financial and construction firms invest in regional projects with the support of regional organizations, RECs and financial institutions. The trade agreements between China and RECs aimed at promoting trade and direct linkages have also acted as an important factor in promoting regional integration in Africa. However, there are still several barriers noted, which have been acting as an impediment to Africa's integration efforts. These must be addressed forthwith if Africa is to be successfully integrated into a single community. Furthermore, China's efforts have to some degree been acting as a stumbling block to Africa's regional integration efforts. China's involvement has been, in many cases, linked to resource exploitation and should thus be carefully managed to avoid challenges that may arise.

NOTES

1. Zhang Jin. "China and Africa regional economic cooperation: History and prospects," *PULA: Botswana Journal of African Studies*, Vol. 29, No. 1 (2015): 8.
2. Ibid.
3. Ibid., 7.
4. Jeremy Youde, "Why Look East? Zimbabwean Foreign Policy and China." *Africa Today*, 53, No. 53 (2007): 4.
5. Victor H Mlambo and Daniel N Mlambo. "Challenge's Impeding Regional Integration in Southern Africa." *Journal of Economics and Behavioural Studies*, Vol. 10, No. 2 (2018): 250–261.
6. The World Bank Group. *Supporting Africa's Transformation: Regional Integration and Cooperation Assistance Strategy*. World Bank: Washington, DC, 2018, 2.

7. Grobbelaar, S.S. and Meyer, I.A. "The Dynamics of Regional Economic Integration: A System Dynamics Analysis of Pathways to the Development of Value Chains in the Southern African Customs Union." *South African Journal of Industrial Engineering*, Vol 28, 1 (2017): 73–89.
8. Mlambo and Mlambo, *Challenge's Impeding Regional Integration in Southern Africa*, 250.
9. Zeb, M. "Native Peoples of the World: An Encyclopaedia of Groups." *Cultures, and Contemporary Issues*, 3 (2012): 674–675.
10. Soderbaum, F. "Modes of Regional Governance in Africa: Neoliberalism, Sovereignty-boosting and Shadow Networks." *Global Governance: A Review of Multilateralism and International Organizations*, 10, 4 (2004): 419–436.
11. Mlambo and Mlambo, *Challenge's Impeding Regional Integration in Southern Africa*, 251.
12. Grobbelaar and Meyer, *The Dynamics of Regional Economic Integration: A System Dynamics Analysis of Pathways to the Development of Value Chains in the Southern African Customs Union*, 73.
13. Richard Schiere, Léonce Ndikumana and Peter Walkenhorst. *China and Africa: An Emerging Partnership for Development?* Tunis: African Development Bank Group. 2011, 91.
14. Centre for Chinese Studies, *China as a driver of regional integration in Africa: Prospects for the future*. Conference Report: A joint conference hosted by The Centre for Chinese Studies and the Development Bank of Southern Africa, 31 March to 1 April 2008 (2008): 3.
15. Clayton H Vhumbunu. *Drawing Lessons for African Integration from Accelerated Development in China*. Stellenbosch: China-Africa Joint Research and Exchange Programme: Forum on China Africa Co-operation (FOCAC), 2014, 21.
16. Ibid.
17. Schiere and Rugamba, *China and Africa: An Emerging Partnership for Development*, 91.
18. Vhumbunu, *Drawing Lessons for African Integration from Accelerated Development in China*, 21.
19. Mzukisi Qobo, The challenges of regional integration in Africa in the context of globalisation and the prospects for a United States of Africa." *Institute for Security Studies*, 145 (2007): 2.
20. Centre for Chinese Studies, *China as a driver of regional integration in Africa: Prospects for the future*, 2.
21. Bertollo, M., O. Appolloni, J.P. Bustamente Izquierdo, F. De Angelis, E. Lelli and S. Vesenjak. "China and the different regional approaches in Africa," *Transition Studies Review* 16, 2 (2009): 404–420.

22. Centre for Chinese Studies, *China as a driver of regional integration in Africa: Prospects for the future*, 3.
23. Jiemian Yang. *China-Africa cooperation in the new decade and the historical mission of think tanks*. 2011. Retrieved from http://edu.zjol.com. cn/05edu/system/2011/10/28/017951382.shtml (accessed 26 February 2019).
24. Jin, *China and Africa regional economic cooperation: History and prospects*, 11.
25. For China's security support to Africa see Chap. 10.
26. Centre for Chinese Studies, *China as a driver of regional integration in Africa: Prospects for the future*, 5.
27. Jin, *China and Africa regional economic cooperation: History and prospects*, 11.
28. MOFCOM. China-Africa economic and trade cooperation, MOFCOM white paper (2013). Available at: http://english.mofcom.gov.cn/article/ newsrelease/press/201309/20130900285772.shtml (accessed 26 February 2019).
29. Moumouni, G. "China's Relations with African Sub-regions: The Case of West Africa." *The Bulletin of Fridays at the Commission (African Union Commission)*, 3, 1 (2010): 25–43.
30. Bertollo et al., *China and the different regional approaches in Africa*.
31. Ibid.
32. Alden, C., China and Africa. *Survival*, 47(3) (2005): 147–164.
33. Daouda Cissé. *China's engagement in Africa: what are the potential impacts on Africa's regional integration?* 2015: 1.
34. Kandiero, T. *Infrastructure investment in Africa*. African Development Bank Development Research Brief No. 10 (2009) Available at: http:// www.afdb.org/fileadmin/uploads/afdb/Documents/ FinancialInformation/Infrastructure%20Investment%20in%20Africa.pdf (accessed 26 February 2019).
35. Centre for Chinese Studies, *China as a driver of regional integration in Africa: Prospects for the future*, 3.
36. Schiere, R. and Rugamba, A. "China and regional integration as drivers of structural transformation in Africa," *ICTSD Bridges Africa Review*, Vol. 2, 6 (2013): 12–14.
37. Forster et al., 2009.
38. Schiere and Rugamba, *China and regional integration as drivers of structural transformation in Africa*, 13.
39. Cisse, *China's engagement in Africa: what are the potential impacts on Africa's regional integration?* 2015: 3.
40. African Union (2012). *Decision on the Programme for Infrastructure Development in Africa*. Retrieved from: http://www.au.int/en/sites/ default/files/ASSEMBLY%20AU%20DEC%20391%20-%20415%20 %28XVIII%29%20_E.pdf (accessed 26 February 2019).

41. Ibid.
42. Jin, *China and Africa regional economic cooperation: History and prospects*, 14.
43. Ministry of Foreign Affairs of China (2012). Comments on the Results Achieved at the Fifth Meeting of BRICS Leaders. *People's Daily*, July 20, p. 2.
44. Vhumbunu, *Drawing Lessons for African Integration from Accelerated Development in China*, 11.
45. Ibid.
46. Jianwu, L. *What is Socialism with Chinese Characteristics?* Paris: Hunan University of Science and Technology, 2007.
47. Jin, *China and Africa regional economic cooperation: History and prospects*, 14.
48. Kritzinger-van Niekerk, L. *Regional integration: Concepts, advantages, disadvantages and lessons of experience.* 2005.
49. Ibid.
50. Daouda Cissé. "China's engagement in Africa: opportunities and challenges for Africa," *African and East Asian Affairs/The China Monitor*, Issue 4 (2013).
51. Grimm, S., R. Rank, M. McDonald and E. Schikerling. *Transparency of Chinese aid: An analysis of the published information on Chinese external financial flows*, Centre for Chinese Studies research report (2011). Available at: http://www.ccs.org.za/wp-content/uploads/2011/09/Transparency-of-ChineseAid_final.pdf (accessed 26 February 2019).
52. Workneh, A. "Eastern Africa's energy and infrastructure boom: Opportunities and risks," *Eurasia Review* (2014).
53. Kühnhardt, L. "African Regional Integration and the Role of the European," Discussion Paper C184-2008, *Centre for African Regional Integration and the role of the European Union*, 2008.
54. United Nations Economic Commission for Africa (UNECA). *Accelerating Regional Integration in Africa*. Addis Ababa: United Nations, 2004.
55. Cisse, *China's engagement in Africa: what are the potential impacts on Africa's regional integration?* 2015: 1.
56. World Bank. *De-fragmenting Africa: deepening regional trade integration in goods and services*. Washington, DC: World Bank, 2012.
57. Mlambo and Mlambo, *Challenge's Impeding Regional Integration in Southern Africa*, 251.
58. Qobo, *The challenges of regional integration in Africa in the context of globalisation and the prospects for a United States of Africa*, 3.
59. The World Bank Group, *Supporting Africa's Transformation: Regional Integration and Cooperation Assistance Strategy*, 16.
60. World Bank. *Political Economy of Regional Integration in Sub-Saharan Africa*. World Bank: Washington, DC, 2016.
61. Ye Wang, Jian. *What drives China's growing role in Africa*. International Monetary Fund (2007): 36.

62. Ye Wang, Jian. *What drives China's growing role in Africa.* International Monetary Fund (2007): 43.
63. Percy Mistry. Africa's record of regional economic integration. *African Affairs*, 99 (2000): 553–573.
64. Schiere et al., *China and Africa: An Emerging Partnership for Development?* 91.
65. Centre for Chinese Studies, *China as a driver of regional integration in Africa: Prospects for the future*, 5.
66. Cisse, *China's engagement in Africa: opportunities and challenges for Africa.*
67. Ibid.
68. Workneh, *Eastern Africa's energy and infrastructure boom: Opportunities and risks.*

CHAPTER 10

China's Military Involvement and Peacekeeping in Africa

INTRODUCTION

Chinese arms show up across the African continent from Liberia to Somalia. The People's Liberation Army (PLA) was allowed to sell weapons in the 1980s and created several export enterprises, most notably, Norinco, Xiangxing, and Poly Group, which have sold weapons to those states that the United States called rogue states, such as Sudan and Zimbabwe, while Chinese weapons were used in the Democratic Republic of Congo, Tanzania, Rwanda, Chad, and Liberia.[1]

The Chinese trades in arms appear to be mostly small arms sales to middlemen arms dealers who in turn sell to both governments and rebels in Africa. The available evidence suggests these amounts are not major, especially compared to the United States' supply of nearly fifty percent of the world's weapons, and that the direct leverage of the Chinese People's Liberation Army (CPLA) or the civilian ministries is modest in most African conflicts. The Stockholm International Research Institute (SIRI) estimates China's 2000–2004 unpublished arms exports at about $1.4 billion, and the United States alone exports about 25.9 billion. A United Nations 2005 arms destruction operation in the Democratic Republic of Congo reported that seventeen percent of them were Chinese made, while the remaining eighty-three percent came from other manufacturers. China also disagrees to sell weapons to unrecognized countries. According to

© The Author(s) 2020
O. Abegunrin, C. Manyeruke, *China's Power in Africa*,
Politics and Development of Contemporary China,
https://doi.org/10.1007/978-3-030-21994-9_10

173

Ernest J. Wilson, on the whole, arms sales have been the least significant factor relative to other instruments of Chinese statecraft.[2]

On the other hand, Chinese arms supplies may be underestimated, both because of parts of these weapons come to Africa through indirect ways, or through uncounted exchange of arms for raw materials, or because Chinese sales numbers are biased downwards. For example, in Liberia, from 2001 to 2003, against a United Nations weapon embargo, Chinese weapons were purchased by Van Kouwenhoven, from the Netherlands, to supply Charles Taylor's army in exchange for lumber.[3] In Zimbabwe, President Mugabe bought $24 million of weapons from China, while Sudan received civil helicopters and planes which were later militarized onsite.[4]

Further, Chinese arms are basically low-cost items, sold in large quantities for relatively low cost. For instance, machetes, low-priced assault rifles like the Type 56, or QLZ87 grenade launcher.[5] These items have a far lower value than a single jetfighter or attack helicopter sold by the United States and can kill far more people. That is what happened during the 1994 Rwanda genocide, with large quantities of *Made in China* machetes. Those light weapons, when supplied in large quantities, become a tool of mass destruction.[6]

EXPANSION OF CHINESE MILITARY PRESENCE IN AFRICA, 1990 TO PRESENT

Africa does not stand at the center of China's security strategies, yet the continent has been and remains a major source for China's commodity stocks. Africa was also seen as an important bid for international legitimacy against the Eastern and Western blocs. In the 1960s, China contributed to Africa's military power by assisting and training Liberation Groups, such as Mugabe's Zimbabwean African National Union (ZANU).[7] In 1958, China quickly recognized Algeria's National Liberation Front (NLF) and provided the new government with small weapons. In 1960, it provided training to the Partido Africano da Independencia da Guine e Cabo Verde (PAIGC) Liberation Organization in Guinea-Bissau, led by Amilcar Cabral. In Mozambique, the Front for the Liberation of Mozambique/ Frente de Libertacaio de Mozambique (FRELIMO) received guerilla training and weapons from China. During the 1960–1970s; China provided military training and weapons to any African country that was not already supported by the Soviet Union. Some military assistance turned out to be failures. For example, after supporting Popular Movement for the Liberation of Angola (MPLA) in Angola, the Chinese authorities switched sides and began supporting National Union for the Total Independence of Angola (UNITA), which never succeeded to grasp power in the country. From 1967 to 1976, China transferred $142 million in arms to Africa and the three major recipients are Congo-Brazzaville, Republic of Tanzania, and Democratic Republic of Congo. During the 1980s, China's sales of arms to African countries dropped significantly.[8]

The Chinese military presence in Africa increased since 1990, when China agreed to join in United Nations peacekeeping operations. In January 2005, 598 Chinese peacekeepers were sent to Liberia. Other Chinese military forces were sent to Western Sahara as part of peacekeeping Operation (MINURSO),[9] to Sierra Leone, the Ivory Coast, and the Democratic Republic of Congo (DRC).[10] This was a carefully handled and largely symbolic move, as China did not want to appear as a new colonialist power overly interfering in internal affairs of African countries. Thus, China always emphasizes the policy of noninterference in the domestic affairs of other nations.

During the Chadian Civil War, China put its weight behind the government of Idriss Deby, gave him diplomatic support, and supplied him with light weapons. And since Chad started producing oil in 2003, China has pursued their national interests in replacing Idriss Deby with a more pro-China leader. The 2006 Chadian coup d'état attempt failed after the French intervention, and Deby then switched his support to the Beijing government, with the apparent defeat becoming a strategic victory for China.

China has military alliances with six African countries, five of which are major oil suppliers to China: Sudan, Algeria, Nigeria, Angola, Chad, and Egypt. However, China's influence remains limited, especially when compared with Western powers such as France, whose military involvement in the 2004 Ivory Coast conflict and the 2006 Chadian conflict was significant. China is particularly unable to compete with the ex-colonial powers in providing military training and educational programs to African countries, given the latter's continuing ties via military academies like, Sandhurst in the United Kingdom and Saint Cyr in France.[11] Despite growing economic interests in Africa, China has just started any military base on the continent. However, a naval logistics center planned to be built in Djibouti raises questions about China's need to set up military bases in Africa. China's increasing reliance on Africa's resources warrants it to hold a stronger military position in the continent.[12]

Tanzania is one of the oldest of China's allies in Africa. The two countries established bilateral relations in 1964. During his first visit to China in 1965, President Nyerere signed a Treaty of Friendship with Beijing.[13] This Treaty of Friendship between China and Tanzania provided support that symbolized China's support to the revolutionist comrades in Africa. "From 1961 to 1971, the People's Republic of China provided $41 million in military aid to Africa, and 82 percent of them went to Tanzania."[14]

Africans, Americans, and Chinese broadly agree on the importance of supporting economic growth and development, combating disease, mitigating conflict, enhancing political stability, and fighting violent extremism and organized crime. Because the basic objectives of China, the United States, and African states overlap, collaboration can offer real benefits to all three. What is more, coordination among Beijing, Washington, and African capitals is not as quixotic as it may sound. Together with the African Union and the subregional Intergovernmental Authority on Development, the United States and China have already been working closely on the peace processes in Sudan and South Sudan, easing the contention between the two countries.

China-Africa Defense Forum

The first-ever China-Africa Forum on defense and security was held from June 26 to July 10, 2018 in Beijing, signaling its deepening engagement in Africa. Ren Guoqiang, the Chinese spokesperson for the Ministry of National Defense, said the aims are, first, to deepen the China-Africa comprehensive strategic partnership; second, to promote building a shared future for China and Africa; and third, to meet the needs of Africa's new security situations and China-Africa defense cooperation. The Forum focused on regional security issues, the self-development of Africa's security capacities, and China-Africa defense cooperation. Participants at the Forum visited the services of the Chinese armed forces—the army, the navy, and the air force.[15]

The Forum comes amid rising Sino-Africa political and economic relations, with growing diplomatic links, investments, and much-needed infrastructure, and training of the next generation of African elites. China is striving to project itself as a responsible global power and to craft a positive image of itself on the world stage. This is especially true in Africa, where it has promoted win-win economic cooperation, mutual assistance in security matters, and solidarity in international affairs. This defense cooperation could also be China's effort to secure its strategic interests abroad, and particularly in Africa. This includes the One Belt One Road Initiative, which calls for $1 trillion of investment infrastructure and other projects along trade routes linking China to Europe, Russia, Central and Southeast Asia, and Africa.[16] This project will cover more than seventy countries.

One way China has fortified its investments in Africa is by gradually taking an active role at the United Nations. According to Theodor Neething, head of the Department of Political Science at the University of Free State in South Africa, "Over the last decade, China has ramped up its role in peacekeeping missions; of the five permanent members of the United Nations Security Council, it is the biggest contributor of peacekeepers, and it is among the world's top 12 largest contributors of the United Nations troops."[17] China has contributed troops to the United Nations missions in South Sudan, where it has oil interests, the Democratic Republic of Congo, which supplies it with cobalt and copper, and Mali, one of China's oldest allies in Africa.

China has framed its partnership in Africa as alliances of equals, built around mutual economic benefit. Currently, China is stepping up its role as a humanitarian actor and protector of world peace. In 2018, China opened its first overseas military base in Djibouti in the Horn of Africa. China has 700 peacekeepers in South Sudan, where it is also sending medical teams and food supplies. The two Chinese peacekeepers that were killed in fighting in South Sudan in 2017, Chinese officials and news media described those two soldiers as heroes and their deaths as the price of China's new status as a major power. Chinese President Xi Jinping has pledged to increase China's peacekeeping force to 8000 troops from 2600 deployed in 2016.[18]

China is providing logistical and defense support to African countries, as part of China's plan of "Projecting itself as the leader of the developing World and a nation that finds itself in solidarity with developing Nations."[19] Most of the African countries can barely finance their own security agenda, and many of them face deficits when it comes to countering terrorism, piracy, and natural disasters. "At a time when the United States and European countries are adopting isolationist policies, Beijing is making power moves abroad, for example by opening up its first overseas military base in Djibouti."[20]

The Chinese military base in Djibouti is causing consternation for the United States. As of now, both China and the United States are operating military bases in Djibouti. Consequently,

American military leaders are worried that China might arm-twist Djibouti into kicking United

> States forces out. Tensions, and feeling of what is happening in the South China Sea, are also escalating, with American accusing China of using military-grade lasers to distract its fighter pilots. Caitlin Talmadge has claimed that, "Chinese fighter jets have intercepted U.S. aircraft in the skies above the South China Sea."[21]

As China is expanding its global military might in Africa, many Americans and Europeans are worried that this might herald colonial ambitions or a new form of United States-style military hegemony. "At the same time many have argued that this should not be a concern: China is certainly acutely aware of the pitfalls associated with the politics of interventionism and neo-colonialism, especially in the developing World."[22]

China-Africa Defense, and Security Forum

From June 26 to July 10, 2018, high-ranking military officials from fifty African countries met in Beijing, attending the first China-Africa Defense and Security Forum.[23] The China-Africa Defense and Security Forum, the first of its kind, was attended by 50 African nations and the African Union and was hosted by China's Ministry of National Defense.[24] The theme of the conference was "*Work Together and assist each Other.*" Major-General Hu Changming, Chief of the Office for International Military Cooperation at the Chinese Central Military Commission, said "he believes the forum will gather helpful advice and suggestions for China-Africa Cooperation in defense and Security, and for building a community with a shared future among them."[25] First, the aim of this military Forum was to increase and strengthen China's military ties with Africa. Second, this forum was an effort to solidify Beijing's role as provider of expertise and technical know-how in a wide variety of areas, including the defense and military arenas. The following are China's defense strategy in Africa, and the broader impact of the defense and security forum.

First, China's Africa policy looks to build strong defense networks. China's bilateral relations with many African countries already include sending military attachés and holding joint drills and lie-fire military exercises. The 2018 China-Africa Defense and Security forum, which ran for two full weeks, is a further sign of China's growing military ties and efforts to deepen professional networks between Chinese officers and their African counterparts. Holding the forum in China allowed the participants to visit multiple People's Liberation Army (PLA), Navy, and Air Force sites. Showcasing technical capacities and meeting defense personnel serve as a marketing strategy to demonstrate that China is a serious security partner.

Second, the Forum was a follow-up on China's pledge to build Africa's defense capacity. In 2015, President Xi Jinping pledged to provide "$100 million of free military assistance to the African Union in the next five years to support the establishment of the African Standby Force and the African Capacity for immediate Response to Crisis."[26] However, the Chinese authorities are still negotiating a plan for disbursement of the assistance. Part of the Chinese government's second African policy paper is a strong focus on the professionalization of training programs in which tens of thousands of African military officials are invited to China for workshops. During the Summit, African military officials toured Chinese military facilities and saw various cities in China, taking in positive impressions of the country's successful development story. The defense and security forum included similar visits.

China's involvement in United Nations peacekeeping operations (PKOs) is a sign of China's commitment. China ranks second after the United States in financial support of the United Nations peacekeeping operations, and first among the United Nations Security Council's permanent members in contributing peacekeepers to African countries. Since President Xi Jinping pledged before the United Nations to further support U.N. Peacekeeping Operations with funds and 8000 troops to the Standby Force, China has been working on training peacekeepers, both national and foreign troops. For instance, Chinese peacekeepers in South Sudan have been engaged in protecting refugee camps, providing medical assistance, repairing broken infrastructures, and facilitating local peace initiatives.[27] According to Colonel Wang Yang, the defense attaché at the Chinese Embassy in Kenya:

China has always been a builder of world peace, a contributor to global development and an upholder of international order. The growth of Chinese military also means the growth of the world peacekeeping force. Among the permanent member states of the United Nations Security Council, China has contributed the largest number of troops to United Nations peacekeeping Missions and the second largest share to the United Nations peacekeeping budget.[28]

Colonel Wang Yang went further and said that:

China has always been insisting on a path of peaceful development and has been pursuing an independent foreign policy of peace and a national defense policy that is purely defensive. China has therefore stepped up the transforming of its armed forces into a world-class military that is ready to fight and win wars as the country will never compromise on defending sovereignty.[29]

Third, China's Defense Strategy in Africa is significantly different from the United States' Strategy in Africa. Beijing has taken a comprehensive approach, blending trade and investment deals and cultural exchanges with arms sales, medical assistance, troops training, anti-piracy drills, and other programs. China has established a military base in Djibouti in 2018 and, according to Chinese officials, this may not be the last, while China's commitments to United Nations peacekeeping forces and its growing arms trade with African nations are watched closely by the West, particularly the United States.

Unlike the United States, the Chinese military base in Djibouti included huge investment deals and development projects that were signed into the base package deal. In March 2018, a United States lawmaker created a diplomatic row when he spoke out against China's investments on the continent and warned that "they [Chinese] come with a price tag following concerns over the Doraleh Port in Djibouti."[30] Thus, China defended its Africa presence and accused the United States of groundless suspicion over its interests. The new Cold War (this is Economic War between China and the United States) between China and the United States may start in Africa over the Chinese and American bases in Djibouti. The choice to set up a military base in Djibouti is the fact that Djibouti is a stable country, which is located at the strategic trading route which links the Suez Canal to the Indian Ocean. From this base, China's maritime aircraft can cover a greater part of the Arabian Peninsula together with northern and central Africa without having to refuel. According to Anthony Kleven, "the port in Djibouti has the capabilities of accommodating Chinese aircraft carriers on top of being close to the United States base where drone attacks on Al Shabab and Al Qaeda are often conducted."[31]

First, Africa's smallest state and one of the poorest, Djibouti, is where the United States has the largest military base in Africa. Second, the most visible U.S. military operation base on the African continent is in this small East African country of Djibouti. Djibouti is roughly the same size as the

Massachusetts state and has a population of about half a million people. It is home to the U.S.-led Horn of Africa anti-terror Combined Joint Task Force-Horn of Africa (CJTF-HOA) headquartered at camp Lemonier in Djibouti.[32]

The United States began initial operations at Camp Lemonier in 2002. The Camp started with 88 acres of land and it has been expanded to about 500 acres since July 2006 and serves nearly 3000 military and civilian personnel. However, the visit to Djibouti by the former U.S. Defense Secretary Leon Panetta in November 2011 seems to be an omen foretelling the rebirth of the U.S. African Command's (AFRICOM) base in the Horn of Africa. Thus, it has been confirmed that "a lot of United States military personnel and equipment is going to be based in Camp Lemonier, Djibouti in short order whether the official African Command (AFRICOM) headquarters is there or not."[33]

Third, United States foreign policy in Africa during the Trump administration, in contrast to Chinese, has involved mixed messages, and sometimes racist. United States policy has mostly focused on U.S.–Africa Command (AFRICOM)[34] missions to counter violent extremism in Africa. In contrast with China's comprehensive approach, the United States, especially, since the Trump administration came into office has adopted a narrow, military-focused approach in Africa.

Fourth, the defense and security forum mirrors another China-Africa Forum, FOCAC. For nearly two decades, the Forum on China-Africa Cooperation (FOCAC), started in 2000, has pursued steady economic and cultural diplomacy. Forum on China-Africa Cooperation meetings have taken place every three years since its inception in 2000, with the location alternating between China and an African country. The continuity and consistency of the Forum helped institutionalize China's multilateral cooperation with African nations.[35]

In addition, the Forum on China-Africa Cooperation also provided Chinese foreign policy makers the experience to apply this forum diplomacy to regions outside Africa, such as the China Arab States Cooperation Forum, initiated in 2004. The security and defense forum will probably be a recurrent element of China-Africa relations as a potential launchpad for China's defense relations to regions beyond Africa. One area of potential increase in military engagement between China and Africa is in providing training for police and Army Units for African Union, as well as bilaterally for interested countries.

For China, the Trump administration's *American First* platform has opened up new opportunities for China to take on a larger global role. The bigger picture here is that China, under President Xi Jinping, is clearly moving ahead to take on that greater global leadership role across many arenas. African countries' leaders are drawing closer ties with Beijing not only in the realm of trade and economic relations but increasingly in defense and military matters as well. The Chinese Minister of Defense, Wei Fenghe concluded that, "China-Africa Defense and Security Forum with an emphasis on South-South Cooperation among developing nations is very important in China's overall foreign policy."[36]

China and Zimbabwe's Security

China's ties with many authoritarian regimes in Africa have continued to receive criticism about its lack of consideration for good governance and human rights issues. However, China maintains a foreign policy position of noninterference in domestic affairs of African countries or any other country thereof, and China's arms sales to certain regimes in Africa have received international criticism. Notable cases are Zimbabwe, Sudan, and Liberia.[37] Zimbabwe is the most trusted Chinese' ally in Africa, thus, Abiodun Alao has described Zimbabwe-China relations as "the steadfastness of a trusted friend."[38] In terms of security and political cooperation, China has traded in weapons with Zimbabwe. Thompson notes that, "Zimbabwe bought, 12 jet fighters and 100 military vehicles valued at $240 million in 2004, six trainer/combat aircraft in 2005 and six additional trainer/combat aircraft in 2006; and 20,000 AK47, and 15 military trucks in 2011."[39] Such military cooperation is beneficial to Zimbabwe considering that the country is under United States and European Union arms embargo, among other restrictions.

South Sudan and China-Africa Security

China has been contributing over US$1 million annually as part of her efforts aimed at supporting the AU's capacity building and peacekeeping operations in Somalia and Sudan.[40] China has dispatched 268 peacekeepers to South Sudan. A battalion was dispatched from Zhengzhou, Henan Province, in two groups on September 11 and September 23, 2018, respectively. The peacekeepers were tasked with repairing roads, bridges, and airports, building facilities for water, power, and heating supplies, and

10 CHINA'S MILITARY INVOLVEMENT AND PEACEKEEPING IN AFRICA   183

providing engineering support in peacekeeping mission areas.[41] In addition, to fulfill the mission in South Sudan, the troops did not only conduct training exercises under combat conditions but also studied international law, diplomatic protocol, the peacekeeping mission area situation, and basic English expressions.

As one of the eight Action Plans of the Forum on China-Africa Cooperation to be implemented (in three years) between 2019 and 2021, on security, China will set up a China-Africa peace and security fund and continue providing free military aid to the African Union. A total of 50 security assistance programs will be carried out in the fields, including United Nations peacekeeping missions, fighting piracy, and combating terrorism in Africa.[42] Thus, China is actively involved in the United Nations Peacekeeping Mission in Africa.

NOTES

1. Michael, Serge; Beuret, Michael; Wood, Paolo, *La Chinafrique: Pékin a la conquête du continent noir*, Arms, Grasset & Fasquelle, 2008, pp. 221–235.
2. Ernest, J. Wilson III, *China's Role in Africa, 2018 the World: Is China A Responsible Stakeholder in Africa?* The U.S.-China Economic and Security Review Commission; Center for International Development and Conflict Management, University of Maryland, College Park, MD: August 3–4, 2006, p. 10 https://www.uscc.gov/hearings/2006hearings/written_testimonies/06_08_3_4_wilson_ernest_statement.pdf)(PDF).Hearing before the U.S. Congress.
3. Dead on Time- Arms Transportation, Brokering and the Threat to Human Rights, Amnesty International, 2006, pp. 22–28.
4. Michael, Serge; Beuret, Michael; Wood, Paolo, *La Chinafrique: Pékin a la conquête du continent noir*, Arms, Grasset & Fasquelle, 2008, pp. 221–235.
5. Michael, Serge; Beuret, Michael; Wood, Paolo, *La Chinafrique: Pékin a la conquête du continent noir*, Arms, Grasset & Fasquelle, 2008, pp. 221–235.
6. Ibid.
7. Olayiwola Abegunrin, *Nigeria and the Struggle for the Liberation of Zimbabwe: A Study of Foreign Policy Decision Making of An Emerging Nation.* Stockholm, *Sweden*: Bethany Books, 1992.
8. Olayiwola Abegunrin, "Soviet and Chinese Military Involvement in Southern Africa," A *Current Bibliography on African Affairs*, Washington, DC: 6, 3, 1983–1984. Also see Robert Rotberg, China into Africa: Trade, Aid, and Influence, Washington, DC: Brookings Institution Press, 2009, p. 156.
9. Lafargue, François, *China's Presence in Africa*, China Perspective, 2005.

10. Michael, Serge; Beuret, Michael; Wood, Paolo, *La Chinafrique: Pékin a la conquête du continent noir*, Grasset & Fasquelle, 2008, pp. 221–235.
11. Ernest, J. Wilson III, *China's Role in the World: Is China A Responsible Stakeholder in Africa?* The U.S.-China Economic and Security Review Commission; Center for International Development and Conflict Management, University of Maryland, College Park, MD: August 3–4, 2006, p. 10 https://www.uscc.gov/hearings/2006hearings/written_testimonies/06_08_3_4_wilson_ernest_statement.pdf) (PDF). U.S. Congress.
12. Privilege Musvanhiri, Hang Shuen Lee, "Economic Interests Push China to increase Military Presence in Africa," December 9, 2015. https://www.dw.com/economic-interests-push-china-to-increase-military-presence-in-africa/a-18900735. Retrieved August 7, 2018.
13. David H. Shinn and Joshua Eisenman, *China and Africa: A Century of Engagement*. Philadelphia, PA: University of Pennsylvania Press, 2012, p. 69.
14. Ibid.
15. Abdi Latif Dahir, "China is Expanding Its Military Footprint in Africa," *Quartz: Africa Weekly Brief*, September 2, 2018.
16. See chapter ten, "China's One Belt, One Road Initiative in Africa." The Chinese Government calls this initiative, "A bid to enhance regional connectivity and embrace a brighter future." Others see it as a push by China to take a larger role in global affairs with a China-centered trading network. "China Unveils Action Plan on Belt and Road Initiative," *Xinhua News Agency*, March 25, 2015.
17. Abdi Latif Dahir, "China is Expanding Its Military Footprint in Africa," *Quartz: Africa Weekly Brief*, September 2, 2018.
18. Lily Kuo, "China's Wolf Warriors two in "war-ravaged Africa," Gives the White Savior Complex a Whole New Meaning: Chinese Exceptionalism," *Quartz Africa Weekly Brief*, August 14, 2017.
19. Ibid.
20. Ibid.
21. The United States is challenging China's right to occupy the South China Sea as part of Chinese territories. See Caitlin Talmadge, "Beijing's Nuclear Option: Why A U.S.-Chinese War Could Spiral Out of Control," *Foreign Affairs*, October 15, 2018.
22. Ibid.
23. Lina Benabdallah, "China-Africa Military Ties Have Deepened. Here are Four Things to Know," *The Washington Post*, July 6, 2018.
24. Ibid.
25. Zheng Yibing, "First China-Africa Defense and Security Forum Kicks Off," China Global Television Network (CGTN), June 26, 2018.
26. "China-Africa Security Forum Concludes in Beijing," *Africa Times*, July 11, 2018.

27. James Morgan, "South Sudan Welcomes China's Peace Mediator Role," *China-Africa Relations*, May 28, 2018.
28. Colonel Wang Yang, "Defense Attache: China is Committed to Military Exchanges, Cooperation," Chinese Embassy, Nairobi, Kenya. Also see *China Daily*, Beijing, August 01, 2018.
29. Ibid.
30. People's Republic of China File, *Ministry of National Defense*, July 11, 2018.
31. Anthony Kleven. "Is China's Maritime Silk Road a Military Strategy?" *The Diplomat*, December 2015, http://thediplomat.com/2015/12/is-china-s-maritime-silkroad-a-military-strategy/ (accessed 22 December 2018).
32. Joseph Giordano, "U.S. Military Plans to Expand Camp Lemonier in Djibouti," *Stars and Stripes Middle East Edition*, July 9, 2006; Djibouti Information from Central Intelligence Agency, "The World Fact book, Djibouti," October 27, 2008, available at www.cia.gov.
33. Thomas C. Mountain, "U.S. AFRICOM Reborn in Djibouti," Retrieved April 20, 2012 at http://www.intrepidreport.com/archives/4935.
34. Olayiwola Abegunrin, "Africa Command Center (AFRICOM) and U.S. Foreign Policy of Militarization of Africa under the Obama Administration," in Adebayo Oyebade, editor, *The United States' Foreign Policy in Africa in the 21st Century: Issues and Perspectives*, Durham, NC: Carolina Academic Press, 2014, pp. 77–97.
35. Shelly Zhao, "The Geopolitics of China-African Oil," *China Briefing*, https://www.china-briefing.com. April 13, 2011.
36. Editor, "China-Africa Defense, and Security Forum Concludes in Beijing," *Africa Times*, July 11, 2018. Also see Chinese Global Television Network (CGTN).
37. Ibid.
38. Abiodun Alao, *Mugabe and the Politics of Security in Zimbabwe*, Montreal: McGill-Queen's University Press, 2012.
39. Reagan Thompson, *Assessing the Chinese Influence in Ghana, Angola, and Zimbabwe: The Impact of Politics, Partners, and Petro*. Stanford University: Centre for International Security and Cooperation (CISAC), 2012, 102. Also see Abiodun Alao, *Mugabe and the Politics of Security in Zimbabwe*, Montreal: McGill-Queen's University Press, 2012.
40. Zhang Jin, "*China and Africa regional economic cooperation: History and prospects*," *PULA: Botswana Journal of African Studies*, Volume 29, No. 1, 2015, 11.
41. ZX, "China to Send 268 Peacekeepers to South Sudan," www.Xinhuanet. news.cn.com, September 5, 2018. Retrieved October 1, 2018.
42. Liangyu, "Xi Jinping Says China to Implement Eight Major Initiatives with African Countries," https://www.xinhuanet.com, September 3, 2018.

CHAPTER 11

China's One Belt One Road Initiative in Africa

INTRODUCTION

As part of its economic transformation, China continues to find new ways to continue its growth. One of the means through which China seeks to guarantee its position as an economic powerhouse is through its policy of looking outwards. China has for the past four decades realized the importance other countries could play in its economic development. It has thus sought to establish strong ties with nations that are strategic and that have a part to play in its intended objectives. Consequently, to achieve these economic objectives, China has come up with its *going global strategy*. This strategy follows the trail of economic transformation and open policy originally promulgated by previous Chinese leaders. Basing on this, China's President Xi Jinping has sought to revive the ancient Silk Road which was a gateway to markets and trade outside China through what is today known as the *One Belt One Road Initiative*. The ancient Silk Road, which was established more than 2000 years ago, was a peaceful way in which interstate commercial activities and cultural exchanges were conducted and it covered more than 10,000 km from China to Rome. The revival of the ancient Silk Road will culminate in the development of the Silk Road Economic Belt and the Twenty-First-Century Maritime Silk Road, as the linchpins of this new initiative. The OBOR initiative is essentially an extension and expansion of China's "opening up" and "going global" strategy, with a regional focus on Asia, Europe, and Africa.

© The Author(s) 2020
O. Abegunrin, C. Manyeruke, *China's Power in Africa*,
Politics and Development of Contemporary China,
https://doi.org/10.1007/978-3-030-21994-9_11

187

Notably, Africa is still part of the important global growth points that China sees as key to achieving its economic goals. This is shown by China's prioritization and interaction with Africa through the Forum on China-Africa Cooperation (FOCAC). This has resulted in more resources being availed to African countries included in the OBOR initiative, in addition to the ones they already have access to under FOCAC. The African Belt and Road Initiative countries will realize benefits from the new connections among the regions that are part of OBOR, for instance an increase in cooperation with nations that lie along the Maritime Silk Road in South Asia and Southeast Asia. Being a part of these potentially emerging new structures will be of huge advantage to all the nations that are part of the OBOR initiative, including those in Africa. However, Africa, at this stage, is still a part player at the periphery of the OBOR initiative, as the initiative links only a few countries in East Africa. The more the OBOR strategy develops, it becomes more vital that the African continent is incorporated more into this grand vision to further strengthen the historical friendship that exists between China and Africa. This chapter therefore seeks to examine China's One Belt and One Road Initiative in Africa in relation to diplomacy, geopolitics, security, economics, and politics on Africa. Implications of this initiative and associated challenges will also be looked at. Answers will be sought in terms of Africa's involvement and place in China's global strategy.

Historical Background

China's "opening and reform" shift from the late 1970s is the beginning of China's economic interest and being a proponent of China's foreign aid and outward look.[1] McFadden notes that China began its policy of opening to the world with the advent of Deng Xiang's reforms in the 1980s.[2] China's "New Silk Road" (One Belt, One Road) initiative is China's new project, which seeks to revive the ancient trade route and commercial network that spans half the world. The first original Silk Road was a network of trade routes, which were formally established during the Han dynasty. This road had its origins in the Chang'an (now Xian) in the east and ended in the Mediterranean in the West, connecting China with the Roman Empire. McFadden further notes that it comprised a series of major trading routes that had an impact in building trade and cultural ties between China, India, Greece, Arabia, Persia, Rome, and the Mediterranean nations.[3] This Silk Road became a conduit for various trade items other than silk, such as jade from the east, wool, silver, and gold from the West together with the transfer of ideas between east and West. The Silk Road was at its peak during the Tang dynasty and declined during the Yuan dynasty.

China's rapid economic growth within a period of three decades has inspired and created a lot of admiration from fellow developing nations, particularly those on the African continent. Economy and Levi assert that the death of Chairman Mao in 1976 and Deng Xiaoping's consolidation of power in 1978 have both been credited with being the key proponents of China's development, especially the way China opened to the outside world.[4] This had the effect of facilitating China's growth into a modern economy. According to Leberthal and Oksenbegerg, China's leadership orchestrated her economic development through key initiatives such as "the great leap outward" and the national development strategy in 1977, spearheaded by Han Guofeng.[5] China's subsequent leaders such as Jiang Zemin and Zhu Rongji continued the path of economic "transformation and open policy." Ehizuelen and Abdi note that China went global through its encouragement of its state-owned enterprises (SOEs) to venture into overseas markets to increase their competitiveness both locally and internationally.[6] To date, China's SOEs continue to play a pivotal and leading role in its economic development. China's "open policy" has been credited with being responsible for increasing China's wealth and power globally, with China today being described as the leading champion in development amongst fellow developing nations.[7]

There is some form of historical significance that connects China and Africa, particularly in terms of what is known as the OBOR (MSRI) initiative, which was originally known as the Silk Road in ancient times. The launch opportunities of China's OBOR initiative can be linked to history, economics, and demography. Sun notes that, historically, in the 1400s, alongside the original European Silk Route, South East, and South Asian destinations, Chinese fleets managed to reach as far as what is known today as the Kenyan Coast.[8] Particularly, China's relationship with Africa has grown exponentially since the Bandung Conference in 1955 and to date China has surpassed the US as Africa's single largest trading partner.[9] Today, Kenya hosts the Mombasa Port, which has become one of the ports on the African continent that is of great significance to the OBOR initiative. Other countries such as Egypt, Djibouti, and Ethiopia are also of strategic importance to the success of China's latest economic undertaking.

OBOR Initiative in Perspective

The One Belt One Road (OBOR) initiative championed by China's President Xi Jinping is an extensive long-term infrastructure initiative, which has been seen by many as the rebirth of the original Silk Road trading routes. The initiative comprises two core components. The first component is the Economic land belt, which links countries by road along the ancient Silk Road through Central Asia, the Middle East, West Africa, and Europe. The second component of the belt is the Maritime Road, which links countries by sea along the Eastern coast of Africa pushing up through the Suez Canal into the Mediterranean Sea. The World Bank states that China has entered into cooperation agreements with 71 countries and international organizations, which, China included, make up sixty-five percent of the world's population and about thirty-four percent of the world's GDP.[10] The total population of all countries connected through this initiative is around 4.4 billion, covering sixty-five percent of the world's inhabitants and accounts for nearly one third of worldwide GDP and about twenty-nine percent of the global economy.[11] The OBOR initiative could result in investment worth about $6 trillion being invested in the coming years and having the effect of reshaping global trade. The introduction of the OBOR initiative in 2013 has further put Africa on China's radar and has resulted in a special relationship between the two.[12] Ehizuelen and Abdi note that the OBOR initiative represents the linchpin of China's foreign policy as envisioned by its leadership.[13] The initiative aims to set a new path for nations of Asia, Oceania, Europe, and Africa to promote improved growth and human development through infrastructural linkages, improved trade, and investment. In terms of economic cooperation, this initiative presents enormous opportunities never experienced before in Africa.

President Xi Jinping has followed the path of economic transformation set forth by his predecessors, when he proclaimed in 2013 the development of the Silk Road Economic Belt and the Twenty-First-Century Maritime Silk Road.[14] The OBOR initiative has thus been labeled as the most ambitious effort by China's new leadership since its election into office at the 18th Congress of China's Communist Party in 2012. As of 2015, the OBOR initiative had expanded exponentially with outward investment set to come from a combination of newly formed funds such as the Asian infrastructure Development Bank, the New Development Bank, and the Silk Road Funds as well as SOEs and private firms.[15] The initiative is a call by China to the international community to work together toward a "harmonious and inclusive" world. It is a proactive move by China's leadership toward meeting the global anticipations concerning China's international obligation and leadership.

Through the OBOR initiative, Africa remains one of the key global growth points which China has prioritized interactions with, through the Forum on China-Africa Cooperation (FOCAC). However, with OBOR, Africa is somewhat of a part player and is at the periphery as OBOR touches mostly on a few countries in East Africa. For those countries in Africa who are part of OBOR, they have readily available access to new resources on top of the ones they enjoy under FOCAC. Africa's role in the OBOR initiative is thus minute as this initiative has been deemed as inadequate when it comes to supporting the importance that China places on Africa. According to the Ministry of Commerce of the People's Republic of China (MOFCOM), China has pledged newly added aid capital to African nations.[16] More so, in contrast to FOCAC, the OBOR initiative is not limited to the bilateral relations between China and African countries but aims to connect Asia, Europe, and Africa collectively, with some African countries essentially benefitting a great deal from this.

Aims of the OBOR Initiative

China aims at exerting a great deal of influence on the international arena, from Latin America, Africa, and all the way up to the Middle East.[17] To achieve this, China has come up with the OBOR initiative, which is essentially a Twenty-First-Century Silk Road and economic belt initiative. According to Chen the OBOR initiative plans to promote infrastructure construction, trade, and investment among other activities.[18]

The OBOR belt is made up of two independent and interrelated concepts, that is, the *Silk Road Economic Belt* and the *Maritime Silk Road*. The belt comprises a road network, rails, power grids, and gas pipelines. The Maritime Silk Road (MSR) is its oceanic counterpart. Breuer notes that the MSR intends to pass through the coast of East Africa, with several ports being constructed.[19] More ports are also under construction on the coasts of Central and West Africa. There are future plans to link some of these ports with roads and railways into Africa's heartland. The African section of the belt covers Kenya, Djibouti, Egypt, and Ethiopia. Mwatela and Changfeng state that world politics have always been characterized by *Power Politics*.[20] The horn of Africa and the Suez Canal have always been under the control of Western countries particularly the United States. Whichever powerful nation has an influence on the security of that region, will also have total control over the maritime trade routes between Asia, Europe, and Africa. China's entry into Djibouti could tilt and realign security partnerships that have influenced global order since 1945.

Egypt has a strategic geographical location at the Suez Canal and could play a central part to the OBOR initiative, hence China cannot proceed with this endeavor without Egypt. Without Egypt the Maritime Silk Road, which is one part of the OBOR initiative, is not feasible in Africa. This is because of the simple reason that the Suez Canal is a critical transit point between the Indian Ocean and the Mediterranean Sea. Consequently, the expansion of the Suez Canal has been initiated. This will be conducted over a period of ten years together with the construction of Egypt's new administrative capital. China will invest USD$ 230 million and USD$45 billion, respectively, to the two projects.[21] The expansion of the Suez Canal will result in enormous benefits for both countries. For Egypt, it will create employment of about 10,000 jobs for the locals. Mwatela and Changfeng further note that China will, on its part, gain substantial influence on power and security dynamics within the region previously dominated by the West through the completion of the expansion and operation of the Suez Canal, which will leave it squarely in the hands of the Chinese.[22]

When it comes to Djibouti, it is simply a case of global dominance and the geopolitics of the horn of Africa. Kenya is also of strategic importance to the OBOR initiative because of its location along the East African Coast of the Indian Ocean in relation to some key China partners. According to Zhou, of interest is the fact that Kenya shares a border with South Sudan, which is an important exporter of oil to China, hence, China needs an alternative route for its oil because of the violent nature of the relations between North and South Sudan.[23] Kenya offers this alternative route. It has been noted that, at some point, China imported five percent of its oil from Sudan.[24] Kenya offers a route for China to import oil from South Sudan without being frustrated by the north, which is a win-win situation for both China and South Sudan. Also, the discovery of oil fields in Uganda, which is a landlocked country, means that she can also export some of this oil to China via Kenya. Through securing the Kenyan route, China has taken care of the prospects for future OBOR expansion into Africa's heartland.[25]

In the light of the EU-Africa Summit 2017 and of the G20 Summit 2017, with Africa being one of the focus areas, China's engagement in

Africa seems more relevant than ever.[26] The "One Belt, One Road" initiative (OBOR) or Silk Road Initiative by China has, at times, been often denoted as a Eurasian infrastructure network initiative, but in fact transcends beyond that. The Maritime Silk Road (MSR) is intended to pass through the coast of East Africa, where construction of a few ports has already begun with the planned construction of more ports and infrastructure soon to follow.[27] In addition, ports have not only been planned and are under construction on the Maritime Silk Road's direct way along Africa's east coast through the Suez Canal, but also on Central and West African coasts. There are plans to connect a number of these ports to Africa's heartland through railways and roads, in some instances, from the east coast all the way to the west coast. The OBOR initiative is thus not only about Eurasia but is also, to a substantial extent, about Africa. There is even a *second belt* on the African continent.

It should be highlighted that the OBOR initiative is not seen as an aid program and China could potentially attain huge economic and financial rewards from it just as the United States of America did in the nineteenth century when it embarked on a huge infrastructure building initiative with the aim of opening novel markets on its Western frontier.[28] The focus of the MSRI is to facilitate and support booming trade growth between Asia and Africa.[29] The OBOR initiative will most likely result in the reduction of the costs of trade to enable China to reap huge benefits from global trade. The OBOR initiative has been dubbed a win-win partnership by some; however, some critics such as the United States have strongly criticized this initiative, arguing that China is exploiting Africa and extracting her resources for its benefit. Naidu asserts that China's engagement with Africa has been labeled by some as new colonialism and neo-imperialism.[30] Verlare and van Putten have a different view from this and argue that the key pillars of the OBOR initiative are "promotion of policy coordination, facilitating connectivity, unimpeded trade, financial integration and people to people bonds."[31] According to McFadden, under the OBOR initiative:[32]

1. Policy coordination entails consultation of issues on an equal footing between the countries along the belt. Development plans and measures for improving cross-national or regional cooperation together with policy support and the implementation of large-scale projects will be jointly formulated.
2. Facilitating connectivity refers to prioritising areas of construction as part of the Belt and Road strategy. There shall be strides made

towards eliminating barriers in the missing sections and bottlenecks in areas of core international transportation passages, advancing the construction of port infrastructure facilities and clearing land-water intermodal transport passages. Through this initiative, efforts will be made to promote the connectivity of infrastructure facilities such as highways, air routes, railways, telecommunications, oil and natural gas pipelines, and ports. All this is aimed at establishing an infrastructure network that will connect Asia, Europe and Africa.[33]

3. Unimpeded trade will be guaranteed through taking steps aimed at resolving trade and investment facilitation issues. Efforts will be made to reduce trade and investment barriers, reduce the costs of investment and trade, and, at the same time, stimulate regional economic integration. There will be efforts to broaden the scope of trade and attempts will be made in a bid to strengthen cooperation in the industry chain with all related countries.

4. Financial integration will involve the enhancement of the coordination in the monetary policy together with the expansion of the scope of local currency settlement and currency exchange in terms of trade and investment between countries along the route. The objective of this is to deepen multilateral and bilateral financial cooperation through setting up of regional development financial institutions.

5. People to people bonds mean that considerable efforts will be made to encourage exchanges between different cultures, strengthen friendly interactions amongst the people of various countries, and heighten mutual understanding and traditional friendships.

Politics, Diplomacy, and Soft Power

From the outset, China's leadership, particularly Hu Jintao, encouraged a three-point proposal on friendly relations with Africa, which encompassed common prosperity and closer cooperation between China and Africa to strengthen bilateral ties between the two. According to Hurst, the idea was to establish close cooperation on the international level to safeguard the rights and interests of developing nations instead of focusing on the political ties alone.[34] To achieve this, diplomacy was used as the preferred tool. Mustafic notes that the level of diplomatic efforts aimed at strengthening China's relationship with Africa, Asia, and European countries has brought astonishing results on almost a daily basis.[35] This has paved the way for Chinese investments in Africa and all over the world. This has led to the belief by many that China has effectively been able to use soft power.

Since China's competitors in global influence have a considerable advantage in Africa due to colonialism, China has been making strides to effectively utilize soft power as a way of attracting partners and gaining an edge over its competitors. According to Joseph Nye, soft power is when "a country gets another country to want what it wants."[36] With soft power, attraction becomes the weapon of choice, instead of the traditional military force or coercion. China has depicted herself as a peace-loving, development-oriented global citizen (power), with noble intentions in relations with other states through her mantra "peaceful development" (*hepingfazhan*). Yuon-kang notes that this, coupled with China's clever use of diplomacy, has gained her a great number of friends within the international arena.[37] It is under this peaceful development strategy that OBOR falls.

China has made the realization that building soft power is perhaps the most effective way through which she can gain the trust of other nations, especially in a world characterized and dominated by US hegemony and influence. This has allowed China to build a modern state in terms of people, the economy, and military. Mwatela and Changfeng argue that any other strategy besides soft power will most likely have a disastrous outcome, as it would trigger US counterbalancing measures.[38] These counterbalancing measures in turn might have undesirable effects through destabilizing Chinese society and leading to civil unrest together with other issues that may affect China's accumulation of power and, consequently, her rise. Focusing primarily on the economy has thus been designed to draw attention away from China's military exploits, which would attract counterbalancing measures and may have the same effect of a collapse of China's empire in the same manner the Soviet Union did.[39] The focus on economic matters allows China to gain allies both regionally and globally. It has been noted that this is one of the chief aims of OBOR. However, compared to other countries, such as the United States, the United Kingdom, Germany, and Japan, China currently has less soft power capabilities in Africa, notably since these countries have been using culture and language, aid and donor agencies for a few years now. The colonial history also gives them an advantage over China.

Geopolitics

Geopolitics can be defined as a combination of practices and representations that transform the built environment and the political organization of space and how different parts of the world are labeled.[40] It is a set of transformative projects that are the product of actions, which require representations and narratives to justify and explain those actions to limit dissent and gain a consensus across a variety of audiences. The Maritime Silk Road Initiative (MSRI), as part of the OBOR initiative, is an expression of geopolitical practices, as investments are made and new port, rail, and road facilities are built. The MSRI is thus a geopolitical project, which has as its goal the construction of building landscapes to guarantee the flow of investment and trade. It is thus a massive geopolitical project based on infrastructure development.

Countries in East Africa such as Djibouti, Egypt, Sudan, and Ethiopia are notably of strategic importance to China, especially for the Maritime Silk Road Initiative due to their geographical location.[41] China is also expanding similar infrastructure networks on Africa's West Coast. China is further making efforts to connect parts of Africa with the inland through railway lines, which provide several benefits for China. These connections make it possible for China to transport products and resources from the inland to the respective coasts so that they can be exported to (inter-alia) China. Cheung and Lee are of the view that the OBOR initiative is a brilliant undertaking, which has the potential to make a historic contribution to the age of globalization capable of laying the seeds for a new geopolitical era.[42] According to Leandro, OBOR is reshaping the maps of the future through the global multidimensional infrastructure network.[43] It holds vast potential to reshape geo-economic maps at the regional, international, and global level. It has been argued that the success of OBOR will be measured by the way maps in the future will be viewed, particularly the Indian-Pacific Oceans, as primary visual reference.

China intends on connecting all countries along the OBOR routes through a complex network of roads, rails, and pipelines.[44] The new ports constructed in Kenya that stretch across from the coast of mainland China through to the South China Sea, the strait of Malacca, across the Indian Ocean, and into the Arabian Sea and the Persian Gulf offer a basis for the construction of new railways that stretch from these ports into the interior of host countries.[45] It is apparent that the Maritime Silk Road Initiative (MSRI) and the Silk Road Economic Belt (SREB) are the two components of the OBOR initiative that each has a potential to transform the global geopolitical landscape. This will be achieved through undertaking inter-related infrastructure projects that include ports, highways, railways, and pipelines.[46] Although it has been argued that the end destination of the MSRI is Europe through the Suez Canal and the Mediterranean, it should be noted that the MSRI will also pass through several Eastern African countries, amongst them Djibouti, Kenya, Madagascar, Mozambique, and Tanzania.[47]

SECURITY

On peace and security under the OBOR initiative, President Xi Jinping stated that China intends on establishing a China-Africa peace and security fund. China will further continue offering free military aid to the African Union. Security assistance programs will be conducted in different areas, including peacekeeping missions, the fight against piracy together with combating any threats posed by terrorism. As part of the OBOR initiative, China is establishing a military base at Port Doraleh in Djibouti with the goal of cushioning the maritime route's security interests in East Africa and the Indian Ocean.[48] According to Linehan, this military base is of crucial and strategic importance to China as it is the first Chinese military base of any kind outside Chinese soil.[49] Mwatela and Changfeng are of the view that the official purpose of this base is to stave off piracy which is rife in the area, but critics have argued that it could be used as a mechanism to safeguard the trade artery, which links Asia and Europe through the Suez Canal and is being expanded and modernized by China.[50] Liu states that the base will cost within the region of US\$590 million and will be financed by China.[51] The base will be of great significance as it will enable China to have a rapid response to emergencies in North Africa, the Middle East, and South Asia.[52] The choice to set up a military base in Djibouti can be explained by a few reasons. Amongst them is the fact that Djibouti is a stable country which is located at the strategic trading route which links the Suez Canal to the Indian Ocean. From this point, China's maritime aircraft can cover a greater part of the Arabian Peninsula together with northern and central Africa without having to refuel. Kleven notes that the port in Djibouti has the capabilities of accommodating Chinese aircraft carriers, on top of being close to the United States base where drone attacks on Al Shabab and Al Qaeda are often conducted.[53] This project has, however, stirred a great deal of controversy and attracted a fair amount of criticism as Yale points out that "despite the claims of peaceful economic development, absent political strings, China has continued to act otherwise."[54] Further, Kleven is of the view that this shows that China has not only been building commercial ports through the OBOR initiative but this could easily turn out to be a military ambition consisting of a series of ports stretching from the South China Sea to Africa's East Coast.[55]

With regard to Egypt, the military cooperation and the economic ties between China and Egypt have been deemed to have reached unprecedented levels.[56] Mustafic notes that China has dedicated US$300 million to help train Egyptian police to strengthen its domestic security.[57] This is strategic, as domestic upheavals in Egypt similar to the Arab Spring will put a dent in China's ambitions and possibly disturb the progress being made in the refurbishment of the Suez Canal. It is thus of paramount importance that Egypt's domestic security is guaranteed and the country remains stable for China to fully realize its ambitions. Although China puts a lot of emphasis on its principles of nonintervention and noninterference, Mustafic further argues that China's military and diplomatic endeavors, interpreted through OBOR, are aimed at assisting China to not only get access to resources but to also solve some of its security issues within its region and beyond.[58]

ECONOMIC

There are huge benefits to be realized by countries that lie along and beyond the Silk Road routes, particularly in terms of imports and exports. Benefits that come with the OBOR initiative can be realized especially in the transport and other infrastructure projects that have been undertaken by the Chinese, especially in East Africa. Notable examples include Kenya and Djibouti, who have had infrastructural projects undertaken with the assistance of Chinese firms with finances being provided by China's Export-Import (Exim) bank. Another similar project is the US$4 billion railroad project, which was officially completed and connected Addis Ababa, Ethiopia's capital, to the port of Doraleh in Djibouti.[59] This project was undertaken using funds partly provided by Chinese companies together with the Chinese government. It is believed that China gave a loan of $2.4 billion to Ethiopia to fund the construction of the railway.[60] The railway is associated with several benefits that it brings in as it spans over 752 kilometers and, at the same time, significantly reduces the travel time between Addis Ababa and the Port of Doraleh to around twelve hours from three days. Future infrastructural projects to be undertaken will aim to connect Mombasa and Uganda, Rwanda and South Sudan, which will set the ground work for economic growth in these countries.

Infrastructure is at the center of the Belt and Road initiative. The OBOR initiative seeks to increase trade and investment cooperation.[61] OBOR will greatly promote Chinese outward foreign direct investment (FDI) in developing nations. China has been making a lot of emphasis on the historical connections between Africa and China to meet its own economic goals. Hurst notes that Chinese officials visiting Africa have increased the frequency of their visits over the past few years with Beijing being depicted as a reliable partner uninterested in lecturing Africa on issues to do with human rights, corruption, and governance.[62] Mustafic states that as a result, under the OBOR initiative, a few African countries are being promoted as important Chinese raw material exporters (particularly oil).[63]

In 2017, China entered into trade and economic cooperation agreements with thirty nations at the first Belt and Road Forum in Beijing; amongst these nations were two African countries, Kenya and Ethiopia.[64] Consequently, the Exim Bank entered into loan agreements with the National Treasury of Kenya, one company from Egypt, and with Ethiopia's Finance Ministry. Through these agreements, China has invested more than any other country in the development of Egypt's Suez Canal corridor. Breuer notes that in Djibouti, the Doraleh port was constructed in less than two years with joint funding from China Merchant Holdings International (CMMHI) and the Djibouti Ports and Free Zone Authority (DPFZA).[65]

To create a connection to South Sudan, the Ethiopia-Djibouti railway will be connected to the Kenyan Standard Gauge railway (SGR). The Mombasa Port will be broadly linked to inland Africa, stretching far beyond Kenya where railway lines shall be created via Nairobi to connect with South Sudan, Uganda, Rwanda, and Burundi. At the 2017 Belt and Road Forum (BRF), China and Kenya entered into an agreement, which facilitated funds in the form of credit worth US$ 3.6 billion for the extension of the Kenyan railway line between Nulvasha near Nairobi and Kisimu.[66] This will create massive economic advantages for Kenya. As part of the second belt, China intends to revitalize the Tanzania-Zambia Railway (TanZam), which was originally constructed in the 1970s with the aid of China. This railway stretches for about 1900 km and since its completion it has served as a symbol of Sino-Africa friendship. Breuer further notes that this is set to ensure that the railway gains renewed vigor. In addition, a 400 km railway from Chipata to Serenye, which connects Zambia to Mozambique, is also being constructed with the aid of China Civil Engineering Construction Company (CCECC).[67] However, it is important to note that Africa is not a major region along the belt and road, hence it is difficult for African states to fully benefit from the initiative.[68]

IMPLICATIONS OF THE OBOR INITIATIVE

The OBOR initiative presents both opportunities and challenges for Africa. According to Ehizuelen and Abdi, Africa has vast needs in terms of infrastructure investment in communication, water, and energy.[69] China's OBOR initiative is thus a strategic vision for strengthening investment and trade flows that lead to a renewed drive for the development trajectories of African, Asian, and European nations.[70] Wolff notes that through OBOR, the costs of importing inputs and favoring participation in the value chain will be reduced and, at the same time, OBOR offers a potential for profits through increasing regional supply networks to sustain competitiveness, low tariff, and non-tariff barriers to trade.[71] The OBOR initiative can stimulate African growth through infrastructure development. Yun Sun is of the view that this means that the OBOR initiative produces various economic opportunities for Africa through bolstering the construction outlooks of African countries situated along the MSRI route through the development of considerable transportation and physical infrastructure.[72] Africa is set to receive US$ 60 billion, which China has pledged to provide, and more than half of this amount will be used for infrastructural development in Africa. The OBOR initiative is set to undeniably revive Eastern and Southern Africa and will further be a new source of motivation.

However, the OBOR initiative is also associated with a range of challenges. The initiative will require careful and shrewd diplomacy to manage the relations and interactions of the many nations together with prudent planning to achieve maximum effectiveness. According to Ehizuelen and Abdi, it will further be challenging to make the initiative work, since it encompasses a vast number of people from different cultural and religious backgrounds who do not speak a common language and who have dissimilar political and economic systems.[73] Combative issues such as tariffs and currencies might have to be determined for everyone to be able to share and enjoy the benefits that come with OBOR. A few countries within the OBOR region are characterized by constant political upheavals and this presents a great challenge since political instability is often at times accompanied by cultural challenges. Henry Chan Lee notes that there has been an evident lack of specialized and qualified personnel in host countries in Africa, which has meant that over a million Chinese citizens have had to move to Africa to fill this gap.[74] Governance failures such as corruption and poor implementation of reforms are serious challenges as well. This, coupled with political tensions in the form of terrorism certainly complicates the situation further as it results in a lot of uncertainty. According to Toogood, conflict has cost African nations an estimated US$ 300 million between 1990 and 2005, an amount which is close to the same amount that these African nations have received in developmental aid.[75] China also faces some challenges when it comes to the quality of manufactured products it sends to African countries. These products have been deemed low cost and substandard. Perhaps the biggest challenge that the OBOR initiative faces is the state of perpetual warfare experienced in African states. Ndhlovhu-Gatsheni propounds that war and conflicts have exacted a heavy toll on Africa's development since time immemorial.[76]

CONCLUSION

The OBOR initiative and MSRI have drawn widespread attention from both academics and policy makers alike and stimulates a great deal of debate among them. Their opinion has varied and ranges from those who support the initiative and view it as part of a benevolent development project spearheaded by China. Some have classified it as a doom-laden geopolitical representation and have depicted the initiative as another step toward a foreseeable confrontation between the United States and China over global hegemony. It is apparent that China still maintains her position as Africa's most important ally to date. The One Belt One Road Initiative (OBOR) clearly offers prospects for the extension of Sino-Africa relations and it will be of great benefit to both parties, hence the Chinese and African leaderships must explore this relationship further. There still exists, however, some prospects for further cooperation. OBOR can be used by China as an opportunity to bring more foreign direct investment onto the continent, which will be to Africa's advantage. The OBOR initiative has clearly been presented to the rest of the world by the Chinese government as an action plan. It has been envisioned as an economic plan that has the potential of propelling Chinese trade and investment with its

African partners at the same time creating positive spillover effects that extend beyond the initial projects (win-win). It is evident that China is making attempts at stimulating shared prosperity with its partners and south/south cooperation. The Belt and Road initiative is to be viewed as a vital initiative for cooperation through an innovative approach aimed toward sharing responsibility, resources, and benefits. Some scholars have already suggested that the successful implementation of OBOR will most likely result in the creation of a single distinct Asian-European-Africa trading bloc, which will offer a stern challenge the present US-centered transatlantic and transpacific trading bloc system. The OBOR initiative will most likely reinforce China's "special role" in the global economy, where developing (especially African) countries have increasingly come to play a significant role. As a result, China has continued to be a crucial and perhaps the most important ally for the African continent to date. The OBOR initiative thus presents an opportunity to strengthen China-Africa cooperation and should be explored further.

However, the OBOR initiative currently has a limited threshold in Africa. As it stands, the OBOR initiative in Africa falls short in terms of mirroring the optimism the China-Africa relations have attracted in recent years, particularly when it is viewed in terms of the importance that China puts in Africa. The truth of the matter is that Africa remains a footnote in China's plans globally and there has been disharmony between the rhetoric regarding the importance and growth in the relationship, vis-à-vis the reality. A limited number of countries are involved in the initiative as compared to other regions and this does not present an optimistic picture. Despite this, the OBOR initiative will generally be a positive strategy for African nations, since Africa is currently in dire need of capital to finance its infrastructure development, and OBOR offers the best platform to achieve this. It is therefore important for African countries to strategically engage China in terms of how OBOR will be implemented to attain all the potential benefits that could be attained from this initiative.

NOTES

1. Lauren, A. Johnston. "The Belt and Road Initiative: What is in it for China," *Asia Pac Policy Stud* (2018):1–19.
2. Danny McFadden. The New Silk Road- China's One Belt One Road Initiative. *Researchgate* (2016): 1.
3. Ibid., 2.

4. Elizabeth C. Economy and Michael Levi. 2014. *Necessary – How China's Resources Quest is changing the World*. Oxford: Oxford University Press, 2014.
5. Kenneth Lieberthal and Michael Oksenberg. *Policy Making in China: Leaders, Structures, and Processes*. Princeton: Princeton University Press, 1988.
6. Michael Mitchell Omoruyi Ehizuelen and Hodan Osman Abdi. Sustaining China-Africa Relations: Slotting Africa into China's One Belt, One Road Initiative makes economic sense. *Asian Journal of Comparative Politics* Vol. 3, no. 4 (2018): 286.
7. Ibid.
8. Lixin Sun. "Chinese maritime concepts." *Asia Europe Journal*, 8(3) (2010): 327–338.
9. Raphael Ziro Mwatela and Zhan Changfeng. "Africa in China's 'One Belt, One Road' Initiative: A Critical Analysis," *IOSR Journal of Humanities and Social Science (IOSR-JHSS)*, Vol. 21, Issue12 (2016): 10.
10. World Bank, Data from the World Bank as of 12/31/2016, retrieved 12/26/2018 (2016).
11. Ehizuelen and Abdi, *Sustaining China-Africa Relations: Slotting Africa into China's One Belt, One Road Initiative makes economic sense*, 286.
12. Kroneshares. *The One Belt One Road Initiative: A New Paradigm in Global Investing: An Overview of the KraneShares MSCI One Belt One Road ETF* (2018).
13. Ehizuelen and Abdi, *Sustaining China-Africa Relations: Slotting Africa into China's One Belt, One Road Initiative makes economic sense*, 285.
14. John Wong. *Reviving the Ancient Silk Road: China's New Economic Diplomacy*. Singapore: East-Asian Institute, 2014, 2.
15. Ehizuelen and Abdi, *Sustaining China-Africa Relations: Slotting Africa into China's One Belt, One Road Initiative makes economic sense*, 286.
16. Ministry of Commerce of the People's Republic of China (MOFCOM). Ministry of Commerce holds briefing on measures for administration of foreign aid, December 10, 2014. http://english.mofcom.gov.cn/article/newsrelease/Press/201412/20141200851923.shtml (accessed 30 December 2018).
17. Mwatela and Changfeng, *Africa in China's 'One Belt, One Road' Initiative: A Critical Analysis*, 10.
18. Huiping Chen. China's 'One Belt, One Road' Initiative and its implications for Sino-African investment relations. Transnational Corporations Review 8(3): 178–182 (2016): 78.
19. Julia Breuer. *Two Belts, One Road? The role of Africa in China's Belt and Road initiative*. Blickwechsel, 2017, 1.

20. Mwatela and Changfeng, *Africa in China's 'One Belt, One Road' Initiative: A Critical Analysis*, 11.
21. Ibid.
22. Mwatela and Changfeng, *Africa in China's 'One Belt, One Road' Initiative: A Critical Analysis*, 13.
23. Hand Zhou. "China and South Sudan: Economic Engagement Continues Amid Conflict," *African Arguments* (2014).
24. David Shinn. "Africa Tests China's Non-Interference Policy," *China US Focus*, http://www.chinausfocus.com/foreign-policy/africa-tests-chinas-non-interferencepolicy/#sthash.8GwI3qi8.dpuf, 2014 (accessed 22 December 2018).
25. Mwatela and Changfeng, *Africa in China's 'One Belt, One Road' Initiative: A Critical Analysis*, 13.
26. Breuer, *Two Belts, One Road? The role of Africa in China's Belt and Road initiative*, 1.
27. Ibid.
28. Ehizuelen and Abdi, *Sustaining China-Africa Relations: Slotting Africa into China's One Belt, One Road Initiative makes economic sense*, 288.
29. Ibid.
30. Sanusha Naidu. The Forum on China-Africa Cooperation (FOCAC): What Does the Future Hold? *China Report*, Vol. 45, No. 3 (2007): 283–296.
31. Jikkie Verlare and Frans Paul van Putten. *One Belt, One Road: An Opportunity for EU's Security Strategy*. Netherlands Institute of International Relations, 2015, 8.
32. McFadden, *The New Silk Road- China's One Belt One Road Initiative*, 6.
33. Ibid., 7.
34. Cindy Hurst. *China's Oil Rush*. Institute for the Analysis of Global Security, 2006, 5.
35. Almir Mustafic. "China's One Belt, One Road and Energy Security Initiatives: A Plan to Conquer the World?" *Inquiry, 2* (2017): 153.
36. J. Nye. Soft Power, Foreign *Policy*, No. 80 (1990): 153–171.
37. Wang Yuon-kang. China's response to the Unipolar World: The Strategic Logic of Peaceful Development, *Journal of Asian and African Studies*, Vol. 45, No. 5 (2010): 554–567.
38. Mwatela and Changfeng, *Africa in China's 'One Belt, One Road' Initiative: A Critical Analysis*, 17.
39. Yuon-kang, *China's response to the Unipolar World: The Strategic Logic of Peaceful Development*.
40. Jean-Marc F. Blanchard and Colin Flint. The Geopolitics of China's Maritime Silk Road Initiative. *Geopolitics, 22* (2017): 223–245.

41. Breuer, *Two Belts, One Road? The role of Africa in China's Belt and Road initiative*, 5.
42. Francis Cheung and A. Lee. Thirty Years of Unprecedented Growth. *CLSA* (2016).
43. Francisco Jose Leandro. "OBOR is reshaping geopolitics," *Macau Functional Subsidiarity* (2016): 163.
44. Elodie Sellier. "China's Mediterranean Odyssey." *The Diplomat*, April 19, 2016. http://thediplomat.com/2016/04/chinas-mediterranean-odyssey/ (accessed 15 December 2018).
45. Ibid.
46. Blanchard and Flint, *The Geopolitics of China's Maritime Silk Road Initiative*, 223.
47. Ibid., 226.
48. Rob Edens, China's Naval Plans for Djibouti: A Road, a Belt, or a string of Pearls? *The Diplomat*, May 14, 2015. www.thediplomat.com (accessed 15 December 2018).
49. Michael Linehan. China's Belt and Road Strategy: Reality vs. Ambition. *Rising Powers* (2016).
50. Mwatela and Changfeng, *Africa in China's 'One Belt, One Road' Initiative: A Critical Analysis*, 13.
51. Zhu Liu. "China starts work on Horn of Africa Military Base in Djibouti, Defence ministry confirms," *South China Morning Post*. http://www.scmp.com/news/china/diplomacy-defence/article/1917210/china-starts-work-horn-africa-military-base-djibouti (accessed 22 December 2018).
52. Ibid.
53. Anthony Kleven. "Is China's Maritime Silk Road a Military Strategy?" *The Diplomat*, December 2015, http://thediplomat.com/2015/12/is-chinas-maritime-silkroad-a-military-strategy/ (accessed 22 December 2018).
54. Yale (2015:2).
55. Ibid., 7.
56. Lin Noueihed and Ali Abdelaty. "China's Xi visits Egypt, offers financial, political support." *Reuters Canada*, April 7, 2016. http://ca.reuters.com/article/topNews/idCAKCN0UZ05I (accessed 22 December 2018).
57. Mustafic, *China's One Belt, One Road and Energy Security Initiatives: A Plan to Conquer the World?* 164.
58. Ibid., 167.
59. Ehizuelen and Abdi, *Sustaining China-Africa Relations: Slotting Africa into China's One Belt, One Road Initiative makes economic sense*, 288.
60. Ibid.

61. Huayong Chen. China's 'One Belt, One Road' Initiative and its implications for Sino-African investment relations. *Transnational Corporations Review* 8, no. 3 (2016):178–182.
62. Hurst, *China's Oil Rush*, 17.
63. Mustafic, *China's One Belt, One Road and Energy Security Initiatives: A Plan to Conquer the World*, 172.
64. Breuer, *Two Belts, One Road? The role of Africa in China's Belt and Road initiative*, 2.
65. Ibid., 4.
66. Ibid.
67. Ibid.
68. Ibid., 180
69. Ehizuelen and Abdi, *Sustaining China-Africa Relations: Slotting Africa into China's One Belt, One Road Initiative makes economic sense*, 300.
70. Ibid.
71. Peter Wolff. China's 'Belt and Road' Initiative - Challenges and Opportunities. Report Prepared for the 2016 Annual Meeting of the Asian Development Bank. German Development Institute. https://www.die-gdi.de/uploads/media/Belt_and_Road_V1.pdf (accessed 15 December 2018).
72. Yun Sun. "Inserting Africa into China's One Belt, One Road strategy: A new opportunity for jobs and infrastructure?" March 2, 2015. http://www.brookings.edu/blogs/africa-in-focus/posts/2015/03/02-africa-china-jobs-infrastructure-sun (accessed 28 December 2018).
73. Ehizuelen and Abdi, *Sustaining China-Africa Relations: Slotting Africa into China's One Belt, One Road Initiative makes economic sense*, 302.
74. Henry Chan Lee. "One Belt, One Road Initiative creates fresh opportunities for Asians investing in Africa," *South China Morning Post*, November 10, 2016. www.scmp.com/specialreports/business/topics/one-belt-one-road/article/2041874/one-belt-one-road-initiative (accessed 19 December 2018).
75. K. Toogood. *Understanding the emerging relationship between China and Africa: The case of Nigeria. Changing landscape of assistance to conflict-affected states: Emerging and traditional donors and opportunities for collaboration policy brief.* London: International Alert, 2016, 32.
76. Sabelo J. Ndhlovhu-Gatsheni. Beyond the Equator There Are No Sins: Coloniality and Violence in Africa, *Journal of Developing Societies*, Vol. 28, No. 4 (2012): 419–440.

CHAPTER 12

Conclusion

China, once in need of international recognition and now in need of raw materials, has walked carefully and humbly toward Africa. Thus, the Chinese President Xi Jinping's first overseas trip was to Africa in March 2013. During this trip to Africa, he doubled Chinese aid commitment to $20 billion from 2013 to 2015.[1] The dynamic evolved into what is now called the *Beijing Consensus*, China's soft power diplomatic policy, entailing a strict respect for African sovereignty and a hands-off approach to internal issues. In short, loans and infrastructure without any political strings about democracy, transparency, or human rights attached.[2]

China's *noninterference* in the internal affairs of other nations model gives African leaders more freedom and the opportunity to work for immediate economic development with China; controversial African leaders face a second or third chance to join in international partnership this time with a successful developing nation; many of these excuses about Western domination, which had been previously used to justify Africa's lack of growth or independence, can no longer be made.

To the West, China's approach threatens the promotion of democracy, transparency, liberalism, and free trade, engaging instead with authoritarianism, economic development at the expense of civil progress, and strengthened ties between political and economic elites over broad social change. To China, who regards the West's human rights discourse as blatantly hypocritical, their involvement with so-called rogue states increases long-term stability and much needed win-win social and economic

© The Author(s) 2020   207
O. Abegunrin, C. Manyeruke, *China's Power in Africa*,
Politics and Development of Contemporary China,
https://doi.org/10.1007/978-3-030-21994-9_12

development. The arrival of a new global actor (China) in Africa has led Western powers to review their own strategies as they analyze Chinese actions in Africa. The Western responses may ultimately aid Africa, as think tanks provide strategic analysis on how African elites can squeeze more out of Chinese investments.[3]

Indeed, it's clearly in the interest of Africa to play one side against the other, and to avoid alliances between China and the West, which might work to decrease raw material prices.[4] Legal power remains in the hands of local African elites, who may or may not decide to enforce laws which would tighten control of resources, or further exploit them. Pursuing democracy and transparency is no longer the sole model[5]; development is for sure, and if African leaders can provide it, their power will be that much assured.

China and Resource Shortage

Although committed to good relations with Africa, in the twenty-first century China finds perhaps the greatest value in Africa as markets and sources of raw materials. The years of solidarity with revolutionary movements in Africa, especially in Southern Africa[6] in the 1950s and 1960s, have long been replaced by efforts to cultivate normal diplomatic and economic relations.

Key reasons of China's interest in Africa are to be found in China itself. Chinese economy, industry, energy, and society have a special interest in Africa. Chinese economy and industry turn toward export markets.[7] These industries and associated works and investment provide the Chinese society the recent two-digit yearly economic growth, job chances, and life standard improvement, but dramatically rely on sources, such as coal, seventy percent and oil, twenty-five percent (these are 2003 figures),[8] as well as other raw materials. Notable are the frequent electricity supply shortages. A United States analyst noticed that energy shortages have already led to rationing of electricity supply, slowing down the manufacturing sector and, consequently, overall economic growth. On other raw materials side, China simply does not have enough natural resources of its own to meet its growing industrial need.[9]

Within China's economic success story, Western scholars noticed that China's quest of wealth has once more led coastal provinces to quickly enrich, while inland provinces or rural areas of China stay relatively poor, an inequality which thus leads to internal social tensions and instability.[10]

12 CONCLUSION 209

Repositioning the African economy is not a short-term task and there are no shortcuts; indeed, there are tough decisions that need to be made, but we have no doubt that focusing on infrastructural investment, revenue mobilization, and value for money in public expenditure will deliver growth, wealth, and opportunity for all Africans.

Forums on China-Africa cooperation, including industrialization, agricultural development, training, job creation, and technology transfer through investment in manufacturing, are very essential. In addition, necessitated by China's rising investment in Africa and the local African security risks associated with them, peace and stability are very important key areas for Chinese-African cooperation.

China has consistently doubled its financing commitment to Africa during the past three Forums on China-Africa Cooperation (FOCAC) meetings, from $5 billion in 2006 to $10 billion in 2009 and $20 billion in 2012. Half of the $20 billion commitment in 2012 had been disbursed by the end of 2013, leading to China increasing the credit line by another $10 billion in 2014. If this pattern serves as any indicator, China announced another impressive line of credits of $60 billion available for Africa during the 2015 Forum on China-Africa Cooperation Summit, and the same amount in the 2018 Summit.[11]

The key questions are what China and Africa will prioritize the new batch of Chinese financing for and how Africa can work with China to maximize the benefits for the continent. Since its inauguration, the President Xi Jinping Administration has emphasized African infrastructure development. This move originates from the negative publicity and frequent criticism of China's traditional emphasis on natural resources. During his May 2014 visit to Africa, Chinese Premier Li Keqiang enthusiastically promoted major projects such as the 461[12] frameworks on China-Africa economic cooperation,[13] and the three networks—the high-speed rail network, the highway network, and the regional aviation network. Many of these plans were supposed to materialize or expand during the 6th Forum on China-Africa Cooperation Summit.

Despite the supposedly cooperative nature of the Forum on China-Africa Cooperation, China has played a larger role in setting and driving the agenda in the past as the financier of the projects. Africa's priorities are in structural reform and a framework of mutually beneficial cooperation. However, since its inauguration, President Xi Jinping's Administration has enhanced its emphasis in the areas in which Africa is most interested. This decision partially reflects China's desire to mitigate the broad criticisms on its mercantilist approach toward Africa and President Xi Jinping's economic charm offensive to boost China's contribution in international development and rising African demands. The 6th Forum on China-Africa Cooperation Meeting included agricultural development, industrialization, training, job creation, and technology transfer through investment in manufacturing industries. In addition, necessitated by China's rising investment in Africa and the local security risks associated with them, peace and stability were the key Areas for discussion at the 6th Forum on China-Africa Cooperation in Johannesburg, South Africa in 2015.

As Africa's largest trading partner and a major investor, China's actions have major implications for the development of the continent. Thus, Africa needs to accurately anticipate and assess the Chinese agenda, weighing the pros and cons, to approach FOCAC with strategies and priorities that will align with that agenda, but also meet African needs. For example, agricultural transformation has been a main priority for Africans to enhance productivity, food security, and inclusive development. In addition, investments are greatly needed to achieve structural transformation and diversify Africa's production and export base. Given the importance of these issues, African countries should be courageous in negotiating with China for direct investment in these areas.

China's response may most likely be that its investment in infrastructure will lay the necessary foundation for both Africa's agricultural transformation and industrial development. However, the key question here is whether such infrastructure deals will bog African countries back down to reliance on natural resources transactions and undermine the momentum for structural reform. The Chinese model of infrastructure development in Africa features resources-backed loans and aid to create business opportunities for Chinese importers and contractors. While it may contribute to the infrastructure needed for economic development, this emphasis does not address Africa's most urgent needs in agricultural transformation, economic structural reform, or human resources capacity building.

Despite, the hope that Beijing will contribute more to areas such as agricultural and industrial development, observers of China-Africa relations are concerned that most of the new financing committed by China in 2014 or those announced in 2015 at the 6th FOCAC meeting followed the traditional trajectory. In fact, according to China's former special envoy for African affairs, China has no intention of breaking away from this old pattern. Commenting on the $10 billion China offered in 2014, the special envoy pointed out that "this funding will be paid back by

African countries with commodities or the franchise (of the infrastructure projects)."[14] Meanwhile, although Beijing has imposed more stringent requirements on Chinese companies in order to improve the companies' records on governance, transparency, and accountability when investing in Africa, few Chinese expect them to completely abandon their suboptimal operation model in the near future. Some Chinese experts have pointed out that private Chinese investors make up about eighty percent of all Chinese entities investing in Africa and, due to their own deficiencies, are less adaptive to the African context.[15] If African governments deem these approaches undesirable, they need to work and negotiate for a change of rules and practices. African regional organizations, such as the African Union (AU), should play the important role in pushing China as well as African countries to sign international agreements on transparency, especially in the natural resource extraction industry, including the Extractive Industry Transparency Initiative (EITI).

China's recent and rising interests in African security affairs has brought more resources and assistance to the table in terms of stabilization and conflict resolution in Africa. China has adjusted its principle of noninterference in other countries' internal affairs in cases such as South Sudan and has enhanced its military assistance to and security cooperation with African countries and regional organizations. For example, China has sent an infantry battalion, the largest combat troop contribution China has made to a United Nations peacekeeping mission, to South Sudan in the beginning of 2015.[16] While China's contribution to African security issues could be positive, Africa needs to understand and prepare for the potential geopolitical implications, and most likely, a heightened sense of competition between China and Western powers if China's political influence and security presence in Africa are to expand.

AFRICAN NEEDS

In 2013, President Xi Jinping announced the One Belt One Road Initiative (OBORI), a trillion-dollar project that aims to connect more than seventy countries across Asia, Africa, and Europe via an overland belt and a maritime road.

In the past Forum on China-Africa Cooperation Summits, China has always set the agenda for the meetings. To level the playing field, African leaders need to carefully strategize and actively voice their demands for China's contribution according to their own needs. They should coordinate their goals and strategies to leverage collective bargaining and binding power vis-à-vis China, through regional and subregional organizations. The African Union has played a key role in harmonizing the positions and development agendas among African countries. Now is the perfect opportunity for the African Union to spearhead discussions with China on how African agendas are incorporated in China's planned activities in the African continent.

As noted above, it remains to be seen whether China will abandon its traditional financing model backed by African resources, despite its new emphasis on African demands. African leaders, therefore, must aim for a more informed understanding of the short-term and long-term consequences of Chinese financing projects in Africa. As most African countries prioritize structural transformation as the central and most critical theme in their economic policies, they need to develop a nuanced assessment of how China's infrastructure financing will contribute or undermine this theme and actively manage the results efficiently.

China has stated a willingness to enhance and improve its input in African capacity building, such as human resources development, technical assistance, and technological transfers. The commitment, indeed, presents an opportunity for African countries to wisely strategize and demand China deliver the investments they need most, including on manufacturing industries and job creation. Africa should not stop with China's piecemeal approach and demonstration projects crafted for public relations purposes. For example, the corporate social responsibility programs operated by Chinese companies are passive rather than active. They are motivated by executive directives by Chinese government agencies and neglect the public relations campaign.[17] Africans should design their own capacity building project guidelines aimed at structural transformation in a comprehensive manner.

China's burgeoning presence in Africa is already shaping and reshaping the future of millions of African peoples; from Senegal to Kenya and from Egypt to South Africa, in creaky trucks and back roads, we have seen the characters of what make up China's dogged emigrant population, entrepreneurs singlehandedly reshaping African infrastructure, and less-lucky migrants barely scraping by, but still convinced of Africa's opportunities. This study/book offers illuminating insight into the most pressing unknowns of modern Sino-Africa relations. And why China is making these cultural and economic incursions into the continent of Africa; what the ramifications for both the Africans and the Chinese and their peoples,

12 CONCLUSION 213

and the whole world is and will be for the foreseeable future. Interest in this subject is enduring. China's foray into Africa will continue to heighten and consequently play an important role in the shaping of contemporary Africa's external relations. Thus, this subject will continue to engage the interest of scholars and policy makers alike. Arthur Kroeber said: "China has emerged from backwardness to become a global economic superpower since economic reforms began under Deng Xiaoping in 1978. The Chinese economy has stumbled, but despite problems, it still spurts ahead at home and abroad. It is changing the world."[18]

There is a leadership deficit. In effect, the economic and development problem of Africa is a problem of governance. When one examines the ease with which African governments mortgage the future of their people for money, sign trade agreements without reading the fine print, settle for raw material based economy, receive exploitative foreign aid, waste their resources on the maintenance of experts from overseas, and continue to cultivate the mentality that whatever comes from outside is better for them, one cannot but conclude that the new generation of African leaders need mental liberation.

One need not wonder then why after over five decades, the Organization of African Unity (OAU), transformed into African Union (AU), has failed to achieve the economic and political freedom and the unity sought for by the pre-independence African elites. When African leaders begin to value their heritage, overcome inferiority complex and the *"theirs is better syndrome,"* realize the wealth at their disposals, refrain from seeking immediate gratifications and short-term gains that mortgage the heritage of their citizens for a bowl of soup, understand the negative impact of *"foreign-aid"* and see their people as assets, and understand that the call to govern is a privilege to serve their people, then the light will dawn on the continent and a new Africa will be born.

The Christian Science Monitor vividly explained China's aim in Africa thus: "China, in both an individual and collective sense, is shrewdly and opportunistically maximizing its relationship with African nations in an effort to extend its economic influence across the world."[19] China is claiming to be in Africa to invest and help Africa, but we should not overlook that, at the same time, this strategy is helping China capture African markets and control her resources. Realistically, until the Africans themselves join hands together and build their own countries, no foreign power, be it China, the United States, Japan, or the European Union, will build Africa for the Africans.

Notes

1. "China's Aid to Africa: Monster or Messiah?" Available at http://www. brookings.edu/research/opinions/2014/02/07-china-aid-africa-sun. Retrieved September 12, 2018.
2. D. Thomson, I. Taylor, D. Shin, J. Eisenman, and Y. Shichor, *China Brief,* Volume 5, Issue 21, Jamestown Foundation, October 13, 2005.
3. Leveraging the Dragon: Towards "An Africa That Can Say No." March 2005.
4. Cindy Hurst, *China's Oil Rush in Africa*, Political-military Research analyst, Foreign Military Studies Office, Institute for the Analysis of Global Security, 2006, pp. 17–18.
5. Ernest, J. Wilson III, *China's Role in the World in 2018: Is China a Responsible Stakeholder in Africa?* The U.S.-China Economic and Security Review Commission; Center for International Development and Conflict Management, University of Maryland, College Park, MD: August 3–4, 2006, p. 10. https://www.uscc.gov/hearings/2006hearings/written_testimonies/06_08_3_4_wilson_ernest_statement.pdf) (PDF). U.S. Congress.
6. Olayiwola Abegunrin, "Soviet and Chinese Military Involvement in Southern Africa," A *Current Bibliography on African Affairs*, Washington, DC, 6, 3 (1983–1984), pp. 52–83.
7. Ian Taylor, "China's Oil Diplomacy," *International Affairs* 82, 5, 2006, p. 937.
8. L. Noronha et al., "India-China Energy Perspectives," *Energy Security Insights*, 2 (2), 2007, p. 28, The Energy and Resources Institute, New Delhi, India.
9. James Reynolds, China in Africa: Developing Ties > Minerals, BBC News, July 2007. https://news.bbc.co.uk/2/hi/asia-pacific/6264476.stm. Retrieved August 16, 2018.
10. G. Friedman, The Next 100 years: A Forecast for the 21st Century, New York, NY: Doubleday, 2009.
11. Peterson Tumwebaze, "Johannesburg Summit of FOCAC 2015 Will Deepen Sino-African Cooperation," *The New Times*, Johannesburg, November 28, 2015. Also see The Forum on China-Africa Cooperation Johannesburg Action Plan, Beijing, 2016–2018.
12. **461** is a cooperation framework proposed by China that includes four principles—(1) equality, (2) solidarity/mutual trust, (3) tolerance in development issues, (4) innovative cooperation. Six major projects are (1) industrial cooperation, (2) financial cooperation, (3) poverty alleviation cooperation, (4) environmental protection cooperation, (5) civil and cultural exchanges cooperation, (6) peace and security cooperation, and one platform Forum on China-Africa Cooperation (FOCAC).

12 CONCLUSION 215

13. Ibid.
14. X. Shang, "Li Kequiang's visit to Africa." *JingHuaShiBao*, May 13, 2014. https://fortune.chinanews.com/gn/2014/05-13/6162221.shtml. Retrieved September 25, 2018.
15. Q. Liu, "Strengthening Corporate Social Responsibility in China," *China Social Sciences Today*, July 25, 2013. https://www.nisd.cass.cn/news/724763.htm. Retrieved September 25, 2018.
16. ZX, "China to Send 268 Peacekeepers to South Sudan," www.Xinhuanet.news.cn.com, September 5, 2018. Retrieved October 1, 2018.
17. Y. Wang, "The Kenya Conundrum of Chinese Companies." *Phoenix Weekly*, August 19, 2014. https://view.inews.qq.com/a/20140819A000KQ00. Retrieved September 25, 2018.
18. Arthur R. Kroeber, *China's Economy: What Everybody Needs to Know*, New York: Oxford University Press, 2016.
19. "China in Africa," *The Christian Science Monitor*, Boston, 2014.

SELECTED BIBLIOGRAPHY

Abegunrin, Olayiwola, *Africa in Global Politics in the Twenty-First Century: A Pan-African Perspective*, New York: Palgrave Macmillan, 2009.

Abegunrin, Olayiwola, and Sabella O. Abidde (co-editor), *African Intellectuals and the State of the Continent: Essays in Honor of Professor Sulayman S. Nyang*, London: Cambridge Scholars Publishing, 2018.

Abegunrin, Olayiwola, "Zimbabwe," in David Levi and Karen Christensen, editors, *Global Perspectives on the United States: A Nation by Nation Survey, Volume 2*, Great Barrington, MA: Berkshire Publishing Group, 2007.

Abegunrin, Olayiwola, *Nigeria and the Struggle for the Liberation of Zimbabwe: A Study of Foreign Policy Decision Making of An Emerging Nation*. Stockholm, Sweden: Bethany Books, 1992.

Abegunrin, Olayiwola, "Soviet and Chinese Military Involvement in Southern Africa," A *Current Bibliography on African Affairs*, Washington, DC: 6, 3, 1983–1984.

Adisu, Kinfu, Thomas Sharkey and Sam C. Okoroafo, "The Impact of Chinese Investment in Africa," *International Journal of Business and Management*, Vol. 5, No. 9, 2010.

Alao, Abiodun, "China and Zimbabwe: The Context and Contents of a Complex Relationship," *Occasional Paper 202; Global Powers and Africa Programme*, 2014.

Alao, Abiodun, *Mugabe and the Politics of Security in Zimbabwe*, Montreal: McGill-Queen's University Press, 2012.

Alden, Chris, editor, *China in Africa*, London: International African Institute, Royal African Society, Zed Books, 2007.

© The Author(s) 2020
O. Abegunrin, C. Manyeruke, *China's Power in Africa*,
Politics and Development of Contemporary China,
https://doi.org/10.1007/978-3-030-21994-9

218 SELECTED BIBLIOGRAPHY

Alden, Chris, Daniel Large, and Ricardo Soares De Oliveira, Editors, China Returns to Africa: A Rising Power and a Continent Embrace, London: Hurst & Company, 2008.

Ashurst, Mark, "China's Ambitions in Africa," BBC News, November 25, 2006. Available on www.bbcnews.com. Accessed on November 27, 2006.

Botha, Ilana. *China in Africa: Friend or Foe? China's Contemporary Political and Economic Relations with Africa,* 2006.

Brautigam, Deborah, *The Dragon's Gift: The Real Story of China in Africa.* Oxford: Oxford University Press, 2009.

Brown, Adam, *CHINA: A History of China and East Asia,* Charleston, SC: CreateSpace Independent Publishing Platform, 2016.

Britz, Anna Christina, *The Struggle for Liberation and the Fight for Democracy: The Impact of Liberation Movement Governance on Democratic Consolidation in Zimbabwe and South Africa,* Johannesburg: Stellenbosch University Press, 2011.

Brzezinski, Zbigniew, Editor, *Africa and the Communist World,* Stanford, CA: Stanford University Press, 1963.

Burdette, Marcia M. *Zambia: Between Two Worlds.* Boulder, Colorado: Westview Press, 1988.

Carmody, Padraig, *The New Scramble for Africa,* Malden, MA: Polity Press, 2013.

Carr, William, H.A., *The Emergence of Red China,* New York, NY: Lancer Books, Inc., 1967.

Chan, Stephen, Editor, *The Morality of China in Africa: The Middle Kingdom and the Dark Continent,* London and New York: Zed Books, 2013.

Cheru, Fantu, *The Silent Revolution in Africa: Debit, Development and Democracy,* London: Zed Books, 1989.

Cheru, Fantu and Cyril Obi, Editors, *The Rise of China and India in Africa,* London: Zed Books, 2010.

"China-Africa Relations: A win, win Strategy," *African Business,* London, March 2007–XXXX.

Chingono, Hebert. Revolutionary *Warfare and the Zimbabwe War of Liberation: A Strategic Analysis.* Washington, DC: National War College, 1999.

Clapham, Christopher. *From Liberation Movement to Government Past Legacies and the Challenge of transition in Africa.* Johannesburg: The Brenthurst Foundation, 2012.

Cohen, Stephen, S., and J. Bradford DeLong, *The End of Influence: What Happens When Other Countries Have the Money,* New York, NY: Basic Books, 2010.

Crilly, Rob, "Oil from Africa Comes with Political Instability," *USA TODAY,* May 1, 2006.

De Lorenzo, M., African Perspective on China. *American Enterprise Institute for Public Policy Research,* 2007.

Dollar, David, *China's Engagement with Africa – from Natural Resources to Human Resources.* New York: Brookings, 2016.

SELECTED BIBLIOGRAPHY 219

Dreyer, June Teufel, *China's Political System: Modernization and Tradition*, Fourth Edition, New York, NY: Pearson Longman, 2004.

Ebangit, Zerubbabel Ojimam, *The Chinese Conception of Economic Development: Its Influence on Development Strategy in Tanzania*, PhD Dissertation, University of Texas at Austin, 1977.

Economy, Elizabeth C. and Michael Levi. *By all Means Necessary: How China's Resources Quest is changing the World*. Oxford: Oxford University Press, 2014.

Edinger, Hannah, and Christopher Burke. *China-Africa Relations: A Research Report on Zimbabwe*, Stellenbosch: Centre for Chinese Studies, University of Stellenbosch, 2008.

Ellis, Stephen. The *Genesis of the ANC's Armed Struggle in South Africa-1961*. Oxford: Oxford University Press, 2011.

Elizabeth, C. Economy and Michael Levi.. *Necessary – How China's Resources Quest is changing the World*. Oxford: Oxford University Press, 2014.

Farrow, Ronan, *War on Peace: The End of Diplomacy and the Decline of American Influence*, New York, NY: W.W. Norton and Company, 2018.

Freeman, Sharon T., *China, Africa, and the African Diaspora: Perspectives*, Washington, DC: AASBEA Publishers, 2009.

French, Howard W., *Everything Under the Heavens: How the Past Helps Shape China's Push for Global Power*, New York, NY: Alfred A. Knopf, 2017.

French, Howard W., *China's Second Continent How A Million Migrants Are Building A New Empire in Africa*, New York, NY: Vintage Books, 2014.

Geda, Alemayehu, and Atnafu G. Meskel, "Impact of China-Africa Investment Relations: Case Study of Ethiopia," *Institute of African Economic Studies, IAES Working Paper Serious No. A04*, 2011.

Grimm, Sven, Yejoo Kim, Ross Anthony, Robert Attwell and Xin Xiao. *South African Relations with China and Taiwan - Economic Realism and the 'One-China' Doctrine*. Johannesburg: Centre for Chinese Studies, Stellenbosch University, 2013.

Haglund, Dan, *Chinese Investors in Zambia; Is it for a Long Term?* Cambridge, UK: Cambridge University Press, 2007.

Halper, Stefan, *The Beijing Consensus: How China's Authoritarian Model Will Dominate the Twenty-First Century*, New York, NY: Basic Books, 2010.

Hanauer, Larry, and Lyle J. Morris, *Chinese Engagement in Africa: Drivers, Reactions, and Implications for U.S. Policy*. Washington, DC: RAND Corporation, 2014.

Hayter, Teresa. *Aid as Imperialism*. Middlesex: Penguin Books, 1971.

Hinton, Harold C. *China's Turbulent Quest: An Analysis of China's Foreign Relations Since 1949*. Bloomington, Indiana University Press, 1970.

Hung, Ho-Fung, *China and the Transformation of Global Capitalism*, Baltimore, MD: The John Hopkins University Press, 2009.

220 SELECTED BIBLIOGRAPHY

Jacques, Martin, When China Rules the World: The End of the Western World and the Birth of a New Global Order, New York, NY: Penguin books, 2012.

Jalata, G. G., "Development Assistance from the South: Comparative Analysis of Chinese and Indian to Ethiopia." *Chinese Studies* 3 (1), 2014.

Johnston, Lauren A. "The Belt and Road Initiative: What is in it for China," *Asia Pac Policy Study*, 2018.

Kahin, George McTurnan, *The Asian-African Conference: Bandung, Indonesia, April 1955*. Port Washington, NY: Kennikat Press, 1956.

Khanna, Parag, *The Future is Asian, Commerce, Conflict, and Culture in the 21*[st] *Century*. New York, Simon and Schuster, 2019.

King, Kenneth, *China's Aid and Soft Power in Africa: The Case of Education and Training*, New York, NY: BOYEG, 2013.

Kissinger, Henry A., *World Order*, New York, NY: Penguin Books, 2014.

Kissinger, Henry A., *On China*, New York, NY: The Penguin Press, 2011.

Langqing, Li, *Breaking Through: The Birth of China's Opening-Up Policy*, New York, NY: Oxford University Press, 2009.

Larkin, Bruce, *China and Africa, 1949–1970: The Foreign Policy of the People's Republic of China*, Berkeley, CA: University of California Press, 1971.

Lawrence, Alan. *China's Foreign Relations Since 1949*. Boston, MA: Routledge & Kegan Paul, 1975.

Le Corre, Philippe, and Jonathan D. Pollack, *China's Global Rise: Can the EU and U.S. Pursue a Coordinated Strategy?* Washington, DC: Brookings Institution, October 2016.

Li, Cheng, Chinese Politics in the Xi Jinping Era: Reassessing Collective Leadership, Washington, DC: Brookings Institution Press, 2016.

Madunagu, Edwin, "China's Return to Africa," *The Guardian*, Lagos, December 14, 2006.

Mandaza, Ibbo, editor, *ZIMBABWE: The Political Economy of Transition 1980–1986*, Dakar, Senegal: CODDESRIA Book Series, 1986.

Manyeruke, Charity, and Mhandara Lawrence, 2011, *"Zimbabwe's Views on Current Transformation of the International System,"* *Global Review*, Shangaai Institute of International Affairs.

Manyeruke, Charity, Mhandara Lawrence, and Nyemba Eve, 2012, *"Debating China's Role in Africa's Political-Economy,"* Centre for Chinese Studies (The China Monitor), Issue 2, June 2013.

Manyeruke, Charity, Chitando Ezra, and Madzokere Amanda, 2014, *"The Concept of Reciprocity in Zimbabwe and Chinese".* Global Review, Shanghai Institute for International Studies.

Marx, Karl, and Friedrich Engels, The Communist Manifesto, New York, NY: Penguin, 1998.

McGreal, Chris, "Hu Jintao Starts Africa Tour with Loans Promise," *Guardian News*. London, January 31, 2007.

SELECTED BIBLIOGRAPHY   221

Meredith, Martin, *MUGABE: Power, Plunder, and the Struggle for Zimbabwe*, New York: Public Affairs, 2007.

Mohan, G. and Kale, D. *The invisible hand of South-South globalization: Chinese migrants in Africa. A Report for the Rockefeller Foundation prepared by The Development Policy and Practice Department.* Milton Keynes: The Open University, 2007.

Tilda Verdonk, *South-South Cooperation-A case study of Ethiopia's political and economic relations with China and Turkey*, Sweden: Linnaeus University, 2017a.

Monson, Jamie. *Africa's Freedom Railway: How a Chinese Development Project Changed Lives and Livelihoods in Tanzania.* Bloomington, Indiana: Indiana University Press, 2009.

Morgenthau, Hans J., and Kenneth W. Thompson, *Politics among nations: the struggle for power and peace.* New York: McGraw-Hill, 1993.

Mubita, Oliver. *Increased Economic Relations Between China And Zambia In The Last Decade: Implications on Zambia's Existing Bilateral Relations with the United States.* Fort Leavenworth: U.S. Army Command and General Staff College, 2013.

Mutukwa, Kasuka S. *Politics of the Tanzania-Zambia Railway Project: A Study of Tanzania-China-Zambia Relations*, Lanham, MD: The University Press of America, 1979.

Naisbitt, John and Doris Naisbitt, China's Megatrends: The 8 Pillars of A New Society, New York, NY: HarperCollins Publishers, 2010.

Ndhlovhu-Gatsheni, Sabelo J., Beyond the Equator there are no Sins Coloniality and Violence in Africa, *Sage*, Vol. 28, No. 4, 2012.

Nkrumah, Kwame, *Neo-Colonialism: The Last Stage of Imperialism.* New York: International Publishers, 1965.

Nye, Joseph, Jr., The Future of Power, New York, NY: Public Affairs, 2014.

Nye, Joseph, Jr., *Soft Power: The Means to Success inworld Politics*, New York, NY: Public Affairs, 2004.

October, Lauren Sue, *Liberation Movements as Governments: Understanding the ANC'S Quality of Government.* Johannesburg: Stellenbosch University Press, 2015.

Olimat, Muhamad S., *China and North Africa Since World War II*, Lanham, MD: Lexington Books, 2014.

Peerenboom, Randall, *CHINA: Modernizes: Threat to the West or Model for the Rest?* New York, NY: Oxford University Press, 2007.

Pillsbury, Michael, *The Hundred-Year Marathon: China's Secret Strategy to Replace America as the Global Power Superpower.*

Prah, D.L.S. Kwesi and Vusi Gumede editors, *Africa-China Partnership and Relations: African Perspectives*, Trenton, NJ: Africa World Press, 2018.

Rodney, Walter, *How Europe Under-Developed Africa*, Washington, DC: Howard University Press, 1994.

222 SELECTED BIBLIOGRAPHY

Roy, D. *China's Foreign Relations*. Basingstock: Macmillan, 1998.

Sachikonye. Lloyd, Crouching Tiger, Hidden Agenda: Zimbabwe-China Relations. South Africa: University of KwaZulu-Natal Press, 2008.

Sata, Michael. *Chinese Investment in Africa and Implications for International Relations, Consolidation of Democracy and Respect for Human Rights: The Case of Zambia*. Cambridge: Harvard University, 2007.

Shinn, David H. and Joshua Eisenman, *China and Africa: A Century of Engagement*, Philadelphia, PA: University of Pennsylvania Press, 2012.

Songwe, Vera and Nelipher Moyo. *China-Africa Relations: Defining New Terms of Engagement*. Pretoria: The Brookings Institution, 2009.

Sörensen, Jen Stilhoff, *Challenging the aid paradigm: Western currents and Asian alternatives*. Basingstoke: Palgrave Macmillan, 2010.

Southall, Roger. *Liberation Movements in Power: Party and State in Southern Africa*. London: Boydell and Brewer, 2013.

Sun, Irene Yuan, *The Next Factory of the World: How Chinese Investment is Reshaping Africa*, Boston, MA: Harvard Business Review Press, 2017.

Tanzania-Zambia Railway Authority. *Ten Years of TAZARA Operations. Review and Perspective*, Dar-es-Salaam, Tanzania: TAZARA Head Office, 1986. www. Info.tazarasite.com.

Taylor, Ian, *China and Africa: Engagement and Compromise*. London: Routledge, 2006.

Taylor, Ian, *NEPAD: Toward Africa's Development or Another False Start?* Boulder, CO: Lynne Rienner Publishers, 2005.

Timberg, Graig, "Hu Jintao Defends China's Role in Africa," *The Washington Post*, February 8, 2007.

Van de Looy, Judith. *Africa and China: A Strategic Partnership*. Leiden: African Studies Centre, 2006.

Toogood, K., *Understanding the emerging relationship between China and Africa: The case of Nigeria. Changing landscape of assistance to conflict-affected states: Emerging and traditional donors and opportunities for collaboration policy brief*. London: International Alert, 2016.

Van Vuuren, Hennie. *Apartheid Guns and Money: A Tale of Profit*. Johannesburg: Vacana Media, 2017.

Verdonk, Tilda, *South-South Cooperation-A case study of Ethiopia's political and economic relations with China and Turkey*, Sweden: Linnaeus University, 2017b.

Vogel, Ezra F., *Deng Xiaoping and the Transformation of China*, Cambridge, MA: The Belknap Press of Harvard University Press, 2011.

Walter, Culter. *The TAZARA Railroad Project: Progress and Prospects*, Senior Seminar in Foreign Policy. Washington, DC: U.S. Department of State, 1973–1974.

Weinstein, Warren. Chinese and Soviet Aid to Africa. New York, NY: Praeger Publishers, 1975.

SELECTED BIBLIOGRAPHY   223

Woldemariam, Kasahun, *The Chinese Eldorado and the Prospects for African Development*, Trenton, NJ: Africa World Press, 2016.

Wolff, Peter, China's 'Belt and Road' Initiative - Challenges and Opportunities. Report Prepared for the 2016 Annual Meeting of the Asian Development Bank. German Development Institute, 2016.

Yew Kuan, Lee, The Grand Master's Insights on China, the United States, and the World, Cambridge, MA: The MIT Press, 2013.

Young, Marilyn, *The Vietnam Wars: 1945–1990*, New York: Harper Perennial, 1991.

Yu, George T. China and Tanzania: A Study in Comparative Interaction. Berkeley, CA: University of California Press, 1970.

Zemene, *An Overview of the Bilateral Relations between the Federal Democratic Republic of Ethiopia and the People's Republic of China*. Addis Ababa: Asia Australasia and the Middle East General Directorate Ministry of Foreign Affairs, Ethiopia, 2006.

Zafar, A., *The Gravity Relationship Between China and Sub-Saharan Africa: Macroeconomics, Trade, Investment and Aid Links.* Oxford: Oxford University Press, 2007.

Zhan, James, et al. "World Investment Report 2018." *United Nations Conference on Trade and Development*, June 2018.

JOURNAL, MAGAZINES AND NEWSPAPERS

African Business, London
African Journal, London
African Business, Kent, United Kingdom
Africa Today, London
African World, London
Business Week, London
China Daily, Beijing
China Watch, Washington, DC
Financial Times, London
Global Review, USA
Guardian News, London
People's Daily, Beijing: Xinhua Press
Quartz Africa Weekly Brief
South China Morning Post, International Edition
The Guardian, Lagos
The New York Times, New York
The Times, London
The Washington Post, Washington, DC
USA Today, New York

INDEX[1]

A

Abegunrin, Olayiwola, 25n45, 25n52, 93n20, 111n1, 183n7, 183n8, 185n34, 214n6

Abuja, 13

Action Plan, 31, 69, 183, 201

Addis Ababa, 21, 27, 39, 137, 138, 198

Adeosun, Kemi (Nigerian Minister of Finance), 68

Africa, 1, 9, 27–52, 59–72, 75, 96, 116, 131, 151–167, 173–183, 187–202, 207

African continent, 1, 4, 5, 9, 10, 14, 22, 29, 31, 35, 40, 43, 45, 46, 61, 65, 70, 75, 76, 80, 92, 102, 108, 115, 173, 180, 188, 189, 193, 202, 212

African Development Bank (ADB), 37, 159

African Growth Opportunity Act (AGOA), 156

African Liberation Movement, 17, 87

African National Congress (of South Africa), 18, 84–85

African peoples, 19, 27, 43, 63, 212

African population, 28, 59, 155

African Safari, 1, 10

African, Caribbean and Pacific Countries (ACP), 163

African Union Conference Center (AUCC), 21, 22

African Union (AU), *see* Organization of African Unity (OAU)

Afro-Asian Conference, 11, 12, 132

Ajuran Empire, 9

Ajuran Sultanate, 9

Alao, Abiodun, 81, 82, 96, 100, 105, 182

Algeria, 11, 38, 39, 59, 174, 175

Algiers, 38

Aluminum, 53n4, 59, 60

Angola, 34, 37, 50, 61, 63, 66–68, 72, 80, 87, 99, 136, 175

Anina, Germaine, 17

Asian countries, 63, 68, 99, 100

---

[1] Note: Page numbers followed by 'n' refer to notes.

© The Author(s) 2020
O. Abegunrin, C. Manyeruke, *China's Power in Africa*,
Politics and Development of Contemporary China,
https://Doi.org/10.1007/978-3-030-21994-9

225

226 INDEX

B

Bandung, 12, 78, 132
Bauxite, 59
Beijing, 11, 13, 15, 20, 22, 31, 37–41,
  46, 48, 67, 68, 70, 71, 76,
  82–86, 89–91, 102, 109, 115,
  158, 175–178, 180, 182, 199,
  210, 211
Beijing Consensus, 5, 133, 161,
  165, 207
Bella, Ahmed Ben (President), 12
Belt and Road Forum (BRF), 199
Belt and Road Initiative (BRI),
  199, 202
  See also One Belt One Road
    Initiative (OBORI)
Botswana, 17, 59
Bouteflika, Abdelaziz (President), 39
Brazil, Russia, India, China and South
  Africa (BRICS), 160
Britain, 37, 116
British rule, 96
Buhari, Muhammadu (President),
  68, 69
Burkina Faso, 13

C

Cairo, 37, 50, 51
Cape Town, 50
Capitalism, 108
Central African Federation
  (CAF), 155
Central Intelligence Agency (CIA),
  53n8, 72n8, 72n10, 185n32
Chad, 50, 63, 69, 173, 175
Chiluba, Frederick (President), 39
China Aero Technology Import-
  Export Cooperation
  (CATIC), 105
China-Africa Cooperation (CAC), 4,
  40, 43, 178, 202

China-Africa Development Fund
  (CADF), 32, 40, 48
China Architecture and Design
  Research Group (CADRG), 21
China Civil Engineering Construction
  Corporation (CCECC), 200
China Global Television Network
  (CGTN), 184n25
China Machine -Building International
  Corporation (CMBIC), 105
China Merchant Holdings
  International (CMHI), 199
China National Offshore Oil
  Corporation (CNOOC), 67, 68
China Non-Ferrous Metal Group
  Company (CNMC), 123, 124
China Open Door Policy, 16
China Railway Engineering
  Corporation (CREC), 138
China's Council for the Promotion
  of International Trade
  (CCPIT), 158
China's National Bureau of Statistics
  (CNBS), 103
China State Construction Engineering
  (CSCE), 21
China-Zimbabwe Friendship, 95–113
Chinese Central Military Commission
  (CCMC), 178
Chinese Communist Party (CCP),
  6n7, 14, 15, 24n23, 84, 86, 91
  See also Communist Party
    of China (CPC)
Chinese Coolies, 17
Chinese Development Bank (CDB),
  36, 48, 142, 160
Chinese National Broadcasting
  Corporation (CNBC), 52
Chinese National Oil Companies
  (CNOC), 61
Chinese People Liberation Army
  (CPLA), 85, 173

INDEX 227

Chinese peoples, 4, 16, 19, 35, 43, 88, 132
Coal, 59, 60, 121, 208
Coal mine, 105
Cobalt, 28, 59–61, 177
Cold War, 1, 29–31, 77, 79, 98, 132, 180
Colonialism, 2, 37, 47, 80, 83, 87, 89, 92, 109, 119, 193, 195
Colonial rule, 11, 12, 80, 81, 91, 116
Coltan, 28, 59
Common External Tariff (CET), 159
Common Market for Eastern and Southern Africa States (COMESA), 155
Communist Party of China (CPC), 6n3
Congo, 59, 60, 63, 125
See also Republic of the Congo
Copper, 34, 59–61, 104, 123, 124, 126, 177
Corruption, 66, 68, 199, 201
Crude oil, 60, 66

D
Dakar, 50
Dar-es-Salaam, 37, 38
Darfur conflict, 69
Democratic Republic of the Congo (DRC), 50, 61, 70, 86, 164, 173, 175, 177
Diamond, 28, 59
Djibouti, 5, 175, 177, 178, 180, 181, 189, 191, 192, 196–199
Djibouti Ports and Free Zone Authority (DPFZA), 199

E
East Africa, 1, 10, 37, 152, 188, 191, 193, 196–198
East African Community (EAC), 155, 158

Economic and trade cooperation zones (ETCZ), 123
Economic Community of West African States (ECOWAS), 155, 158, 159
Economic Partnership Agreements (EPA), 156
Egypt, 5, 9, 11, 23n15, 51, 70, 71, 152, 175, 189, 191, 192, 196, 198, 199, 212
Equatorial Guinea, 59, 61, 125
eSwatini, 13, 23n19
Ethiopia, 11, 18, 21, 23n15, 27, 39, 72, 131–146, 189, 191, 196, 198, 199
European Union (EU), 30, 32, 63, 71, 97, 103, 110, 136, 140, 156, 165, 182, 213
EXIM BANK of China-Export-Import Bank of China, 29, 35
Export-Import Bank of China (EIBC), 142
Extractive Industry Transparency Initiative (EITI), 211
ExxonMobil, 66

F
Factory, 31, 126
Foreign investment, 29
Foreign policy, 77, 98–100, 118, 119, 132, 133, 180–182, 190
Forum on China-Africa Cooperation (FOCAC), 3–5, 20, 31, 39–40, 42–47, 49, 68, 69, 98, 101, 102, 117, 119, 121–123, 127, 153, 157, 166, 181, 183, 188, 191, 209, 210
France, 14, 17, 28, 35, 37, 70, 175
French, 22, 175
Front for the Liberation of Mozambique (FRELIMO) (Frente de Libertacaio de Mozambique), 76, 87–90, 174

228 INDEX

G
Gabon, 17, 34, 59
Gamedze, Mgwagwa, 13
General Assembly, 12
Geneva, 11
Geneva Conference, 11
Germany, 28, 37, 195
Ghaddafi, Muammar, 25n52
Ghana, 11, 82
Global economy, 16, 115, 131, 133, 152, 190, 202
Global order, 192
  See also New Global Order
Gold, 28, 59, 60, 72, 189
Greater Nile Petroleum Operating Company (GNPOC), 69
Great Wall Industry Corporation (GWIC), 68
Greece, 188
Gross Domestic Products (GDP), 5, 28, 30, 31, 47, 125, 143, 190
Guinea, 11, 59, 60, 63

H
Harare, 111n4
Huawei Technologies Limited (HUAWEI), 68

I
Ibn Battuta, 9
Imperialism, 2, 37, 65, 77, 96, 108, 109
India, 10, 17, 22, 23n15, 51, 70, 137, 160, 188
Indian Ocean, 1, 9, 180, 192, 196, 197
Indonesia, 10, 12, 23n15, 78
Ing-Wen, Tsai (President), 13, 14
International Energy Agency (IEA), 60, 67
International Monetary Fund (IMF), 70

Investment, 2, 5, 13, 14, 16, 19, 20, 29–31, 36, 38, 40–42, 46, 48–50, 52, 65–72, 95–98, 100, 101, 104, 115, 116, 118–122, 124–126, 128, 131–146, 154, 156, 158–160, 162–165, 176, 177, 180, 190, 191, 194–196, 199–201, 208–210, 212
Iran, 23n15, 61
Iraq, 23n15, 61
Iron ore, 59, 60, 72

J
Japan, 14, 16, 17, 23n15, 32, 195, 213
Jiabao, Wen (Premier), 39–41
Jiang Zemin (President), 3, 27, 29, 39, 107, 189
Jinping, Xi (President), 3, 5, 19–21, 42, 45, 46, 52, 68, 69, 177, 179, 182, 187, 190, 197, 207, 209–211
Jintao, Hu (President), 3, 32, 39, 40, 194
Johannesburg, 4, 5, 35, 42–46, 210
Joint Task Force for the Horn of Africa (CJTF-HOA), 181

K
Kaunda, Kenneth (President), 37, 38
Kenya, 5, 9, 34, 136, 179, 189; 191, 192, 196–199, 212
Korean War, 11

L
Lagos, 50
Land reform program, 95, 97, 100, 103, 110
Langqing, Li, 12
Liberia, 61, 173–175, 182

INDEX   229

Libya, 23n15, 59
Look East Policy, 96, 97, 99–102,
    104, 110
Lusaka, 38, 85, 115

M
Madagascar, 10, 17, 60, 197
Malawi, 121
Malaysia, 47
Mali, 11, 59, 177
Manganese, 59
Manufacturing, 4, 29, 32–34, 43,
    65, 71, 104, 119, 120, 123,
    135–137, 140, 143,
    208–210, 212
Mao Zedong (Chairman), 2, 3, 6n7,
    10, 12, 14–16, 18, 24n23, 38,
    82–84, 116, 189
Maritime Road, 190, 211
Maritime Silk Road (MSR), 187, 188,
    190–193, 196
Marxism-Leninism, 14
Mauritania, 59
Mauritius, 17, 34
Mediterranean Sea, 190, 192
Meles Zenawi (Prime Minister), 39
Middle East, 60, 61, 68, 85, 190,
    191, 197
Mineral resources, 50, 70, 104, 123
Mining, 60, 96, 101, 104–105, 116,
    119, 120, 123–124, 126, 133
Ministry of Commerce of the
    People's Republic of China
    (MOFCOM), 191
Mkapa, Benjamin William
    (President), 39
Mnangagwa, Emmerson Dambudzo
    (President), 103
Mogadishu, 9, 11
Mombasa, 50, 189, 199
Morocco, 11

Mozambique, 9, 59, 60, 71, 75, 76,
    78, 80, 87–91, 105, 121, 174,
    197, 200
Mozambique Revolutionary
    Committee (COREMO), 76,
    88–90
Mugabe, Robert G. (President), 95,
    106, 174
Multi-Facility Economic Zones
    (MFEZ), 123

N
Nairobi, 199
Namibia, 59, 80, 87
National Information and
    Communication Technology
    Infrastructure Backbone
    (NICTIB), 68
National interest, 175
National security, 60
National Union for the Total
    Independence of Angola
    (UNITA), 175
Natural gas, 60, 194
Natural resources, 4, 27, 29, 31, 34,
    43, 50, 59, 63, 71, 99, 101, 104,
    107, 117, 118, 122, 123, 125,
    126, 131, 132, 134, 135, 138,
    153, 165, 208–211
N'Djamena, 50
New Asian-African Strategic
    Partnership (NAASP), 157, 159
New Global Order, 52n2
New Partnership for African
    Development (NEPAD), 41, 159
Niger Delta, 66
Nigeria, 13, 34, 59–61, 63, 66–70,
    72, 99, 164, 175
Nigerian Naira (Nigerian currency), 69
Nigerian Oil, 68–69
Nixon, Richard (President), 11–13

230 INDEX

Nkrumah, Kwame (President), 108, 109
Non-Ferrous Metals Corporation of Africa (NFCA), 123, 124, 126
North Africa, 9, 63, 197
Nyerere, Julius (President), 37, 38, 176

O
Obama, Barack (President), 185n34
Obama Administration, 185n34
Ogooue-Maritime Province, 17
Oil, 19, 28, 34, 53n4, 59–72, 99, 117, 133, 136, 144, 175, 177, 192, 194, 199, 208
Oil Diplomacy, 59–72
Omboue, Etimbwe Department, 17
One Belt One Road Initiative (OBORI), 3, 5, 20, 47, 50, 52, 69, 177, 184n16, 187–202, 211
One China Policy, 13, 105
Organization of African Unity (OAU), 39, 80, 81, 85, 153, 157, 213
Organization of Economic Cooperation and Development (OECD), 138

P
Pakistan, 23n15, 47
Pan-Africanist Congress of South Africa (PAC), 76, 83–86, 90
Pan-African road, 50
Partido Africano do Independencia da Guine e Cabo Verde (PAIGC), 174
Peacekeeping operation (PKO), 158, 175, 179, 182
People's Liberation Army (PLA), 15, 85, 173, 179

People's Republic of China (PRC), 4, 10, 12, 13, 16–18, 28–30, 32, 36, 37, 39, 40, 42, 53n4, 65, 66, 81, 87, 132, 176
Petroleum, 34, 35, 59, 60, 67
Ping, Jean, 17
Platinum, 59, 60, 99, 103, 104, 124
Popular Movement for the Liberation of Angola (MPLA), 175
Program for Infrastructure Development for Africa (PIDA), 160–161

R
Railroad, 17, 18, 27, 35, 37, 38, 51, 198
Regional Economic Communities (REC), 151, 156, 159, 163
Republic of China (Taiwan/ROC), 13, 18, 90
Rhodes, Cecil, 37, 51
Rhodesia, 51
Northern Rhodesia, 37
Southern Rhodesia, 37
Rome, 187, 188

S
Salim, Ahmed Salim, 39
Sao Tome and Principe, 14
School of International Relations and Public Affairs (SIRPA), (China Fudan University), 148n39, 148n47
Senegal, 50, 52, 60, 212
Shanghai, 6n7, 12, 13, 15, 22, 24n23, 86
Shanghai Communique, 13
Sharm El-Sheikh, 40–41
Sierra Leone, 59, 175

INDEX 231

Silk Road Economic Belt (SREB), 187, 190, 191, 196
Singapore, 70
Sino-African Relations, 30, 118
Slavery, 17
Socialism, 16, 28, 161
Somalia, 1, 9–11, 134, 141, 158, 164, 173, 182
Somalia Empire, 9
Song Dynasty, 9
South Africa, 17, 18, 34, 35, 37, 42–46, 50, 51, 60, 70, 75–78, 80, 81, 83–87, 90–92, 99, 103, 105, 110, 177, 210, 212
South African Communist Party (SACP), 84
South African Liberation Movement (SALM), 83
South China Sea, 178, 184n21, 196, 198
Southern African Customs Union (SACU), 153, 155, 156, 158
Southern African Development Community (SADC), 155, 158
Southern Development Coordination Conference (SADCC), 155
South Sudan, 61, 176, 177, 179, 182–183, 192, 199, 211
Special economic zone (SEZ), 38, 67, 119
Sri Lanka, 23n15
State-owned Enterprises (SOE), 34, 189, 190
Stockholm International Research Institute (SIRI), 173
Sub-Saharan Africa (SSA), 117, 135, 160
Sudan, 11, 23n15, 60, 61, 63, 64, 66, 67, 69, 72, 99, 134, 141, 158, 164, 173–176, 182, 192, 196
Sun, Irene Yuan, 31, 189
Swaziland, 13, 14, 46
See also eSwatini

T
Taipei, 13, 92
Taiwan, 12–14, 17, 28, 46, 90, 102, 108, 117
See also Republic of China (Taiwan/ROC)
Taiwanese, 13
Tang Dynasty, 9, 189
Tanzania (Tanganyika), 11, 18, 37–39, 71, 72, 80–82, 87, 88, 98, 115, 173, 175, 176, 197, 199
Tanzania-Zambian Railway (TAZARA or TAZAM), 25n40, 37, 38, 55n37, 55n42, 115, 116, 121
Thailand, 10
Tiananmen Square, 3, 29, 106
Total oil, 66
Trans-African Highway Network, 50–52
See also Pan-African Highway
Tunisia, 11

U
Uganda, 136, 192, 199
Uhuru/freedom Railway, 37
Union of Soviet Socialist Republics (USSR), 16, 18, 76, 77, 79, 82–84, 86, 87, 90, 106, 132
United Kingdom, 28, 70, 175, 195
United Nations Conference on Trade and Development (UNCTAD), 70
United Nations Economic Commission for Africa (UNECA), 50, 163
United Nations Security Council (UNSC), 37, 95, 99, 100, 106, 152, 179
Uranium, 28, 60
U.S. African Command (AFRICOM), 181, 185n34
USSR, *see* Union of Soviet Socialist Republics

232 INDEX

V

Vatican City, 14

W

Washington Consensus, 5, 134, 161
West Africa, 10, 70, 190, 191
West African Economic Community
(WAEC), 155
World Bank (WB), 36, 37, 63, 134,
135, 138, 143, 153, 163, 190
World population, 44
World Trade Organization (WTO),
30, 35, 109

X

Xiaoping, Deng (President), 2, 3,
14–16, 18, 28, 29, 189, 213

Y

Yi, Chen, 11
Yuan Dynasty, 1, 10, 189

Z

Zambia, 17, 18, 37–39, 50, 60, 61,
98, 115–128, 199, 200
Zambia-China Cooperation Zone
(ZCCZ), 123
Zambian Electricity Supply
Corporation (ZESCO), 121
Zanzibar, 9, 11
Zheng He, Chinese Admiral, 1, 9, 10
Zhiping, Cheng, 17
Zhou Enlai (Premier), 1, 3, 10–12,
15, 18, 88, 192
Zhu Siben, 1, 10
Zimbabwe, 37, 75, 76, 78, 80–83, 87,
90–92, 95–110, 173, 174, 182
Zimbabwean African National
Liberation Army (ZANLA),
81–83, 87, 107
Zimbabwean African People's Union
(ZAPU), 81–83
Zimbabwean Electricity State
Association (ZESA), 105
Zimbabwean Iron and Steel Company
(ZISCO), 101, 103
Zuma, Jacob (President), 42